Years of
No Decision

Years of
No Decision

Muhammad El-Farra
Former Jordanian Ambassador to the United Nations

Earth is sick;
And Heaven is weary of the hollow words
Which States and Kingdoms utter
When they speak of Truth and Justice

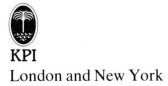

KPI

London and New York

First published in 1987 by KPI Limited
11 New Fetter Lane, London EC4P 4EE

Reprinted 1988

Distributed by
Routledge & Kegan Paul,
Associated Book Publishers (UK) Ltd.
11 New Fetter Lane, London EC4P 4EE

Methuen Inc., Routledge & Kegan Paul
29 West 35th Street
New York, NY 10001, USA

Routledge & Kegan Paul
Methuen Law Book Company
44 Waterloo Road
North Ryde, NSW 2113
Australia

Produced by Worts-Power Associates

Set in 11/12 Times New Roman
by The Design Team, Ascot, Berkshire
and printed in Great Britain
by Dotesios Printers Ltd, Bradford-on-Avon,
Wiltshire

ISBN 07103 0215-0

Contents

We are grateful for permission to reprint passages from the
following:
Doubleday New York for extracts from Harry S. Truman, *Years of
Trial and Hope*; Macmillan Publishers, Ontario for extracts from C.
R. Sulzberger, *A Long Row of Candles*; The Middle East Journal;
Norton & Co for passages from W. C. Eveland, *Ropes of Sand*;
Oxford University Press for passages from A. Toynbee, *Experiences*
and Isaac Deutscher, *The Non-Jewish Jew*; Pan Books for
quotations from L. Collins and D. Lapierre, *O Jerusalem*; Quartet
Books, A. Pearson, *Conspiracy of Silence*.

Photo credits:

United Nations, New York: nos. 4, 7, 8, 9, 10, 12, 14, 16
UNWRA, Vienna, photo by M. Nasr: no. 3
Max Machol: no. 5
Leo Rosenthal: no. 6
Associated Press, London: no. 11
Camera Press, London, photo by Daniel Drooz 1977: no. 13
New York Times: no. 15

Dedication

I spent a long time at the United Nations. My first assignment occupied four years. The second, seven. I have often felt that the second term was not in fact seven, but seventy.

So many problems and so many violations of the Armistice Agreements by Israel took place during this period: so many attacks against innocent civilians in their villages or farmers on their farms or children in their schools occurred. All of them I sought to bring before one organ or another of the United Nations. These atrocities were, of course, in addition to attacks against Syrian or Egyptian territory. In every protest raised at the U.N. Jordan, which I represented, had to participate.

Because of the seven hours difference in time between New York and Jordan I would sometimes receive instructions to go to the Security Council very early in the morning. Many times I had to wake up my poor secretary Rula Kana, at 3 a.m. and ask her to leave both daughter and husband to rush to the office to work on a speech to the Security Council. Her salary was modest, but her nationalist feeling was unbounded.

With all this hectic work I neglected many so-called "normal" duties towards myself as an individual. I did not, for example, get married. I was in fact hesitant to take such a step. It was difficult for me, a Palestinian, a man without a country, to think of marriage. I never had any feeling of security. I was worried. I did not own a house. I did not have sufficient income. The job I had did not appear to be permanent. I therefore remained unenthusiastic about entering what is called "the golden cage" of marriage.

Equally, I considered that the positions I constantly adopted on world problems might bring about pressure for my removal from my post. And although such attempts failed, there was always the possibility that one would be successful. As I saw it, I had no reason to make a wife and children suffer because of all this. Yet, marriage was my mother's desire and my brother's promise and assurance to her regarding my future.

I did not come to a final conclusion until I left the U.N. I eventually married Salma Shihabi in 1971. I now have two children, a girl Heba twelve years of age and a boy, Hadi, who is seven. I feel I owe them an explanation, for the writing of this book has deprived them of much of my time.

It is to them, the Palestinians of the future, and to the hundreds of thousands of young sons and daughters of Palestine who are today growing up stateless, that I dedicate this book. If there is any justice in this world the day will come when they step into the heritage of a home, freedom, land and statehood, promised to every man under the United Nations Charter.

Preface

Only part of my experiences in the international field are covered in this book, in which I show British, American and Israeli practices in the Arab East. I explain these countries' attitude in the United Nations towards the Palestine problem and the role of the United States vis-à-vis every Arab-Israeli war. I have for many years debated various aspects of the Palestine question before the several organs of the United Nations. This book is written on the basis of those debates as well as the many documents relevant to, and minutes of, other meetings in which I participated.

I have attempted to acquaint the reader with the reasons why all the years I spent in the United Nations representing Jordan were years of no decision, why the debates were mere exercises in futility. I have done much research on related matters in order to familiarize him with the background of every issue raised, whether in the United Nations Security Council, the General Assembly or elsewhere. For this reason I have lived with this book for over seven years.

It must be a truism of Middle East politics that international peace initiatives in the area are as old as the creation of the State of Israel. The Partition of Palestine in November 1947, against the will of many of its people but recommended by the United Nations as a solution to the "Jewish Problem", was a resolution adopted to help a Jewish minority to acquire a place to call their homeland. The later resolution of May 1949 admitting Israel to the family of nations was adopted on the understanding that she was "peace-loving" and "able and willing" to carry out the obligations contained in the Charter.

This understanding has been betrayed not once but many times by Israel and the undertaking to stand by the Charter of the United Nations has been proved not once but repeatedly to be an ill-kept promise. While accepting a homeland for themselves, the Jews have never sought to consider the pain and suffering they have caused to those whom they dispossessed of houses, farmsteads, villages and territory which had been theirs for centuries, leaving the Palestinians a people wronged in the name of right.

This is a problem of which we must all be aware and for which we must all struggle to achieve a just solution, not simply because of the moral issue at stake, but because the consequences of Israeli actions touch us all. The welfare of the people of Palestine is as fundamental to peace in the world as it is to the people themselves and so their problem is one in which we must all be not only informed but also involved. This active participation must be immediate, before the children of the new generation either inflict more damage or suffer it, not deferred to some indefinite future date.

That the Palestinian people should share the same rights as every other people on this earth must be an undisputed truth, but the fact remains that their cause is not fairly championed by the countries in whose power it lies to help them. Neither do these same countries condemn the consistent and persistent aggression of Israel in terms which would leave no room for the Israeli government or any Israeli to doubt that they have wilfully flouted the conditions of their admission to the United Nations and have forfeited the good will of the world without whose assistance it would be they who were the homeless ones.

Peace plans for the Middle East have not been lacking. What is common to the failure of all of them is the attitude first of Israel which is always the aggressor and secondly of the world, the western world, in which I include the United States, in particular.

The reader will find that I have focussed on the role of the United States because it is the United States which, in one way or another, has accommodated every Israeli war, each Israeli expansion and every other illegal Israeli practice. Consequently it is the United States which can help bring peace with justice to the Holy Land.

I hope the points raised in this book will make readers realise that the basic concept of Zionism is wrong. It has created an exclusively Jewish State on land purloined by force. It assumes a "Master Race" based on a particular religion and it preaches a militant expansionist policy, to be implemented with total disregard of the national rights of others. With this concept and the behaviour to which it leads, how can there be any peace?

There are many whom I should like to thank for their assistance. I acknowledge my great indebtedness to Claud Morris and Layla El-Farra for their counsel and advice. Rafif Mattar was the first to read the original draft of the manuscript. For her encouragement and invaluable advice I am most grateful. I am indebted also to Sabri Jiryis for providing helpful material.

My nephew, Dr Munir, was with me in all my visits to London. He heard the comments of many friends about the idea of publishing the book. He spent many nights listening to me reading chapters of the work, offering his own suggestions and constructive ideas. Unfortunately Munir passed away on Tuesday March 11th 1986 and I am deeply grieved that he did not live to see the finished work to which he contributed so much.

I am indebted also to the wise insight of many other friends which greatly assisted the shaping of the book. I shall refrain from naming them to avoid associating them with the views I express, all of which are my own.

Chapter 1

Boy with a Horn

"We are a small people but a great people, an ugly and yet a beautiful people; a creative and a destructive people — a people in whom genius and folly are equally co-mingled. We are an impetuous people who have time and again repudiated and wrecked what our ancestors built. For God's sake let us not allow the breach in the wall to swallow us."

Chaim Weizmann

When I was twelve I owned a musical instrument, called a "Barazan", a kind of horn which my father had picked up from the Turks when Palestine was part of the Ottoman Empire. Its sound reached every corner in the small town where I was brought up: Khan-Yunis, in the southern district of Palestine, less than ten miles south of Gaza and only seven miles from the Egyptian border. The Barazan was my constant companion. I had no close friends of my own age. My father had died six months before my birth, leaving my mother, then a young woman, to bring up four children.

One evening in the autumn of 1936 my Uncle Tewfic came to mother and asked her to let me go with him on a "special mission".

My mother laughed. "You want this child on a 'special mission'?" She knew that my uncle was with the Palestine Resistance, at that time struggling against the British occupying forces. "How can a child be of help to you?"

"I want him together with his horn — the Barazan," he replied, adding some other remark which I could not hear.

Mother smiled and turned. "Son, you are going to be important

1

tonight. You will serve your country. Go with your Uncle Tewfic. Do what he tells you and make sure not to be naughty."

I wanted to follow Uncle Tewfic straightaway but he turned, "No, not now. I'll come and fetch you in two or three hours. You can sleep now for a couple of hours if you wish."

Of course, I could not sleep. I was too excited.

Uncle Tewfic came to fetch me three hours later. I sat behind him on a back of a white donkey. We travelled for some fifteen to twenty minutes, something like four miles away from the town. He did not take the usual road. Instead, he selected a small, narrow path which I had never even seen before. When he reached the place he wanted, Uncle Tewfic asked me to crouch in a small ditch which had apparently been prepared earlier for this purpose. He had a torch and showed me where to squat. No one else was there. Tewfic pulled out a watch with a phosphorous-illuminated dial. He said that at midnight I would see a convoy of military tanks travelling in our direction, coming from the north towards the south. I was to wait ten minutes. I would then see the military convoy on the main road reaching a position almost facing me. I was then to blow my horn. After that I would hear much firing. Bullets would fly from every direction, but I was not to be afraid. Tewfic added that I would also hear bombs exploding but that I should stay put until he came to fetch me, even though the moon would shine an hour later. I was not to move.

While he was talking I remembered what I had heard about our people who were fighting the British soldiers for independence, although I did not know at the time what the word "independence" meant.

Every night this convoy crossed Palestine from the north to the south. We children of the town used to go up to the roof of our houses to see it and its searchlights. We frequently heard occasional firing. I had never realised who was doing the firing, nor thought I would ever become a part of it.

But that night, crouched in the narrow ditch, clutching my Barazan, I was excited and full of joy.

Uncle Tewfic had departed, leaving me to my thoughts. I sat in that ditch surrounded by trees bearing almonds, apricots, plums, figs, and grapes. The land was fenced with cactus. I waited impatiently for the convoy to arrive. Everything was quiet. The birds slept and so did the people who during the day worked in the fields round about. But I was alone, sitting in the dark, ready to fulfill the mission entrusted to me. I thought time would pass quickly but the wait for midnight seemed endless. I was constantly looking at the watch with its magic phosphorous dial, putting it to my ear thinking that it had stopped.

Suddenly I saw a light appear in the distance. I looked at the watch. It was not yet midnight. Fifteen minutes later I could see the convoy getting nearer. A few minutes later the convoy reached the exact place fixed for me by Uncle Tewfic. I started to blow my horn with all my strength. Immediately, firing began from both sides of the road. The convoy returned the fire. Bombs planted in the middle of the road exploded as the tanks were passing. I could hear shouting and screaming. Searchlights swivelled in every direction. I could hear the bullets and almost feel them swishing over my head. I was as though anchored to my ditch and made no movement. I was scared.

The firing stopped, though the screaming of wounded soldiers continued. Then, suddenly, everything was quiet.

I did not know what had happened. My Uncle did not return and I soon started to worry. An hour passed. Still nobody appeared. No one but Tewfic knew about my being in this ditch.

Suppose he had been killed? What would happen to me? Afraid to stay alone in the dark, still more afraid to make a single move even after the moon came out, I decided to stay where I was until the morning. Then I could walk home and go to school.

Two hours later I heard a donkey bray. In a few minutes Uncle Tewfic appeared riding his white donkey. I was at that moment the happiest boy in Palestine. "You did a good job. You are a man," he said.

"What happened?" I asked.

"Two tanks were destroyed and many soldiers killed."

"But why?" I questioned.

"The occupiers (the British) wanted to give our land to the Jews. We had to make them leave before they put the Jews in," he explained.

I asked him why he had wanted me to blow my Barazan. He said this was to give the impression that we were a well-organised movement and had a perfect organisation. In fact, we had no organisation, though everyone fought to defend his land. He added: "When you grow up you will realise the importance of a homeland, and also the importance of having your soil free from trespassers. You know, in these orchards that belong to us, we own the land all the way up to heaven."

I gaped. "You mean we own the land up to that shining moon!"

"Of course," he said, "You will understand this later. Now you are too young."

At home I found my mother waiting a little way from our house. My uncle greeted her.

"Here is Muhammad. You should be proud of him. He is a man."

She embraced me with all the love of a mother for her child. There was a warm hug and a big kiss.

"My son, you have brought me pride and happiness."

We walked to the house. Tewfic told my mother to tell me not to disclose what had happened to any of my class mates at school. Mother asked him to stay for some food. He said no because he had some other work to attend to. He drank a cup of coffee, then left.

As a reward for my part in the ambush of the British convoy, my mother had prepared my favourite dish for me — stuffed pigeon. She asked me not to tell anybody what happened during the night, saying: "You will see the young students gathering at school during the play break. Don't stand with them. Don't show you know anything."

This was all a disappointment to me. I was excited and wanted to tell my class-mates everything.

I asked mother: "Why not?"

She explained how harmful this would be to both me, my uncle and all members of his group. She thus taught me how to keep a secret at this tender age. The British response the next day seemed to me to be beyond belief.

Two uncles of mine, the Mayor of Khan-Yunis, Abdul Rahman El-Farra, the Mukhtar of the town, Mustafa Hassan El-Farra, together with the former Mayor of Khan-Yunis, Haj Saleem El-Agha and Sheikh Said Hamdan El-Agha, were exiled for six months to northern Palestine for their alleged part in the attack. Abdul Rahman and Haj Saleem were exiled to the village of Samakh while Mustafa and Sheikh Said were sent to the town of Baisan. All were ordered to report to the police three times a day, later reduced to twice a day. The intention was not only to intimidate them but to enable the British authorities to have complete control over their activities and ensure their presence in their places of exile. Other dignitaries from the town were also either detained for some time or exiled to different places, all accused of being part of the resistance.

It was only later that I learned that many of the detainees, including my own relatives, had indeed been working with the resistance. There was no indication that they were anything other than ordinary citizens, for by day they went about their normal business, only after dark becoming involved in activities connected with the resistance against the British Occupation. When I did finally learn it was all the more amusing because the British District Commissioner, Sir Aubrey Leese, used to call at my uncle's office and go on from there, with my brother Qassim, to my uncle's house for lunch. Young though I was, the Commissioner used to insist on my being with them and he used to speak to me in perfect Arabic.

Shortly after this episode Sir Aubrey Leese was transferred to Jaffa, apparently because he could not play an effective role in stopping the resistance, but my uncles continued to serve out their year of exile. It was a long time and my brother Qassim and cousin Adel decided to try to do something to release them. They went to Jaffa, taking me with them so that all of us could ask Sir Aubrey to intervene to obtain the release of our uncles. It was a rainy day. He was kind to us but firm about his refusal to intervene. He emphasized the role of our uncles in the resistance, implying: "let them stay where they are. There is nothing that I want to do to release them." He apparently was not happy about the whole affair although he showed understanding of our cause and was not at all pro-Zionist.

Abdul Rahman and Mustafa witnessed the creation of the Jewish State on the soil of their homeland before their death; some of their children continued resistance to the foreign invader, this time the Jews. Abdul Rahman's son was arrested after 1967, accused of resisting Israeli occupation. In an arbitrary trial he was sentenced to twenty-five years imprisonment. The Israelis promised his father to release him if he signed an undertaking that the son would not get involved again in resistance activities. Abdul Rahman came to Amman to consult me. He was then about eighty years old. I asked him: "Uncle, do you want to sign this document?" He answered with firmness "Fasharo!" (Over my dead body!)

He added: "I just want to make sure that you, as our Ambassador, approve of my stand." I kissed his hand, thanked him for his wisdom, and asked him to stay with me for a few days. He then went back to Khan-Yunis, where he died before his son completed his prison term. His son was brought, chained wrist and ankle, to attend the funeral. Only later was he released after experiencing all kinds of physical ill-treatment.

2

When I was in the seventh elementary grade the teacher asked every one in the class to write an essay describing his future plans and what he would like to be. I wrote that I intended to visit the big country that Christopher Columbus had discovered – America.

5

The teacher read my essay, gave me a good mark, then said: "Just like that. You want to go all the way to America." I answered: "Yes, sir." He laughed.

After finishing my elementary education in the town of Khan-Yunis I moved to Jaffa, where I received my high school education. My dream was to become a lawyer. Before going to America I worked in Shihadeh and Nasser's law firm in Jaffa. I was planning to finish my legal studies and then join the same firm. I obtained my degree, but Jaffa had been taken by the Israelis before I could return and its inhabitants expelled so that my dream was never fulfilled.

Until I finished school I stayed with my elder brother Abdul Salam, who was a merchant there. He had married and had one daughter, Saheer. My mother stayed with my other brother and sister back in Khan-Yunis, though she occasionally visited us.

One afternoon in the late summer of 1938, around four o'clock, Abdul Salam took me to the Jaffa mosque for prayer. On our way we met a huge protest demonstration against the British occupation. Before we knew it, we were in the middle. British troops came to break up the crowd and people started running. My brother, who had nothing to do with the demonstration, was still taking it calmly. He kept walking slowly. I was doing the same, a look of bewilderment on my face. A soldier suddenly rushed up to him and hit him on the back of the head with his rifle butt. His skull was smashed, and he fell to the ground. I ran away and the soldier could not catch me.

I returned moments later. It was a horrific scene with so many bodies lying on the ground. I was helpless and didn't know what to do, though a little later ambulances came to take the wounded to hospital.

It was a tragic experience for me. I was all alone in the city. I wondered how all this could happen to a peaceful man going to the mosque for prayer. I rushed to my sister-in-law and she asked my brother's business partner to find out his whereabouts.

Eventually we discovered that my brother had been taken to the City hospital in the Ajami Quarter overlooking the Mediterranean. "An operation has been performed on Abdul Salam El-Farra, and he is in a very critical condition", we were told.

We begged the nurse to let us see him, even from a distance. He lay there, unconscious, wrapped in white. The nurse said that we could visit him after one full week.

After that week, he was taken off the danger list. Only then were we allowed to enter the room and sit with him. I remember when we we allowed to enter the room and sit with him. I remember when we walked in we found him on a chair near his bed. He looked at me. "I meditate a great deal, but I have been unable to pray since the day we were together." I smiled and wished him a speedy recovery so that we could go again together to the Mosque.

It was a moving and tragic scene at the hospital. I saw a whole row of faces in my brother's ward — all struck down during the demonstration.

A few weeks later more Jewish immigrants came to Palestine and this resulted in more demonstrations, more bloodshed and more acts of resistance. Unable to arrest all the freedom fighters, the Military Governor imposed a curfew in Jaffa from six p.m. to six a.m. When this remedy failed the Governor ordered everyone in the Nuzha Quarter to assemble in El-Bassa field, surrounded by orange groves and usually used by young boys for football. Each of us was cross-examined, and then two hundred men and boys were moved to a jailyard. My brother and I were among those unfortunates. I still do not know what were the criteria for such detention. Abdul Salam was never interested in politics. I was merely a high-school boy, and, except for my part as a horn-blower back in Khan-Yunis, had never taken part in anything political. And no British official could possibly have guessed my role in that incident.

We spent one night in detention. I was scared. The officer in charge marked each of us with an ink-stamp on the back of our hands which was impossible to wash off. It took days to fade. I could not make anything out of it, although I rightly guessed it to be a means of pressure and intimidation.

As the years passed we saw the Jewish terrorist gangs create their groups to cause terror amongst our peaceful people, who were thus compelled to abandon their lands and homes and become refugees. We felt that some form of defence was badly needed to reassure the people. The young generation must be trained to defend themselves if and when attacked by the Jewish terrorists. This was almost a year before the United Nations recommended the partition of Palestine on 29 November 1947. The idea of self-defence emerged as we saw what the Jewish settlers in Palestine were preparing immediately prior to partition. Many Jews were not in favour of terrorism as means for dividing the land against the will of the majority of its people. Leading scholars such as Judah Magnus, Rabbi Berger and others opposed partition, saying that it would not bring peace to the Holy Land nor serve world Jewry. Even then some leading Jewish scholars were saying that partition might fuel anti-semitism.

A few members of the Jaffa Sporting Club on Jamel Pasha Street in the heart of the city met one afternoon to discuss the threat posed to every Palestinian by the Stern, Irgun, Haganah and other terrorist gangs. All saw the need for a Palestinian organisation which would train its members to defend themselves against Jewish terrorism. I was one of those who attended the first meeting. We agreed that the organisation would be called *Al-Najjadah*. The first article in its constitution emphasized that *Al-Najjaddah* was not a party and belonged to no party; it was not part of any religious group and did not base itself on any family grouping.

All Palestinians sought unity and gave it the highest priority, regardless of their religious or political affiliation or family considerations, in order to face the Zionist invasion. It was natural for every one to join *Al-Najjadah*. In a few months there was a branch in every village, town and city. In its first year, almost every young man was given basic training for defending his home and homeland. *Al-Najjadah* had its first annual rally, at which every village, town and city was represented, in El-Bassa field where many of the Jaffa youth had been detained a few years earlier; it was symbolic of the growth of our movement for independence that those young men detained by the British in El-Bassa field were later to meet there again, as members of an organisation devoted to the defence of their homeland against foreign invaders, British or Zionists.

A similar organisation, *Futowwah,* had also been formed and, to preserve unity, it was agreed to merge both in one body called the "Arab Youth Organisation", with its headquarters in Jaffa. The word "Arab" was used because of our conviction that the movement was an Arab movement intended to serve Arabism. It was not linked to any Government, party or religious community.

There was some disagreement over who should be the head of the new organisation. The overwhelming majority objected to having one of the two heads of the merged organisations as their leader. They did not want a politician but sought a man with a military background. Since none of the members had that qualification, they turned to Egypt for help, and asked an Egyptian, General Mahmoud Labbib, to lead the organisation. He had just retired from military service and was a man dedicated to the Palestinian cause. He would do anything to save Jerusalem.

I was chosen unanimously as the Secretary of the organisation. For me that was the highest honour, a tribute from my young colleagues of *Al-Najjadah* and *Futowwah,* now merged as the Arab Youth Organisation. In later life I was elected to many posts including President of the Arab Unity Council in 1965; and

Vice-President of the United Nations General Assembly in the years that followed, while I also served as President of the United Nations Security Council in March 1966. Never did I feel as honoured as when my fellow Palestinians entrusted me with that first post. I delayed my college education in the United States for a year to serve the young organisation.

We dedicated young Palestinians intended to defend our home-land and challenged the Zionist acts of lawlessness. We felt that our people knew their land best; that they should defend the homeland; that Arab help was necessary but that the leading role should be Palestinian. All Palestinian political leaders were of the same opinion and it was unfortunate that the Palestinians were given only a secondary role in the 1948 Israeli War. The war ended in Israel's favour and the Arab Youth Organisation was dissolved. Most members became either martyrs or refugees, scattered across the world. By the end of 1947 I prepared to leave for the United States. What had been a joke to my seventh grade teacher become a reality ten years later. Against all odds, I completed the requirements for admission to an American college and applied to at least ten universities. I received acceptances from three, in Massachusetts, Missouri and California.

3

There was a time when I had difficulty in spelling the name "Massachusetts"; amusing that I should end up at the University of Suffolk in that State. It was early 1948, and I had little money. Behind me was the determination of a tightly-knit Palestinian family to pool their resources and see the "baby" of the family educated. My adventure as a Palestinian-in-exile was about to begin.

My passage to the United States was from Haifa on the *Marine Carp,* a naval vessel converted into a civilian passenger vessel. The journey from Jaffa was risky. Fighting between Palestinians and Jews in Palestine had started. My brother Abdul Salam hired a taxi, at a high price, in order to take me to Haifa. He and my other brother, Qassim, insisted on coming all the way, a three hours' ride. To go to Haifa one had to pass through many Jewish settlements. A friend of mine, Fareed Khoursheed was also coming with me on this hazardous journey to America. His father, aware of the risks, cut the paper carrying a phrase from the Quran into two parts. He kept one and gave Fareed the other. This was based on the belief that the son would return home after that long trip carrying his part of the phrase to rejoin it with the scrap held by his father. Abdul Salam

9

took a different view and believed that, if God willed, the trip would be safe.

We set out. After half an hour, the Jews residing in settlements to the east of the road started shooting at our passing taxi. One bullet hit a tyre. The taxi driver stopped in order to change it. The four of us rushed to hide behind some rocks until the driver finished. I started to worry about my brothers. What would happen when they got back to Jaffa after seeing me off? The driver finished and asked us to take our seats as the car set off. Firing could still be heard from different directions, but we got through all the various fusillades as the Jewish settlers took pot shots at us.

Despite this, the journey from Jaffa to Haifa was lovely. The scent of orange blossoms coming from the groves surrounding Jaffa was out of this world. I can still remember how at sunrise all the Palestinian farmers were greeting the day with national Arab songs while cultivating the land and watering the orange trees. It was the kind of Palestinian labour and care in cultivation that had rightly made the Jaffa orange famous. Those farmers had acquired this experience long before Jewish immigration to the Holy Land. These memories are still vivid in my mind although I have not been to that part of Palestine since that day.

We stayed in Haifa for two nights. It was extremely dangerous in the city itself, with Jewish terrorists firing at both Palestinian Arabs and British soldiers throughout the night.

We had to confirm my ticket for the voyage, but the offices of the shipping company were in the Jewish sector of Haifa. My brother Qassim asked my elder brother and I to stay in the hotel while he fetched my ticket. I said: "I should do it by myself. You should all stay in the hotel."

Each of us wanted to make a sacrifice for his brothers. Finally the three of us and Fareed went together to the shipping offices, crossing through the very unsafe parts of Haifa simply because we had no alternative. My eldest brother was wearing a red tarbouch. We asked him to take it off in order not to be a target for Jewish bullets. He refused. He said:"God will protect us. Don't worry. I am confident that everything will be all right." We arrived safely at the shipping office to collect my ticket and the other necessary information.

The *Marine Carp* set sail on 17th December 1947. My brothers came with me to the port. The ship was anchored offshore and we had to take a small boat out to it. My two brothers insisted on coming with me all the way. We hugged and kissed as we parted. It was a very sentimental occasion. All was in a state of confusion. The bullets were all over, for me at least, but the future was vague. What would happen to Palestine was anybody's guess. Would we meet again? And in Palestine? Such doubts made our farewell unusual and my passage troubled as I spent a lot of time worrying about my brothers' return to Jaffa.

I carried with me a semi-circular piece of marble given me by my sister-in-law, Qassim's wife Layla, engraved with the words: "Never despair." I put it on a small table next to my bed in the cabin. It gave me hope and a kind of comfort.

I reached New York at the end of the first week of January 1948. It was something of a shock to me, full of surprises and new experiences. It was my first experience of the varied life-stream that floods the streets of a great modern city! Raucous Italian taxi-drivers, hard-living Irish cops, the sleazy side-streets of Broadway as well as the excitement of Times Square. It was a revelation to one who had never in his life tasted a hot dog.

Two days later I took the train to Boston where I stayed at the Y.M.C.A. When I arrived I remembered that I had forgotten my marble "never despair" which I placed near my bed. The same night I travelled all the way back to New York. The hotel manager was astonished and asked why I had not phoned him to ask for it to be sent "special delivery". He did not know that I was a newcomer who lacked such experience.

The following morning I returned to Boston carrying my precious bit of marble and registered at Suffolk University Law School. My college life had started. My happiness increased when, a week later, I received a cable from my two brothers saying that they had reached Jaffa safely.

4

My first few weeks in Boston were puzzling. Here I was, a stranger "in paradise", trying to adjust to my new life. I found many things that were different. Every morning I bought all the Boston newspapers to read the news about Palestine. I examined every one of them column by column, so that I could subscribe to the best. I settled on the *Christian Science Monitor.*It was objective and it had a fine philosophical and religious article every morning about the beauty of life and how to enjoy it.

I sensed that the other newspapers did not print correct information about the Arabs. There was a false image of the Arab in the U.S., which I picked up from Arab friends I met as well as from the press reports I read. The presentation of our case vis-à-vis the

Jews in Palestine was much distorted. In my inexperience I thought that this was due to lack of information, and felt it my duty to correct these errors. One day I wrote a letter to an editor. It was never published. I tried another newspaper with the same result. I decided finally to go myself to the *Christian Science Monitor*. I asked to see the man in charge of the Middle East section. I was then introduced to a Mr Reuben Markham.

Mr Markham was very pleasant and took me to one of the paper's conference rooms. He asked me to tell him about myself. I explained my disappointment about the American papers, and about the letters I had written asking for the correction of published distortions. They had not been published. Yet, I said, "we are told that freedom of expression is a constitutional right. At least this was what we were taught in school."

Mr Markham laughed and then explained to me the influence of the Zionists in the United States. He asked what I had written and I took from my pocket a letter I had prepared for possible publication in the *Monitor*. He read it and then promised me to publish it, on the understanding, however that he would have a Jew publish his version on the matter. Both contributions, from Arab and Jew, would be published on the day and on the same page. I kept a copy of that page in my special file.

Mr Markham invited me to his home along with some of his friends for me to meet. I formed the impression that the Americans are a good-hearted friendly people and I was beginning to understand something of American psychology and attitudes. That meeting also reinforced my conviction that the Americans were very scared about Communism and wanted to know about the Arab stand on that issue.

5

In the early summer of that year, 1948, the Jewish settlers in Palestine occupied most of Palestine with the help of the American President Harry S. Truman, (in an election year) and the Zionist movement abroad. The war continued. I lost all contact with my family. The money I had would hardly cover my expenses for the year and I did not know anybody well enough to ask for a loan.

This, I realised, must be the problem of every Palestinian student in the United States. I started wondering how to solve it and discussed the matter with two fellow students. One was a classmate and a good friend, Salam Dajani. We had been brought up together, had planned to come to the States about the same time, and were now in the same law school. I suggested to Salam that we should establish an Arab student organisation. At that first meeting, amongst a good deal of bravado, we formed the organisation. One of us was "elected" president. A second was "elected " vice-president and a third became treasurer!

We collected a list of Palestinian students and wrote asking that they inform us if they had any financial difficulty, and that they contact their colleagues and friends and urge them to write to us too. In a short time, we received scores of letters requesting membership and asking for help in obtaining postponement of payment of university fees. One letter was sent by my old friend Fareed. Everyone explained his financial situation. We built up a big file which we took on behalf of the "Organisation" to the Arab ambassadors at the United Nations in New York.

A few agreed to meet us, amongst them Faris Bey El-Khouri of Syria. One of my fellow students was very undiplomatic with this diplomat. He angrily proclaimed that the Arab governments were responsible for the Palestinian tragedy and were consequently responsible for the students' difficulty. The governments should help students financially so that they could finish their studies. Faris Bey was patient. He realised our agony and did not take my colleague's outburst the wrong way. He asked whether we could join him for lunch. The others could not make it since they had to go back to Boston, but I accepted his kind invitation.

He offered to take me to the United Nations Security Council to attend a meeting on Palestine and hear a speech he was about to make. I was thrilled for I had heard a great deal about the U.N., but this was my first opportunity to visit it. After lunch a big black Cadillac took us to the U.N. Faris Bey said to me that he was not happy about the Arabs accepting the 1948 cease-fire in the area and that he had advised various governments not to do so. He said: "The Israelis will not abide by it. They always adopt a *fait accompli* policy."

He then asked me what I was studying at university. He did not like the idea of my studying law. Instead he wanted more agricultural and other engineers together with geologists and people who would learn more about the land. He clearly felt the Arab nation needed students concerned with such subjects as irrigation and farming rather than law.

In the Security Council before the meeting, Faris Bey introduced me to members of his delegation — the Syrians. He asked me to sit behind him. I heard his speech, all on Palestine, Then and there I resolved to finish my college education and work at the United

Nations, thinking this to be my way to serve my homeland. But I did not know how to do it. The U.N. was, after all, for delegates from member states and I was a man without a country.

6

Until that day of my visit to Faris Bey and the Security Council I had known little about Zionism; what I heard about it then was an eye-opener. I decided to chase up these ideas and find out all I could. The Boston Public Library gave me the help I needed and in a book called *European Ideologies,* I read about the first Zionist Congress which had taken place in Basle in 1897.[1] The programme accepted at this Congress had been decisive. The words were precise: "the aim of Zionism is to create for the Jewish people a home in Palestine secured by public law." The part explaining the means of attaining the objectives of Zionism attracted my attention in particular. It read as follows:

"1. The systematic promotion of the settlement of Palestine with Jewish agriculturists, artisans and craftsmen.
2. The Organisation and federation of all Jewry by means of local and general institutions in conformity with the local laws.
3. The strengthening of Jewish sentiments and national consciousness.
4. Preparatory steps for procuring of such government assents as are necessary for achieving the object of Zionism."

I also learned that the critical period in the growth of Zionism had coincided with the tremendous growth of revolutionary trends in Russia. I read:

"The Jews were strongly attracted by the Russian Revolution. Hopes for political emancipation and even for broader national rights became so widespread that even extreme Zionist circles embraced this blinding illusion. The Socialist-Zionist parties actively participated in the revolution itself. The Russian General Zionist Organisation was then the strongest and most influential of the parties within the World Zionist Organisation

---

1.   *European Ideologies, a survey of twentieth century political ideas,* ed. Feliks Gross, New York, 1948, chapter XV.

and initiated a broad national programme of activity in the Diaspora."

7

But it was at this time that I was finding it especially hard to survive at University. My brother Abdul Salam and his family had been forced to leave their home in Jaffa as a result of Zionist pressure against the people of the city. He was rescued by my other brother, Qassim, who came by boat from Khan-Yunis to salvage what he could, suffering terrible seasickness. I had counted on my two brothers to meet all my financial needs — now the elder brother had to leave everything behind. Our family property in Jaffa and Abu Swairih was confiscated by the Zionists. We were all in trouble.

Facing up to our grim financial situation the three "founding members" of the Students' Organisation now got together and decided to spend the summer in Chicago looking for work. We were told that this industrial city; the "Windy City", had more opportunities than any other place. Some American classmates scared us by saying that the city was known for the many crimes committed in it and called it the city of the gangsters. However, this did not change our minds. We wrote to all members of our organisation informing them of our endeavours with the Arab governments. We explained that these would take a long time to come to fruition and suggested they join us in Chicago during this summer and also look for work there. Many came. Later on, my classmate Salam decided to go to New York.

On arrival many of my colleagues started looking at the 'job advertisements' in the *Chicago Tribune*. One advertisement was very tempting. It invited students to sit for an examination and, if passed, they would join a big firm and make 97 dollars or even double that amount every week. To all of us that was too good to be true. One of us did sit for the exam, passed it, and received a cable for training the following day. The same ad appeared in the *Tribune* the following day. We all sat for the exam. We all passed and received the same cables, and joined for training. We had our breakfast in the firm then turned to the Training Centre. Only then did we realise what it was all about.

We were to be trained as salesmen of the 'Filter Queen' vacuum cleaner. The instructor explained to us that every one should go carrying a machine from house to house, knock at the door, and when the lady of the house opened the door he should smile. When he was allowed to enter, and before starting the demonstration of the machine, he should admire the place and the good taste of the lady because that psychological move would encourage the lady and help the salesman. The instructor added that even if the door was slammed in our faces we should take it 'with a smile'.

I doubted that I could succeed in this kind of work and had to quit after the first breakfast and first lesson. Other colleagues continued for the three days of training and tried to promote the sales of the 'Filter Queen' without success. We all returned to square one . . . looking for jobs carrying with us what little experience we had gained since our arrival in the 'Windy City' while hunting for jobs and facing many difficulties and we would tell each other: 'Keep smiling!'

I started working as a pipe welder in a factory making army beds. The American boss, a patient and friendly man, taught me how to do it. It was easy and I grasped the knack without much difficulty. Of course, I spoiled many pieces of pipe before mastering the job, but the boss was very understanding. The only problem was its effect on the eyes. The boss warned me about this and asked me to use the special mask all the time. The mask covered the eyes and face. I worked for one month and then decided to quit. I remember that my superior was sad to see me leave them. He was familiar with the difficulties of the Palestinian students in America and apprecia- tive of my work.

I ended up working in a factory cutting iron bars into different sizes. The income from this job during the summer was more than enough to cover my expenses and college fees for a whole year. The work was very hard and I was not used to it. It was also a very hot summer.

There was another machine in the factory used for making screws. It had many gadgets but was very simple to handle and, also, very safe. No one working on it would leave it for another machine. I asked Sam the foreman to let me have it. He promised to write to me any summer that particular machine would be available.

Sam was an American of Italian origin. He was in his late forties. He was husky and looked like a rustler. He would move all day in his navy blue safari suit to watch the work with a big Havana cigar in his mouth. He would always look at the counter in every machine to make sure that the right production was made. But with time and the tolerance and understanding of my American boss I gained experience. It was very dangerous, and I had to be alert all the time. The machine that weighs four tons and that comes down to chop the iron bars needed much attention. When it cut the bar you had to push the piece which the machine had already cut out of the way to make room for the following one. If you failed to synchronise your hand movements with those of the machine it would chop your hand or fingers off.

One evening a student friend of mine, Jalal came to see me. He had met an American girl. They had become good friends and then he had fallen madly in love with her. She wrote him beautiful love letters in green ink. She ended every letter with a request. "Please send some money for 'Wanda's' food." Jalal told me that Wanda was his girlfriend's dog. Every time he visited me, Jalal, who had no work, asked me to read the love letter he had received. Naturally I used to read it with much interest.

After showing me each letter Jalal would say: "She said so and so and I believe her. What do you think?" I would answer: "Since you believe her why ask me?" Whenever she wanted money for "Wanda" Jalal would come to me for a loan. I never rejected his request, for I knew that one day he would pay me back. This was my weakness — I could never say no to a man who was a stranger in a foreign land, because I had also passed through this experience.

One evening Jalal while walking on West Windsor Street in up-town Chicago was hit on the head by a gangster. He was robbed of his watch and the little money he had borrowed from me for "Wanda" and he was taken to hospital where he received seven stitches. I went to see him and assured him that, since the police had arrested the criminal who came from a rich family, Jalal would himself be a rich man soon. The Court would compensate him with a huge amount of money, but he should not waive his rights in the police station or in court.

He said: "Never."

The following day two pretty young ladies visited Jalal in his room. They gave him back his watch, money and other personal things the gangster took from him, and apologised for what happened. They asked him to go with them to the police station in order to sign a paper and waive his rights.

Sure enough, Jalal went. When I saw him that afternoon he told me what had happened. When I criticised him severely for waiving his rights, he answered back saying: "The girls entered my house. I had to be kind and hospitable to them. Don't forget I am an Arab!" He was emphasising the traditional Arab hospitality to guests. It was almost the last I saw of him for when the summer was over, we all went back to our colleges.

Fareed Khoursheed who was my neighbour in the Nuzha Quarter in the city of Jaffa and who was with me on the ship, got his degree in engineering. His city and home having being taken by the Israelis,

Fareed got married and resided in Washington D.C. In December 1984 I attended a reception given by Farouk Taji, a leading businessman, and saw Fareed there. It was a pleasant surprise for both of us. We had not seen each other for over twenty years. We reflected on old memories all evening with mixed feelings for both of us, like many others, had ended up without either home or country. Like many others, we feel like exiles and, despite success, long to go home.

8

I finished the requirements for my LL.B and graduated, but did not know where to go. I was a man without a country. Since no opportunity beckoned, I decided to work for my Master's degree. I finished that at Boston University Law School in one year. Then I was again faced with the same problem. What to do? Where to go? Again, I had no answer and little advice to give to Sabri, Uncle Mustafa's son, who came at this time to study medicine in the States. He was followed by his brother Mahmoud. Sabri became a leading doctor in Hollywood, Mahmoud a businessman in the same State, California. I decided to work for my Doctor's degree. I was offered a scholarship from the University of Pennsylvania and registered for that degree at the University of Pennsylvania Law School and resided in Philadelphia. A few months later I received a letter from Ambassador Farid Zeineddine, the Permanent Representative of Syria at the United Nations, asking me to see him in his office in New York. I learned that my friend and class mate, Salam Dajani, who was working at the U.N. information department had recommended me to him as a research officer.

I was happy to meet the Ambassador but I explained to him that it would be difficult for me to work with him since I was a candidate for my Doctor's degree. I would have accepted his offer had it not been for my new commitment. The law school required one year's residence.

He came up with a suggestion. He said he would arrange with the President of the University to have me reside half of the week in Philadelphia and the other half in New York and to extend the time of residence for two years, not one. This was an unprecedented arrangement made by the university as a courtesy to the Government of Syria.

I was now happy. I was studying for my Doctor's degree. I liked my job. It was certainly very different from the previous summer work in the Chicago factory. It was a little funny that at almost the same time I received an invitation from Sam, the American factory manager, to work on the screw machine. Sam fulfilled his promise but that was a little late. I wrote to him thanking him for his courtesy.

The minute I walked into the United Nations building in early 1952 I remembered Faris Bey El-Khouri and how he had taken me to the session that had so impressed me.

Ambassador Zeineddine, an able statesman and brilliant diplomat, had a high regard for me and gave me the authority to participate in U.N. debates. I started practising my academic knowledge at the United Nations. My favourite subject was the item called 'International Covenants on Human Rights.' The fact that the people of Palestine were deprived of exercising this right made it of special interest to me.

I finished my J.S.D. degree in 1958 and started lecturing as part of my work at many American universities on Arab problems — Morocco, Tunisia, Algeria, Oman and Palestine. In the five years I did this I visited many states and got to know more about the American people. I owed a great deal to American institutions and hoped one day that the good-hearted Americans would understand our cause and apply their great traditions and values to our problems. I felt that the values of Presidents Washington and Jefferson should be the guiding star of all American behaviour and practice in the world, because it was those values that had made America great.

In 1959 the Jordanian Ambassador in Washington, Madhat Juma'a, received a cable from Samir Bey Rifai, then Prime Minister of Jordan, offering me a job in Jordan's Foreign Service with the rank of Counsellor. The Prime Minister met me only once, but my name had been suggested to him by my good friends Abdul Monem Rifai and Zaid Rifai. The first was Samir Bey's brother and the second his son. Both later became Prime Ministers in Jordan.

I received this offer at a time when Arab differences were reaching at their sharpest and I was not in a mood to work for any government. But I was most grateful to the Prime Minister and to my friends for their thoughtfulness. I asked for more time to think the matter over. I then consulted my brother Qassim and my friend Ambassador Zeineddine; both encouraged me to accept. Qassim had been the one to encourage me to work for my Doctor's degree.

I agreed to join the Jordanian Foreign Service. My first assignment was the United Nations. In less than a year, however, there was a change of government in Jordan. The Rifai government was replaced by Hazza Majali's government. Subsequently I was transferred to Amman.

I met the new Prime Minister and he was kind to me. He said that he had transferred me because he wanted to reinforce the Division of his Foreign Office concerned with international conferences. He added that he wanted me to attend every Arab international conference on Palestine. In less than two years in 1961 I was transferred back to New York to be the second man in the U.N. delegation. Ambassador Abdul Monem Rifai, a very able and experienced diplomat was its head.

9

One evening in 1961 after the General Assembly adjourned I went home for a dinner party there in honour of a visiting colleague from Jordan. Ten couples had accepted my invitation. Before going up to my apartment I passed by my private mail box in the building and found a thick letter awaiting me. It was from my brother Qassim who, as a rule, did not write long letters. This time it was very long and I wondered why. Should I read the letter or keep it until my party was over? The guests would arrive in a few minutes. I decided to read the letter.

It started with some unusual observations about my childhood. Its memories were most pleasant to me and I love them. Qassim mentioned my school and the night of the ambush when I took my horn and went with Uncle Tewfic into the fields. He mentioned the horses I loved. Then he spoke about my mother. Her special love for me, being the one son who never saw his father.

I started thinking again about the reason for all this history. Why now?

The letter continued saying more about my mother, explaining many little things I had almost forgotten. I started to worry about her. I didn't want her to die while I was far away across the ocean. I wanted to see more of her. When I reached the last two pages I felt that all the emphasis was on the last few days and what my mother was doing. Qassim was apparently coming to the end of his narrative. I reached the conclusion that my mother was no more. He was giving the news gradually so I would not have a shock. And by the time I reached the last line of the letter I realised that our dear mother had had a stroke and passed away. He added:

"I am writing this to you immediately after the funeral. Mother had a haemorrhage. After a few hours she had a stroke and died. She could not speak after she had this stroke. She kept looking at me and saying: 'MMMMMM'. I did not know what she meant. She pointed at the dress she was wearing which you had brought her from the United States of America. I then realised that she meant you. I said to her: 'you mean Muhammad?' She had a big smile on her face and answered with a nod saying 'yes'. I told her not to worry. 'I know it was your hope to see Muhammad married. He will get married this year. I promise you.' She had the same big smile on her face and looked happy. A few seconds later she died."

Before I had folded the letter, the door bell rang. I left the letter on my bed and rushed to open the door. My guests were arriving. I showed them all hospitality. Oriental music was playing all the time. I asked the ladies to choose any other records they liked. They were very happy, laughing and chattering at the top of their voices. They had a very good time and thought I was the happiest of hosts all that night. We had dinner which my cook Elizabeth had prepared. I had promised my guests and a few friends to take them to see the sights of Greenwich Village, so they could see what kind of place it was. We stayed there till late.

We came home at 2.00 a.m. All my guests left, except for my friend, the guest of honour, Hasan Ibrahim, later Foreign Minister, who was staying in my apartment that night. I said "good night" to him and we retired.

I saw the letter still lying on my bed. I could not control my emotions any more. The memory of my life with mother came back to me in one second. I cried and my guest heard me. He came rushing out. He could not understand what had happened. Then he saw the letter lying on my bed and read it. He was both sad and astonished. He could not understand how I had been able to control myself all that time. Six hours of acting, hiding my feelings to make my guests happy. How could I have done it, he asked.

I asked him to forget it and go to sleep. I stayed up by myself, lying on my bed. I was looking at the ceiling and reflecting on my childhood, youth and manhood. I saw her there all the time. I saw that great woman who had devoted her life for the sake of her children and for my sake in particular. I had never seen my father. I had lost my country and now I had lost the dearest person in the world — my mother.

All night long I reflected on my memories of mother. Now she was no more. I felt so lonely and so discouraged.

Not having attended her funeral I could not believe that my mother was dead. Why I was not asked to attend mother's funeral is another story. According to the Moslem religion the dead should be buried as soon as possible, usually within twenty-four hours. For me to come from the United States together with the formalities and processing to enter my own town would have taken a long time. And it had been my mother's wish to be buried quickly, because she was very religious.

The last time I had seen mother was in 1960. She was everything to me. My father had died when she was very young and beautiful. She never married again. She would look at me when I was a child and say "this will be my man. He is everything to me." She would then hug me and kiss me. I remembered her warmth and genuine love.

I was so attached to her and was with her all the time. While sitting to prepare something for the house I used to put my head on her knee. She would start singing so I could sleep. Her songs were always very sad. Many times her tears would drop on my cheek. They were hot. They would wake me up when they fell on my cheek. I never knew what made her tears drop. But I do remember she was singing something about life and her own destiny in particular. Many times she would hug, squeeze and kiss me.

When I came to the United States I wrote my mother many letters. Her answers were full of wisdom and encouragement. She was always telling me how to endure difficulties. In one of her letters she said that nothing was impossible. "Anything others can do you also can do."

Now it is my desire to visit my mother's grave in our family's cemetery. I want to walk in that cemetery and feel I am walking in mother's funeral. I want to sit by her grave and recite phrases from the Quran. I want to sit in that quietness of the grave for an hour or more. But even today, this is impossible. My homeland is occupied by Israeli forces, and even the cemetery is not quiet any more. I cannot cross to that part of the occupied territories. The Israelis are there.

Chapter 2

The Palestinian Case and the Israeli Problem

"Nothing can replace the need of the people to organise into a state in the territory in which they live and which belongs to them."

Jacobo Timerman, Jewish author
and Argentine newspaper editor
and columnist.

In this book, I am trying to relate some of my experiences in the United Nations concerning the Palestine Question. It is not an autobiography in the real sense. The book embodies the experiences of just one phase in my life, and reflects many years of the diaspora and unrest which the people of Palestine have endured.

I shall take the reader through the mountains and hills of Palestine; I will walk with him through the gates and streets of the Holy City; look at the areas in the Holy Land where Palestinian men, women and children have suffered much humiliation and deprivation of their elementary human rights; visit places of massacres and destruction such as Deir Yassin, Kufr Kasim, Khan-Yunis, Bedrus, Imwas, Yalu and Beit Nuba. I shall then take the reader to what I call "The theatre of Reality", the United Nations, where he will acquaint himself with the arm twisting and political expediency that has for so long played its role in making the Palestinians without hope.

The reader will walk with me on this long and difficult way.

besides familiarising himself with all those human problems, he will come to know some aspects of the Palestine problem. I feel I owe it to him, at this stage, therefore, to explain the background to that problem.

Having become a representative of a member state at the U.N. authorised to speak in any debate and before any organ of the organisation, I spent much time going to the roots of the Palestinian-Jewish conflict. I studied all phases of the problem very thoroughly. To me the historical background was very clear.

Since time immemorial, Palestinians have lived in the Holy Land with no distinction as to race or religion.

They lived happily in their homeland as might any other people. It is a mistake to think that the only connection that the Palestinian Arabs have with Palestine came about since the advent of Islam. They are mentioned in history under different names according to whichever tribe or personality was prevailing at the time. The inhabitants of Palestine, like those of neighbouring countries, were of Arab stock. Thus Palestine had been the homeland of the Palestinians before some Jews came to live in it. A few Jews — mainly religious — have always lived peaceably in Palestine, in harmony for centuries. Since the first Zionist Congress in 1897, however, Zionist leaders have completely ignored the rights of the Palestinians. Theodor Herzl took advantage of the financial problems facing the Ottoman Empire, of which Palestine was part, and began negotiations with the Sultan, Abdul Hamid, seeking the Sultan's approval for mass immigration of Jews into Palestine. The Sultan realised what Herzl was after. Despite his financial difficulties, however, Abdul Hamid perceived Herzl's objectives and rejected his offer, making the well-known statement: "I cannot give you what you want. You want the land. The land is not mine but my people's."

Herzl wanted a state anywhere and at any price and at one desperate point he considered a British offer of territory in Uganda. When World War I broke out Weizmann and other Zionist leaders wasted no time contacting Great Britain, saying that if and when the Allies won the war, the Jewish people would like a homeland in Palestine. Only 50,000 Jews were then living in Palestine. All the other inhabitants were Palestinian Arabs.

On 2nd November 1917 the British Government, ignoring the national rights of the Palestinians, unlike the Ottoman Sultan, issued the Balfour Declaration in which it supported the establishment of a Jewish national home. There was a special proviso attached to that promise which the Zionist leaders deliberately disregarded. It emphasised that nothing in the declaration should affect the civil and religious rights of the non-Jewish communitites in Palestine. This was a specific reference to Moslem and Christian Palestinians. The full text of the Balfour Declaration is as follows:

Foreign Office,
November 2nd, 1917

Dear Lord Rothschild,
I have much pleasure in conveying to you, on behalf of His Majesty's Government, the following declaration of sympathy with Jewish Zionist aspirations which has been submitted to, and approved by, the Cabinet.
"His Majesty's Government view with favour the establishment in Palestine of a national home for the Jewish people, and will use their best endeavours to facilitate the achievement of this object, it being clearly understood that nothing shall be done which may prejudice the civil and religious rights of existing non-Jewish communities in Palestine, or the rights and political status enjoyed by Jews in any other country."
I should be grateful if you would bring this declaration to the knowledge of the Zionist Federation.

Signed: Arthur J. Balfour[1]

The legal material I read on this promise was important. I found that judicial experts and leading lawyers from different parts of the world stated clearly that Balfour, an Englishman, owned nothing in Palestine which he could convey to the Jews. What is more, the Palestinians themselves were never consulted. The British Government made no effort to consider, let alone to satisfy, Palestinian national rights.

How on earth could a British Cabinet dispose of the legitimate rights of others without their consent? The British Government could, if it wanted, promise the leaders of Zionism a home or even a "state" in its own British Isles, but not in what was, after all, the "homeland" of the people of Palestine.

Regardless of the legality of the Balfour Declaration the question

---

1. *The Balfour Declaration*, Leonard Stein, Simon and Schuster, New York, 1961, p.ii.

arises; Did Britain intend to establish a Jewish State and thus bring about the displacement of Palestinians and confiscation of all their property?

The answer is "No". The proviso in the Balfour Declaration affirms the civil and religious rights of the Palestinians.

Needless to say, however, that the promise conflicts with the British Government's other promise made earlier to Sharif Hussain, the Sharif of Mecca, which promised the Arab peoples complete independence in all regions within the frontier requested by the Sharif of Mecca. Sir Arthur McMahon emphasized that no peace treaty would be concluded unless it embodied the freedom to all Arab peoples together with their complete independence from the authority of both Germans and Turks. Certainly the people of Palestine were among the peoples covered by McMahon promise, made on behalf of the government of Great Britain.[2]

America's President Woodrow Wilson, in an address on 4th July 1918, laid down the following as one of the four great objectives for which the Allies in World War I were fighting:

> "The Settlement of every question, whether of territory, of sovereignty, of economic arrangement or of political relationship, upon the basis of the free acceptance of that settlement by the people immediately concerned, and not upon the basis of the material interest or advantage of any other nation or people which may desire a different settlement for the sake of its own exterior influence or mastery."[3]

Of all the people in the world the Palestinians did not benefit from the rights embodied in the Wilson Declaration.

Even prior to the Wilson Declaration, and on 25th January 1916, McMahon said that "now that Arab countries have decided to enter with us the war (against Germany and Turkey), we hope that this will bring happiness and welfare to all." I often wonder how much happiness and welfare the people of Palestine are enjoying now.[4]

I also found that in a British Government White Paper of 1922

---

2. *Hussain-McMahon Correspondence*, Cmd. 5957, 1939, letter no.4 from McMahon to Hussain, dated 24th October 1915 and no.6, 14th December 1915.

3. See W. Wilson: "Four Factors of World Peace", in *Selected Addresses and Public Papers of Woodrow Wilson*, A.B. Hart Edition 1918, p. 266.

4. Ibid, letter no.8, 25th January 1916.

Winston Churchill, then Colonial Secretary, made it clear that, in accepting the Mandate for Palestine, confirmed by the League of Nations, Great Britain intended to establish a cultural home for Jews in Palestine. This was reaffirmed in the Report of the High Commissioner, Sir Herbert Samuel, an influential British Zionist.[5]

Samuel's view and true intention, however, was a very clear statement made three years before the Balfour declaration was issued. In a conversation in November 1914, Samuel stated the case of Zionism in the following terms:

> "If a Jewish State were established in Palestine, it might
> become the centre of a new culture. The Jewish Brain is rather
> a remarkable thing and under national auspices the State might
> become a fountain of enlightenment and a source of a great
> literature and art and development of science."[6]

Thus, not lack of desire on Samuel's part, but the fact that the majority of the inhabitants in Palestine were Arabs made him feel that immediate political privileges for the Jews in Palestine would be impossible, "partly because the Jews in Palestine were a small minority . . . and partly because any attempt at a Jewish State would at this moment fail with very great scandal to the whole of Jewry."[7]

The first High Commissioner to be appointed after the British occupied Palestine, Herbert Samuel, rendered many services to help bring about the creation of a Jewish State. The Zionists took advantage of the Balfour Declaration and with the help of Herbert Samuel, tens of thousands of Jewish immigrants started to arrive in Palestine. Through this immigration, arranged with the collusion of the British Government, the number of Jews steadily increased. Then, helped by successive British High Commissioners and with the steady increase in their number, they said openly: "We want a state in Palestine, as purely Jewish as England is English." Of course, the Palestinians resisted this, with all their limited means. It was difficult, however, for the Palestinians, a small people, to defeat both the British Empire and the World Zionist Movement. The aggression continued.

---

5. *Report of the High Commissioner on the Administration of Palestine, 1920-1925,* London, Colonial Office, 1925 p. 24

6. H. Samuel, *Memoirs,* London, Gresset Press, 1945, p. 140

7. *The Balfour Declaration,* Leonard Stein, New York, Simon and Schuster, 1961 p. 107

While studying the problem I found that in 1937, twenty years after the Balfour Declaration was issued, the Palestine Royal Commission after a thorough examination of the records bearing on the question, came to the conclusion that:

> "His Majesty's Government could not commit itself to the establishment of a Jewish State. It could only undertake to facilitate the growth of a Home. It would depend mainly on the zeal and enterprise of the Jews whether the Home would grow big enough to become a State."[8]

Certainly the Zionist leaders used their zeal and enterprise for the usurpation of Palestine. They organised campaigns of Political action, fund raising and propaganda which ignored all Palestinian rights, including the reservations embodied in the Balfour Declaration that:

> "Nothing shall be done which may prejudice the civil and religious rights of exisiting non-Jewish communities in Palestine or the rights and political status enjoyed by Jews in any other country."

The Arab peoples, of course, were among those who fought alongside the Allies in the First World War and were promised complete independence, only to be betrayed later on by those whom they aided.

Zionism, the expressed aim of making into Jewish territory the area from the Euphrates to the Nile, is a concept which has sustained Jews only for the past ninety years or so. It was formulated less from a deep-rooted desire to acquire this land than from the influence of the revolutionary climate of thought at work on Jewish communities in Eastern Europe then ruled by the Czar. It originated not out of a psychological need for land, for many of those who subscribed to the idea were settled members of their communities, but from intellectual forces at work on a few at the end of last century. For a long time there was no concrete backing for the idea. Those who believed in it sufficiently to make the long and arduous journey to "the Promised Land" were more often disillusioned and disappointed than delighted.

---

8. Palestine Royal Commission, Report, CMD No.5479 (1937) at 24

External circumstances — the advent of the Bolsheviks to power in Russia, the rise of Hitler and the Nazis in western Europe — had the effect of forcing into concrete shape what for fifty years had been a nebulous dream. The massive wave of immigrants into Palestine in the 1930s, whether legal or illegal, together with those who entered immediately after 1945, laid a viable, if questionable, foundation for the declaration of a state.

In 1947, the British Government, having committed many blunders, surrendered its mandate over Palestine to the United Nations. In a letter to the Secretary-General dated April 1947, the United Kingdom requested that the question be placed on the agenda of the next regular session of the General Assembly, at which time the United Kingdom would submit an account of its administration of the League of Nations mandate over Palestine. The United Kingdom also requested the convening of a special session which would appoint and instruct a special committee to make a study of the question preparatory to the convening of the regular session.

After a majority of the member states had approved the proposal to hold a special session, it met in New York between April 28 and May 15 1947. The only item on its agenda was the one proposed by the United Kingdom for constituting and instructing a special committee to make a preliminary study of the Palestine question. Egypt, Iraq, Lebanon, Saudi Arabia and Syria requested the inclusion of an additional item — the termination of the mandate over Palestine and the declaration of its independence, but this item was rejected by the Assembly; this special committee was constituted and recommended the partition of Palestine into two states, one Jewish and the other Arab. Lengthy debates followed in which many member states emphasised that the phrase "national home of the Jewish people" in the Balfour Declaration, whether intended to mean a "Jewish state" or a "homeland" conflicted with Arab national rights. Nevertheless the General Assembly by a vote of 33 in favour, 13 against and 10 abstentions[9] recommended the partition

---

9. *In favour : 33*
Australia, Belgium, Bolivia, Brazil, Byelorussian S.S.R., Canada, Costa Rica, Czechoslovakia, Denmark, Dominican Republic, Ecuador, France, Guatemala, Haiti, Iceland, Liberia, Luxembourg, Netherlands, New Zealand, Nicaragua, Norway, Panama, Paraguay, Peru, Philippines, Poland, Sweden, Ukrainian S.S.R., Union of South Africa, U.S.A., U.S.S.R., Uruguay, Venezuela.

CONTINUED

of Palestine into two states, one Jewish and the other Arab on 29th November 1947. The Jewish minority established its state through force and aggression in May 1948. The Palestinians, convinced that the United Nations recommendation was illegal and unjust, challenged its legality and asked that the matter be referred to the International Court of Justice for an advisory opinion. However, because of pressure from the United States, their request was defeated.

Why did the Palestinians want to go to the International Court of Justice? They maintained that the partition was illegal; that it violated the United Nations Charter and especially the right of self-determination embodied in that Charter, and that the ideal solution would be the creation of a secular state — a single Arab-Jewish state in Palestine. They wanted the Court to decide, therefore, whether it was legitimate to deprive a people of the right to self-determination.

Meanwhile, the Israelis started expanding through the use of force. They immediately occupied important parts of the area that had been allotted to the Palestinian Arab State. Their campaign to displace the Palestinian people continued. So also did the Palestinian resistance to foreign occupation.

Today, the whole of Palestine is under Israeli control, together with other Arab territories in Syria and Lebanon. The Palestinians are now victims of a new diaspora. They are either under Israeli military occupation or having been forcibly expelled by them, they are refugees in the four corners of the earth, dispossessed, dispersed, denied and deprived of their inalienable rights.

This, in short, is the background to the wars of the past thirty-eight years. The part played by the Palestinian people is no more than legitimate resistance to Israeli illegitimate occupation.

I shall discuss the Six-Day-War later. I simply want to mention it at this stage that on 21st October 1969, the Israeli Ambassador

---

CONTINUED

Against : 13
Afghanistan, Cuba, Egypt, Greece, India, Iran, Iraq, Lebanon, Pakistan, Saudi Arabia, Syria, Turkey, Yemen.

Abstained : 10
Argentina, Chile, China, Colombia, El Salvador, Ethiopia, Honduras, Mexico, United Kingdom, Yugoslavia.

See United Nations General Assembly Resolution No.181 dated 29th November 1947.

repeated in the United Nations General Assembly his favourite expression that we (Arabs) "started the 1967 War". He kept repeating the myth that all three wars, in 1948, in 1956 and in 1967, were started by the Arabs. In fact, exactly the reverse is true. The truth is that the Israelis chose the occasion of the run up to the American elections in 1947, 1955 and 1967 to start the wars and have since admitted this themselves.

The Israeli initiation of the 1967 war is now well known. Brigadier Mordecai Hod, the Commander of the Israeli Air Force, told the *Sunday Times* of London on 16th July 1967 about the plan for invading the Arab territories:

> "Sixteen years' planning has gone into those initial eighty minutes. We lived with the plan, we slept on the plan, we ate the plan. Constantly we perfected it."

This explains the crux of the Palestinian issue. It has a history of a chain of acts of injustice, committed against an innocent people who had no lobby in Washington and did not possess the means Israel had to make their voice heard. Trouble started even before the state of Israel was born.

2

One of the earliest massacres of the Palestinians took place at Deir Yassin even before the Israelis declared their state. In the book *O Jerusalem* French and American writers explain how the Jewish "commandos" of the Irgun and Stern gang prepared the assault against Deir Yassin, a suburb of Jerusalem, the Holy City.[10] They wanted to frighten the population of the village, and other neighbouring towns and villages, so they would flee from their homes and leave them for occupation by Israeli settlers.

Eye-witnesses explained how one of those "heroes"shot a bullet into the neck of a woman who was nine months pregnant. Then he cut her stomach open with a knife. Another was killed when she tried to extricate the unborn infant from the dead mother's womb. Other tragic scenes took place, in house after house. The writers say: "bit by bit Deir Yassin was submerged in a hell of screams, exploding grenades, the stench of blood, gun powder and smoke. Its

---

10. *O Jerusalem*, Larry Collins and Dominque Lapierre, Granada Publishing, 1981.

assailants killed, they looted, and finally they raped."

The Irgun and Stern gang leadership which included both Menachem Begin and Yitzhak Shamir, did not deny responsibility. The writers took their information from the report of Jacques de Reynier of the International Red Cross and three reports on the incident forwarded to the Chief Secretary of the Palestine British government by the Assistant Inspector General of the C.I.D. on 13th, 15th and 16th April 1948. To avoid any doubt the writers cited the number of the "Secret" dossier. A British interrogating officer visited a neighbouring village called Silwan, where there were two to three hundred refugees from Deir Yassin, and interviewed many of the women. He said "those women are very shy and reluctant to relate their experiences, especially in matters concerning sexual assault. They need great coaxing before they will divulge any information. The recording of statements is also hampered by the hysterical state of the women who often break down many times whilst the statement is being recorded."

The writers concluded: "There is, however, no doubt that many sexual atrocities were committed by the attacking Jews. Many young school girls were raped and later slaughtered. Old women were also molested. One story is current concerning a case in which a young girl was literally torn in two. Many infants were also butchered and killed. I also saw one old woman who gave her age as 104. She had been severely beaten about the head with rifle butts. Women had bracelets torn from their arms and rings from their fingers. Parts of some of the women's ears were severed in order to remove earrings."

This is documentary evidence, reported in a book which was a best-seller in America and elsewhere so let us go further and study what Mr Reynier, the Red Cross Representative who was on the spot, writes in his diary about what he saw:-

"The first thing I saw were people running everywhere, rushing in and out of houses, carrying Sten guns, rifles, pistols and long, ornate Arab knives. They seemed half-mad. I saw a beautiful girl carrying a dagger still covered with blood. I heard screams. 'We are still mopping up', my German friend [who intervened to let Reynier visit the village because he owed his life to the Red Cross] explained. All I could think of was the S.S. troops I had seen in Athens."

Then, to his horror, Reynier noted, he saw:

"a young woman stab an elderly man and woman cowering on the doorstep of their hut."

The two authors of *O Jerusalem* continued:

"Still dazed by that sight, Reynier pushed his way into the first house he reached." This is what he noted in his diary. "Everything had been ripped apart and torn upside down. There were bodies strewn about. They had done their 'cleaning up' with guns and knives, anyone could see that."

Mr Reynier saw something moving in the shadows. "Bending down, he discovered a little foot, still warm. It belonged to a ten year old girl, still alive despite her wounds. Reynier picked her up and ordered his German escort to carry her to an ambulance. He then furiously demanded he be allowed to continue his search for wounded. He found two more, an elderly woman half paralysed with fear hiding behind a woodpile, and a dying man. In all, he estimated he had seen two hundred corpses. One of them belonged, his diary would record "to a woman who must have been eight months pregnant," who had been hit in the stomach, with powder burns on her dress indicating she had been shot point blank."

Mr Reynier could not complete his findings because his presence embarrassed the Irgun and Stern leaders who ordered him to go back to Jerusalem. He returned, together with the wounded he had managed to save from the ruins. Many others were left to die for lack of treatment.

3

The same year another horrific event took place — the murder of Count Bernadotte, the Swedish U.N. Mediator whose presence in the area was made necessary by the outright Israeli hostilities. It was a well-calculated move to cultivate support for a 'Greater Israel'. The motives of the murders have not been disclosed in full.

In his book C. L. Sulzberger of the *New York Times* quoted the following from his diary of 24th July 1948, written in Tel Aviv, only seventy days after the de facto establishment of the Jewish state:

Tel Aviv, July 24th 1948.
"A most extraordinary thing happened today. I was typing in our room and Alexis (who is a very late sleeper) was still in bed with the sheet wrapped round his head to keep out the light. A knock at the door and a message was handed to me: a name I did not recognise. Downstairs were two handsome, tall young fellows in khaki shorts and light coloured shirts. They shook hands and suggested we go out for a coffee because they had something to say. It turned out they were South African Jews who had come here since the war and were not only ardent Zionists, but members of the Stern Gang. They told me not to bother remembering their names (including the one on

the message) because the names were phoney.

"They discussed the aims of the Sternists and, among other things, horrified me by warning that the organisation intended to assassinate Count Bernadotte and other advisers on the UN Mission just the way Sternists had murdered (my word, not theirs) Lord Moyne [in Cairo, Egypt] because it was necessary to frustrate the UN effort to confine Israel within artificially constricted borders. At first I couldn't believe them. When I was convinced I took them upstairs, awakened Alexis and, as I pulled him up by the hair, said; 'This is my brother-in-law. He works for the UN and I don't want him murdered by mistake; he is not important enough for any deliberate murdering. Remember this face.' Alexis looked bewildered. My visitors nodded amiably and departed. After they left I told Alexis what it was all about. We both inclined to dismiss this as just another one of the absurdities that are so commonplace here. Nevertheless, I suggested he tell the UN people and I intend to pass it on to Reuven Zaslani (later Shiloah), Ben Gurion's high muckamuck in secret service and dirty tricks, if I can get him on this trip."[11]

"Menachem Begin, head of the semi-secret extremist organisation, Irgun Zvai Leumi, refused to see me but sent me a written declaration which included the following points: Irgun claims for Israel all of former Palestine plus all of Trans-Jordan as 'Eretz Israel'. If 'Britain's desert puppet, Abdullah, is not removed, we shall be transformed into something resembling a ghetto, with its curtailed human rights and, in the course of time, even pushed into the sea.'

"Irgun will try and take control of the Government after permanent peace, but 'by ballots, not bullets.' There is 'no possibility of any treaty with England which is still the enemy of our people and country.'

"Irgun respects no territorial limitations imposed by Palestine's partition. 'We do not recognize nor consent to partition. We consider both to be illegal, and in no way binding on our people.' "[12]

Count Bernadotte was assassinated on 17th September 1948 by the Stern Gang. According to Sulzberger's Diary for 24th August 1948 Bernadotte had told a few people confidentially in Rhodes on 22nd

---

11. C. L. Sulzberger, *A Long Row of Candles — Memoirs and Diaries 1934-1954*, Macmillan, Ontario 1969, pp. 402-404 July 24 1948.

12. Ibid, p.402-403

July that he foresaw the following ultimate solution for Palestine:

"There will be a Jewish State, no matter what else happens. Its boundaries will have to be radically altered to provide a more compact and workable state. Its Arab neighbours must be given an ironclad UN guarantee against any move to expand."[13]

Sulzberger also reported that Trygve Lie, the then UN Secretary-General, had assured him that "the late Count Bernadotte had ascertained both British and American views on Palestine. 'In effect, Bernadotte based his report on their recommendations. He thought this was the only way to get practical results. Bernadotte was pro-Jewish by bias, according to Lie." [14] Yet Bernadotte was murdered by the Stern Gang ! And the Security Council reaction next day to this grave event was "a very silly meeting in which they passed a resolution that his funeral expenses would be paid."[15]

Harry S. Truman in his memoirs stated that Bernadotte proposed in September 1948 that there should be a different kind of partition.[16] He would give West Galilee in the north of Palestine to Israel but let the Negeb in the south to the Arabs. Truman said: "I did not like this change. It looked to me like a fast reshuffle that gave to the Arabs the Negeb area, which still remained to be fully settled. If, however, one looked only at the map and how the two partition proposals appeared there, the Bernadotte plan may have seemed an improvement; it seemed to reduce the number of friction points along a long frontier between the Jews and Arabs. In any case, Secretary Marshall informed the UN that it seemed to him that it was a fair and sound proposal."

In July 1974, Menachem Begin at last came to power in his own right, not as a member of a coalition. The man wanted by Britain for being a terrorist was received in London and Washington with all official courtesies and honour. He continued to work for expansion, openly calling the Palestinian territories on the West Bank and Gaza Strip part of *Eretz Israel*. He annexed the Syrian Golan Heights, claiming that they were needed to protect Israel's 'security'. He then

---

13.   Ibid, p.405

14.   Ibid, p.409-10

15.   Ibid, p.412; Security Council Resolution No. 57, dated 18th September 1948

16.   Harry S. Truman, The Memoirs of Harry S. Truman, *Years of Trial and Hope, 1946-1952*, Doubleday, Inc. New York, 1956, vol.ii, p.166.

prepared another war in Lebanon, sending in his armies in June 1982. Since the invasion, Israel has begun to lay the groundwork for permanent control over Southern Lebanon, under the pretext that its rivers, springs and fertile areas are necessary for her security. Leading Israeli politicians are openly calling Jordan part of the Israeli homeland.

Chapter 3

The Massacre of Kufr Kasim and the Shooting in Bedrus

"In days to come, no doubt, young Israelis in search of a picnic site will take the ancient road to Imwas and spread themselves under those trees and laugh and take their ease, but there will be ghosts among the branches, for here, if anywhere, stood their neighbour's landmark."

Michael Adams, British
author and contributor to
the London *Guardian*.

The 1948 war ended with four Armistice Agreements signed by the four Arab adjacent states to Israel. They were purely military, and not meant to embody any political settlement. Since signing those agreements many violations were committed by Israel, and many complaints were presented to the Mixed Armistice Commission, created by the Agreements to handle such complaints. In most cases the Commission, which was headed by a United Nations officer, condemned Israel. On each serious case, Jordan carried the findings of the Commission to the Security Council for action. It wanted the Council to take more effective steps against Israel so that such serious violations would not be repeated. The Security Council either endorsed the findings of the Commission or used stronger terms of condemnation.

The Security Council is authorised to impose sanctions by virtue of chapter VII of the U.N. Charter. Because of political considerations in the Security Council and the special relationship between Israel and the United States, which had a veto power, no such measures against Israel were used. The most Jordan could get from the Council was condemnation "in the strongest terms" and a warning to Israel that the Council may consider further measures as embodied in the Charter, if such violations were repeated. This lack of serious action encouraged Israel to defy the Council and ignore its obligations.

To acquaint myself with serious violations of the Armistice Agreement, I used to go to Jordan and see on the spot what happened; this was helpful in presenting other complaints to the Council. Seeing Israeli practices at first hand, not just learning about them through my Government's reports, was of great assistance to me in the Security Council. I used to go every single year to the Armistice demarcation line, cross the hills of Jerusalem, the valleys and mountains of Hebron and Nabius and visit the farmers and other inhabitants in order to get firsthand information. I was humbled every year when I visited those lovely places of the Holy Land, more so when I saw how the people were determined to preserve their identity and keep their land.

The chairman of the Jordanian delegation to the Mixed Armistice Commission, a high ranking officer in the Jordanian Army, prepared a jeep and accompanied me to every single village on the demarcation line from Samou', in the south, to Hemma, in the North. People would explain to me what happened during the year. This farmer would show me how a few of his olive trees had been annexed by force into lands controlled by Israeli farmers; another would show me how his crop which he spent all year cultivating was taken by the Israelis. Another farmer would show me how the area declared by the Armistice as "no man's land" was forcibly used by the Israelis as if it was theirs.

On 31st May 1967, exactly five days before what the Israelis called "The Six Day War" I found myself explaining to the Security Council my visit to the village of Bedrus on the West Bank of Jordan.[1]

When I arrived in Bedrus I visited a school of little children, adjacent to the Armistice demarcation line. Some of the children, young boys of nine and ten, had been hit by the bullets of Israeli

---

1. Israeli troops occupied Bedrus during that so called war. I do not much care to use the phrase "I told you so", but hope that concerned Israelis will read the record of the 1345th meeting of the Security Council dated 31st May 1967.

soldiers shooting at them across the line. While the children were playing in the school yard, Israeli soldiers took pot shots at them as if they were birds in a hunting game. I met some of those boys; and they showed me their wounds. Most of them refused to leave their classes to visit the playground, afraid of yet more Israeli bullets. Those children were the victims of fear and suffering and I believe the worst crime is to make innocent children suffer. I warned the Security Council then that those children would grow up with bitter recollections. I remember putting the question to the Israeli Ambassador: "Would it be surprising if many of those boys join the Resistance?"

Five days later the Israeli army invaded and occupied that remaining part of Palestine. Friends who visited the area told me that the school of those children simply ceased to exist. The Israelis destroyed it. The neighbouring villages of Imwas, Yalu and Beit Nuba were completely destroyed immediately after the 1967 occupation. Bulldozers erased those villages and no trace of those villages can now be found. Even their names were crossed off the Israeli map and the names exist today only in the Holy Bible.

The British journalist, Michael Adams, after visiting the sites of these villages, said in an article in the London *Guardian*:

"In days to come, no doubt, young Israelis in search of a picnic site will take the ancient road to Imwas and spread themselves under these trees and laugh and take their ease. But there will be ghosts among the branches, for here, if anywhere, stood their neighbour's landmark."

I reminded the Israeli Ambassador during the debate of these words in the Security Council and later in the General Assembly of the United Nations: "The Bible will be a permanent reminder not only to the Israelis but to the Christian conscience in the world at large. The Ambassador may want to know that most of the boys I met at Bedrus school, together with their parents and most of the inhabitants of those villages, are now, I am told, part of the Resistance."

2

The case of Bedrus village is not the only tragedy in the annals of Israeli practices against the Palestinians in the Holy Land. It reminded me of the massacre of Kufr Kasim which stands as another example.

In October 1956, hours before Israel started the Sinai aggression, just before sunset when the villagers were coming from their farms to their village, Israeli soldiers met them at the outskirts of the village and deliberately, in cold blood, murdered or seriously wounded every one of them. The whole world condemned this act. World pressure on Israel increased and the Israeli government had, therefore, to bring a few of the culprits to trial — a show of justice.

What are the facts as established by an Israeli District Court? In October 1956, Israel planned to invade Egypt. The twenty-ninth day of October was set for that purpose. On the eve of the invasion a battalion was ordered to defend the Israeli-Jordanian border. A unit of the Israeli Frontier Guard was attached to that battalion. Its commander, Major Melinki, was placed under the orders of Brigadier Shadmi, the Battalion Commander. That morning the Commander of the Central area, Major General Zvi Tsur, informed Shadmi and the other battalion commanders of the policy it had been decided to adopt towards the Arab population. Brigadier Shadmi asked that he be empowered to impose a night curfew on the Palestinian villages in the area under his command. His request was granted. He immediately summoned Major Melinki and gave instructions to impose the curfew from 5 p.m. to 6 a.m. in Kufr Kasim and other neighbouring villages. Shadmi emphasised to Melinki that the curfew must be extremely strict. Those who broke it must be shot. As he outlined:

> "In explanation 'a dead man' (or, according to other evidence 'a few dead men') are better than the complications of detention."
>
> Melinki asked: "How about people returning from the fields without knowing about the curfew?" Shadmi replied: "I don't want any sentimentality, that is just too bad for them." He was asked about the dead or the wounded and said: "Take no notice of them." According to other evidence he said: "There will not be any wounded."
>
> Another question was asked: "What about women and children?" Major Melinki replied: "They are to be treated like anybody else." Another question "What about people returning from their work?" Milinki replied: "It will be just too bad for them, as the Commander said."

The Arab Mukhtar of the village was informed of the curfew which was to come into force at 5 p.m., only half an hour earlier, i.e. at 4.30. He protested that it was humanly impossible to notify everybody within thirty minutes. He added that there were almost four hundred villagers working outside the village and that he could not inform them all of the curfew in time.

This did not help. A bitter fate awaited the farmers when they returned from their fields after a hard day's work. Within the first hour forty-seven Palestinians were killed. Many of them were boys and girls. Nine were women of all ages. All of them returned by the main road, on foot, on bicycles, in mule carts or on horses. They were lined up for the "crime" of breaking a curfew they did not know existed. The order to fire was given. Shots were fired at short range. The proportion of those killed was, therefore, very high. These facts, together with more details about the killing, the names, the numbers, are incorporated in the judgement of the Israeli Military Court.[2]

Judgement of the District Court 17, 190. The court found Major Melinki and Lt. Dahhan guilty of killing forty-three Palestinians. It sentenced the former to seventeen years imprisonment and the latter to fifteen years. Sergeant Ofer, who perpetrated most of the killings, was found guilty of killing forty-one Palestinians and sentenced to fifteen years imprisonment. Other soldiers were found guilty of killing twenty-two Palestinians, while still others were found guilty of killing seventeen Palestinians. Each was sentenced to seven years' imprisonment and deprived of rank.

The sentences of the Israeli District Court were, by any standards in any part of the world, lenient for premeditated murder. In spite of that, they were considered harsh by the Israeli Supreme Court and were later reduced. Melinki's sentence was reduced to fourteen years, Dahhan's to ten years, and Ofer's to nine years.

The Chief of Staff then used his authority and reduced Melinki's sentence to ten years, Dahhan's to eight years and the sentences of the other killers to four years each. There appeared to be competition amongst Israel's leaders. Everyone wanted to play his part in paying tribute to the "heroes" of Kufr Kasim by reducing their sentences. Finally, the Head of State took over and decided that "justice required" that he should reduce the sentences, too. He therefore reduced the sentences of Melinki and Dahhan to five years each.

Was that all? No, The Committee for the Release of Prisoners later ordered the remission of a third of the prison sentences of all those convicted. This meant that only three and a half years after

---

2. File No. M.D./57/3 – The Military Prosecutor Vs. Major Melinki.

the massacre all those who committed it were free, walking in the streets with pride and joy. And to add insult to injury, Dahhan, who killed forty-three Palestinians in one hour, was appointed as the officer responsible for Arab affairs in the Municipality of the Arab town of Ramleh, an act of extraordinary sensitivity.

While these acts of genocide were committed in Kufr Kasim in the east, other Israeli troops invaded the Gaza Strip in the south, occupied my town of Khan-Yunis, and killed every young man they could find. United Nations observers witnessed this killing, and the United Nations Secretary-General Dag Hammarskjöld intervened and sent special observers in an attempt to stop it.

When I raised this matter at the United Nations I attempted to make the Americans realise that, through their political support and tax-exempt donations and all kinds of accommodation to Israel, they were accomplices in Israeli aggression, encouraging their crimes and feeding their arrogance.

I wonder about Israeli cruelty. Why do they kill innocent civilians? Why do they kill in cold blood men and women coming home from their farms? Why do their soldiers shoot at farmers in their fields and children in their school? It is because they feel that only through the complete destruction of the people of Palestine can they have safety and security in the beloved Palestinian homeland.

3

But I wonder if they realise the full extent of the suffering they cause. One example will perhaps make my point. In time it begins in 1948; it came to my attention in 1965 when I was at the Jordanian Embassy in Cairo and its end, as known to me for perhaps it still continues, comes in 1967.

As I opened the window of my office one day in 1965 I saw a car draw up outside. Hurriedly, an old man clothed in a long Arab dress with his head covered by a kuffiyah stepped out. I saw him rushing towards my office. Depsite the heavy burden of age he ascended the winding stairs of the building with astonishing agility. He entered the office and emotional threw himself at my feet. I found he was crying, with tears falling on his long thick silver beard. I felt perplexed and overwhelmed by this dignified man with tears flowing from his eyes. His look was that of a distracted heart-broken human being, lost in a world full of cruelty and pain. I began by calming him.

He started telling me a tragic story. In the next hour I heard a tale which filled me with diverse emotion: sometimes calm, sometimes rebellious. His name, he told me, was Abu Falah. He said: "My tale opens at the moment Palestine was lost on 15th of May 1948. The area around my village, El-Sheikh Muannis, was occupied. Words reached us of savagery, assaults on women, and the murder of children. We panicked. Our tribe started to move out. Evacuating the women and the children was our first duty.

"It was fated that my pregnant wife should at that moment give birth to a girl, Alia, My wife died a few hours later. I was lost in a whirlpool of tragedies. My wife must be quickly buried in her birthplace. The child in the cradle was in immediate need of nursing. There were also other children awaiting departure. And there I was standing in despair, not knowing where to start and how to find a solution. What to do? Where to go? My mind was going round in a vicious circle.

"My neighbour, an Egyptian Haj Husein, who used to come annually during the orange season and live on my land free, while in search of a livelihood, came and said: 'Do not worry. Attend to the burial of your wife and give the child to me. My wife will care for her and consider her as her own child, for she is mother to another nursing infant.'

"He then repeated: 'do not despair. Do not be sad. God is bountiful. Your kindnesses toward me have been many. I assure you that Alia will receive the best of care and supervision. Whatsoever God wills for us will be for her, too. Now go. God be with you.'

"I kissed Alia who was wrapped in a half-metre of black cloth, and gave her to him.

"A few hours later, pressure had increased. Word of murder, torture, and terrorism found its way to us. We escaped and scattered. Later saw me in the refugee camp in Nablus. No more than three days had passed since my wife's death, but I knew absolutely nothing of where my daughter Alia had ended up.

"For years I lived the life of the tents, of humiliation and of need. I awaited news of Alia, my daughter. Where was she? How was she? I would wake up at night and talk of my woe to the stars scattered in the skies. I would ask in the night's darkness: Where are you, Alia? and how are you Alia?' And I would talk to myself in the darkness of many things. I would end up by saying that one place could reunite me, my village of Sheikh Muannis. There we had parted and there we would sometime meet again.

"Our stay away from our homeland was prolonged, our return delayed. My daughter Alia was growing up in a world I knew not. I was lost not knowing where to turn. I knew, of course, that she was with the Egyptian family somewhere in the Sinai desert. I therefore spread word among all those leaving for the Gaza area, adjacent to Sinai, to enquire about my daughter.

"Finally, after fifteen years, a refugee came to inform me that my daughter Alia was in Egypt living in a farm called Axe in Mansoura. He told me that he had met her adopted father in one of the cotton fields. He had seen her there collecting cotton with some other refugees who had come to earn their bread, just as Haj Husein, the Egyptian step-father, used to do in the orange groves of my own beautiful country. I found myself jumping to my feet joyfully embracing this herald of good tidings.

"I collected my clothes and took a little money from my son, then a soldier on the battlefield, and prepared to leave for Egypt. Suddenly, however, I found myself in a dilemma. The relations between two countries in one Arab homeland did not allow travel. The journey must be postponed. I then considered authorizing someone to bring the girl to me. I thought that it was that easy.

"I sent a proxy to a relative of mine. After receiving permission to cross the borders and to overcome impediments, he made use of the police, and my daughter was brought to him under police protection. It disturbed her that her first contact with her father should be through police and security forces. She pictured her father as a merciless, cruel man who knew no affection. Immediately upon her arrival at the police station she declared that she had no other father but her adopted one, and that she wanted no substitute for him. Being mature now, Alia was given freedom of choice. The police escorted her back to the farm in Mansoura.

"The news of her rejection of her true father reached me and my unhappiness increased. Sorrows, memories, and despair again shared my life. Again I started living in an atmosphere of pain, amidst the fears and regrets of the past. I would look up at the sky's justice and say: 'my wife lost her life, my daughter Alia has denounced me and decided not to return". Thus the cruelty of fate had it appeared snatched my land, wife, daughter and all I owned in the world from me.

"I realized that the only chance left was to try again, but this time by myself. Perhaps God would will success for me. But this trial needed travel, and travel was tied up by the change in relationship between two Arab countries in the one homeland.

"The days passed and the impact of my disaster increased. I would wake up each morning to listen to the news broadcast from Cairo and Amman. I would walk around the camp. Whenever I found a refugee reading a newspaper I would stop and beg him in the name of God and His greatness to read me what news there was of the relations between the country I was staying in and the country my daughter Alia was in.

"Two whole years passed and at long last the first rays of hope began to appear. Things eased between the two Arab countries. I came to Cairo and here I am before you. This is my story. Here is my daughter's address. I plead with you, help me for I cannot sojourn here too long. I only have limited funds and do not want to be a burden to anyone. God has deprived me of everything but my pride. You would not want to deny me this and let me lose my self-respect at this advanced age, I beg you."

This is a literal translation of what the old man, Abu Falah told me. His story pained me.

When the next morning started drawing its first breath, I was with this virtuous man driving quickly to Mansoura. In my pocket I was carrying a letter from the Egyptian Ministry of Interior to the authorities in Mansoura to facilitate my mission.

The authorities sent for Alia. They were careful to be especially nice to her.

Hours passed. We kept waiting. Everytime a girl came by, Abu Falah, Alia's father, would jump to greet her, then say, "this cannot be my daughter!". Later Alia arrived and immediately her father recognized her. How, I did not know.

Maybe it was the "call of blood" as we Arabs say. She did not recognize him. Her father broke down crying when he saw her. She rejected him and refused the relationship. She declared that she did not know or want him — he had on the previous occasion sent police with rifles to fetch her, she had on that occasion spent several hours among women of bad reputation.

The old man's tears increased. It distressed him that Alia knew nothing of his own story.

Alia said: "If you are in truth my father, why did you not seek me previously? Why did you remain silent for seventeen years before remembering me? Was it because I am now grown up and can be of help to you that you now came? No, I do not want you."

Slowly the local Mansoura police officer, a kind and experienced man, familiar with the peasant's mentality, began explaining to Alia what had happened — the suffering her father had gone through, the long tiresome days, the restlessness, his sleepless nights and his agony. I, too, started telling her of the disaster, of the circumstances and of her share in it all. I reassured her that she would not be taken by force or be abducted as she imagined. I told her that I would protect her against any violence — the police would not interfere save for her own good. Her father and I would not take her except following her full consent and positive willingness, and only after a written guarantee and commitment to secure her safety had been obtained. This calmed the girl tremendously.

Then came Haj Husein, the Egyptian 'step father'. He was no longer able to walk without the help of a long stick cut from a branch of an olive tree. He wore a white gallabiyya, his head covered with a woollen cap wrapped in a scarf made of smooth, translucent cotton. He had a long mustache and a short beard. The years had disabled and weakened him; the needs and requirements of life had broken him! His eyesight had become weak. He could see but little. He whispered in my ear that he was Alia's adopted father. I thanked him for all what he did for Alia. He smiled and said:

"Alia is now everything to us. It is she that cares for me, an old and disabled man. She also cares for my wife who nursed her and brought her up. She is the organiser of our life and the one that waits on our comfort. You can see what pain her departure would cause us after she has grown up and matured among us, after we have learned to depend only upon God and her. But despite all this, she is, after all, the trust left in our hands, after the Zionists had displaced her father, the Palestinian Abu Falah. Today she is as my own flesh, blood and honour. She is a trust for whose protection I would give my life. I would not give her up for anything. Every year I, myself an old and disabled man, would journey to Cairo to renew her permit of residence, for she is a Palestinian. I would save piasters all year round to cover the expenses of the journey and for payment of the fees. I would go through these difficulties, and I am such an old man as you see before you, for no other reason but to protect her real name and nationality for I expected a day such as this one. Her father, Abu Falah, is a kind man; he was generous to me in Palestine in the old days and treated me well. What is the reward for kindness but kindness? I am happy and joyous for seeing him but nonetheless I am sad and I feel the whole world with its horizons is closing in on me because Alia's departure is now obvious. My one request however is that you should not take the girl against her will. Let her father live with us for two or three weeks. His daughter will see him daily and will grow accustomed to him. He could give her clothing for the Bairam feast, and fatherly presents. Then he should leave and start corresponding with her. She will get used to him and her fear will soften. I guarantee success and God be with you."

I was impressed with this wise Egyptian. He was rather slow of speech, but had the wisdom of the old. Abu Falah lived with his daughter for a few days, then returned to his own camp, leaving the girl behind. I would take the girl's cousin to the farm in Mansoura once in a while till Alia realised the truth of her situation and stopped asking difficult questions. Strangely enough, this girl, though illiterate, was worrying all the time that she, her absent father and the whole refugee camp he lived in would be thrown in the arms of Israeli occupation. She was the victim of fear all the time. Later, she started asking about her real father. She began to miss him. Finally, she asked that Abu Falah should come back to take her to the camps of the 'returning'.

Many other developments added to the complications and I need not mention them here — problems of identity, passport, visa, departure etc., but suffice to say that Abu Falah came and took his daughter back to the Palestinian camp. Haj Husein refused to accept any money for the maintenance of Alia all this time. His only request was that Alia should come and visit them every year during the Bairam. The father promised Haj Husein that Alia would come to him during the feast each year. I also assured Haj Husein that I would see to it that the promise would be fulfilled.

The day that Alia departed was a kind of feast for the little village of Mansoura with mixed feelings to its people. All rose crying together, then singing, and then laughing at one another. With sunlight beating down on them, their sad sweet and pure voices cried: "Good-bye Alia, God be with you, Alia, go with peace, Alia, remember us, Alia!" The mayor and the Chief of the Ghafar (the village police), came out, expressing words of congratulation and phrases of joy, mingled with the sadness of parting. Everyone was calling out good-bye to their beloved Alia; the whole farm and the hearts of the good hearted Egyptians were celebrating Alia's rejoicing.

The tale did not end at this point. The same year, late 1965, I was transferred to New York as Ambassador and Permanent Representative of Jordan to the United Nations. I was still there when, on the occasion of the first Bairam after Alia had left the house of Haj Husein, I received a letter from the disabled adopted father, Haj. It requested me to fulfil my promise "pledge is a responsibility" the letter said. His step-daughter had not come to Mansoura from her camp as he had been expecting.

The poor man did not know that on 5th June 1967 Israeli forces occupied the remaining parts of Palestine, thus making travel to Cairo difficult if not impossible. What that simple, illiterate, innocent, girl predicted had come true. Haj Husein did not know that Alia's residence and the whole area was cut off from other parts of the Arab homeland; that Alia now lived behind barbed wire, that Israel had committed another act of aggression and occupied more Palestinian land and displaced more people.

Haj Husein said in his letter that he wanted to see Alia again before he died. He wanted me to fulfil my pledge, reciting from the Quran: "a pledge is a responsibility that has to be met."

I could not answer his request because the Israelis had the answer. Haj Husein died two years later. He never saw his step-daughter and I never told him why she did not show up. I wanted to explain this to him in person when I visited him. But when I went to him he was dead.

What happened to Alia? I do not know. Hers remains a typical and poignant true story of a Palestinian child of her day, one of many hundreds.

Yet it seems that the effects of their actions leave the Israelis untouched and by some compulsion they are driven to continue with the policies of their leaders who cannot, or will not, curb their cupidity even though it must be clear that they cannot take from the Palestinians their determination to survive.

4

To quote Jacobo Timerman, an Argentianian-born Israeli writer:

> "Nothing can replace the need of a people to organize into a state in the territory in which they live and which belongs to them. The alternative our government offers, no matter how it masks it, is to continue repressing the Palestinian people until we destroy their will to live and liquidate their national identity. It's incredible that such a policy is being considered by the very people who demonstrated that this is impossible, that it is immoral, that it is criminal."[3]

One wonders if the Israelis want to treat the Palestinians in the same way that the Americans treated the Red Indians, by virtually eliminating them. But there are four million Palestinians. I don't know whether the Israelis who committed those crimes realise that the children of their victims in Bedrus, Kufr Kasim, Khan-Yunis

---

3. *The Longest War, Israel in Lebanon,* Jacobo Timerman, Vintage Books, New York, 1982, p. 77

and Deir Yassin are today grown up. As I predicted in that Security Council debate, many of these children have joined the Palestinian resistance in South Lebanon.

They were united in their suffering, conviction and determination to crush Israeli might, to put an end to Israeli arrogance and liberate their homeland from Zionism so that the Holy Land might become a land of peace for Jew and Gentile alike. They realised that Zionist occupation was a new kind of colonialism. They were young and fresh. Some had only High School education. Others left their refugee camps, obtained their university degrees and came back to fight for their homeland with better technique and expertise.

I hate to see such people die. I hate to see other people die in senseless war.

Many young Palestinian fighters have never known a proper home or shelter. They have been born in either a hut or a tent, living on seven cents a day offered by the United Nations, while the Israelis enjoyed their homes and farms, picking the fruits of trees they never planted in lands they never owned. These young men open their eyes every morning and look across electric barbed wire to see the Israelis trespassing on their land, dwelling in their houses and making a mockery of United Nations resolutions. A fence separates them, the owners, from the Israelis the trespassers. If any Palestinian crosses that fence to pick fruits of which he is the legitimate owner he finds a Zionist bullet waiting for him. Who, I wonder, is the thief and who is the victim?

Chapter 4

The 1967 War and the Refugee Problem

"Sixteen years planning has gone into those initial eighty minutes. We lived with the plan, we slept on the plan, we ate the plan. Constantly we perfected it."

Brigadier Mordecai Hod
(Commander of the Israeli Air
Force 1967)

On 5th June 1967 Israel, in surprise attacks, destroyed the Egyptian Air Force as well as those of Jordan and Syria. The basic facts of this crisis were the same as those of the 1956 attack — the invasion, the occupation, the designs, the tactics and the planning.

Both invasions were intended to bring about further expansion. There was very little difference between this attack and that of 1956 in this respect except for the occupation of Jordanian and Syrian territories in addition to Sinai and the Gaza Strip which had also been occupied in 1956.

During this so-called Six Day War action by the U.N. Security Council was very slow but the meetings were continuous. The curtains were closed and the lights inside the Chamber burned constantly. Most of the time we in the Security Council did not know whether it was night or day. Far away war was raging and minute by minute the situation was deteriorating.

As in the 1948 war, when I had been a student living in Boston, I was again cut off from my family back in occupied Palestine. I did not know what had happened to them.

U Thant, Secretary-General of the United Nations, volunteered to ask General Rijke of the United Nations Emergency Force to visit my home in Khan-Yunis and report about my immediate family. He did. The following morning Dr Ralph Bunche, then the U.N. Under-Secretary for Political Affairs said to me: "U Thant has good news for you." He said nothing more. I kept wondering whether the good news had anything to do with the war itself now going on or concerned my family. A few minutes later U Thant took me aside in the Security Council Chamber and handed me a cable he had received from General Rijke. I thanked U Thant for his thoughtfulness. He was as happy as I was about the cable, which indicated that my immediate family were safe.

The following day reports arrived that some relatives had, however, beeen killed in cold blood. U.N. colleagues and friends offered their condolences. More reports started coming about Israeli occupation of the West Bank, where Israeli atrocities were numerous and Jordanian casualties high. Later reports spoke about the retreat of the Jordanian army.

I studied all the news and came in the afternoon to attend the Security Council meeting, greeting my friends and colleagues with a smile. I shook hands and chatted with this delegate and that, with high faith and spirits. On my way to my seat in the Security Council I saw Lord Caradon, the British representative, sitting waiting for the Council to convene. I chatted with him for a minute. He saw my smile and could not resist saying: "You amaze me. This morning you received reports about members of your family being killed in the war. Later you got reports that a substantial part of your country is now under Israeli occupation. Despite this gloomy picture I was watching you earlier, smiling to your colleagues. Here you are, still smiling. How can you do it?"

I replied: "Let me remind you of something in the history of your ancestors in the United States. One day, after bitter fighting with Red Indians, both parties called a cease-fire in order to collect their dead. A team of doctors and soldiers arrived to do the job. While separating the Indians from the Americans, a doctor heard a sound coming from one of the soldiers he had supposed to be dead. He rushed over to find him still alive, with an arrow stuck deep in his chest. The doctor started pulling it out. While doing this, he asked the soldier: 'Does it hurt?' The soldier answered: 'Only when I smile, Sir.'" I added: "And I am still smiling." My colleague got the message. The Security Council took no immediate action on the war, and I kept smiling!

2

Time passed as I waited for the Security Council to take action to halt this savage war. Despite the gravity and the nature of the Israeli attack however, nothing happened. We wanted a decision calling for a cease-fire and immediate withdrawal. The U.S. showed no wish to support this. Why, we wondered? There was no hostile reaction at all in the United States to the Israeli aggression and we knew that without genuine U.S. support no action would ever be taken by the Council.

In one of my speeches before the Security Council I made a comparison between world action in the United Nations vis-à-vis the 1956 Israeli invasion and the present one. There was no difference between the two invasions, but a marked difference in the behaviour of some of the Big Powers. For example, international law, which was upheld in 1956, was trampled on in 1967.

In the Sinai invasion of 1956 firm and strict adherence to the rule of the U.N. Charter was championed by the overwhelming majority of members of the United Nations, with the United States playing a leading role. In the words of President Eisenhower, "As I review the march of world events in recent years I am ever more deeply convinced that the processes of the United Nations represent the soundest hope for peace in the world."[1]

Neither Zionist pressure, in an election year, nor any other consideration, was able to prevail in substituting political expedience for accepted norms of international law.

The 1956 Sinai campaign had been preceded by Israeli attacks on Gaza in February 1955, which led to a United Nations resolution calling once more upon Israel to take all necessary measures to prevent the recurrence of such actions.[2]

The 1967 Israeli invasion of the three Arab territories was preceded by many acts of Israeli provocation culminating in the invasion of Samou' in the West Bank of Jordan in November 1966, which led to a United Nations resolution of condemnation censuring Israel for "this large scale military action."[3]

In both 1956 and 1967, Israel tried to retain control of the newly occupied areas. In 1956 the attempt failed. The outcome of the 1967

---

1. See Public Papers of the President of the United States: Dwight D. Eisenhower; 1956-1965 at 1065.

2. See Security Council Resolution No: 106/1955, dated 29th March 1955.

3. See Security Council Resolution No: 228/1966, dated 25th November 1966.

attempt is still, after the passing of over eighteen years, pending before the Security Council. One wonders whether it would be in the interest of the United States to be part of such an attempt, or to lend its support to it; I say this because the United States is not just one of those members of the United Nations. It is a Super Power which feeds Israeli arrogance and, through the provision of the most sophisticated weapons, protects Israeli conquests.

3

This 1967 Israeli invasion and occupation brought in its wake another refugee problem. I have already mentioned the treatment of the inhabitants of Palestine by the Israeli authorities. I did not mention the plight of the Palestinians displaced since 1948. I did not do so because the refugee problem should be well known to world public opinion. For more than thirty-seven years this problem has been debated every year in the United Nations. A call for their repatriation to their homes in Palestine is made by the United Nations General Assembly annually, but is rejected by Israel.

Israel refuses to repatriate these refugees, while inviting millions of Jews to come from Russia and other places to settle in Palestine. As a result over two million Palestinians are still living in huts or tents, a prey to hunger and misery. Another two million Palestinians are living in various parts of the world. Now we must remember also the new wave of Palestinian refugees Israel expelled as a result of the 1967 war.

During 1967 Israel resorted to the same tactics they had employed in 1948 at Deir Yassin. The Zionist leaders wanted the remaining Palestinians in the West Bank and the Gaza Strip to evacuate their homes and lands. They almost succeeded, through intimidation and pressuring the people to flee.

While attending the Security Council debate on the 1967 war I received reports on this from my Foreign Minister. I could see Deir Yassin, the tragedy of 1948, being repeated. With that in mind I interrupted the deliberations of the Council on the war itself and asked it to consider, as an urgent matter, the serious new development which, if permitted to continue, would create another huge humanitarian problem.

I said, in part:

"In today's press it was clearly stated that Israeli military authorities had started to evict the native Arab population from the occupied part of Jordan, west of the River Jordan.

Over 13,000 persons — men, women and children — are
reported to have already moved to an area on the other side of
the Jordan River, controlled by Jordanian troops. They are all
in a terrible state, hungry, emaciated, downcast. The women
carry children in their arms while their menfolk carry baskets
and bundles with the few possessions which they have been
able to take with them."

I reminded the Security Council that the tactics used in the Holy
Land in 1967 and 1948 were those of the Nazis in Germany. I went
on:-

"Then, in March, April and May 1948, they started massacres
such as that of Deir Yassin and others . . . Unless the Security
Council takes an immediate measure now on this humanitarian
aspect of the problem . . . Unless we treat this problem right
now with the utmost urgency and adopt a measure which would
prevent further atrocities, further exodus, we will be facing
more problems in the very near future. Is it too much to ask
this Security Council right now to adopt an effective measure
to cope with this humanitarian problem?"[4]

My statement was very short. Time was of the essence and I was
more concerned to achieve some action by the Council. Every
minute that passed was important.

Lord Caradon asked for the floor. He told his fellow delegates:

"When we speak in the Council we speak for our Government,
and it is right that we should do so. Therefore, Mr President, I
would ask for your special indulgence for a minute or two this
morning to permit me to say a personal word. I feel
constrained to do so after listening to the speech just made by
the representative of Jordan."
"I myself many years ago had the privilege of living and
working amongst the people of Nablus, Jenin and Tulkam
before I had the privilege of spending some years in the
country of my friend Ambassador El-Farra. I feel with him, as
I believe we must all feel, great concern today for the people of
those beautiful villages . . . Many of them have suffered before
through no fault of their own. As I said the other day, it is very

---

4. Security Council Meeting no. 1355, 10th June 1967.

often the most innocent who suffer most and suffer worst. We gratefully hope — and I am sure we all join in hoping — that these fine people will not suffer again . . . I would be rash enough to go further in this respect and say that if the voices here can be heard so far away, I would greatly hope that the people of the hills of Samaria would stay where they are. I believe that they would suffer much more if they left.

"I apologise for having intervened on a particular subject, but it is a subject which none of us can disregard, and I believe that whatever we may do in our other tasks and however we fulfil them, it would be well to turn our mind to this humanitarian task at once."[5]

Others spoke on the serious nature of this development. Many people remembered the tragedy of 1948. After spending twenty-four hours scattered under the olive trees of Jenin, Tulkarm, Nablus, Ramallah and other towns and villages of Palestine, they decided to go back. When I visited Amman a few months later I met the Mukhtars of Yalu and Beit Nuba. They said to me that they had heard the Security Council debate and most of those who had not already crossed the Jordan River decided to go back home. So did the people of other parts of the West Bank. These two Mukhtars and their villages, however, could not return because they were pushed out of the West Bank by military forces. I have already explained how Bulldozers came and razed their villages to the ground.

These people, together with the refugees of 1948 whom Israel expelled for the second time from their camps on the West Bank during the 1967 war, now live in Jordan. It was their children, and others, Lebanese and Palestinian, who later challenged the Israeli invasion of Lebanon and who still resist Israeli presence in south Lebanon.

The Israeli Ambassador to the U.N. had attempted, like many of his predecessors before him, to convince the world that the Palestinian refugees had left their homes voluntarily. What he failed to do, however, was to explain why anyone would voluntarily become a stateless refugee.

During the Second World War, hundreds of thousands of Europeans left their homes because of the War and acts of genocide. But Frenchmen, Dutchmen, Belgians and Norwegians

---

5. Ibid.

were allowed to go back when the War was over. Why should the Palestinians be the exception to this rule? Do the Israelis not believe that the elementary requirements of peace dictate that they permit "re-patriation, or compensation" to those who choose not to go back?

Such are, in fact, the precise words of the U.N. General Assembly resolution No.194 on this question which is reiterated annually. Paragraph 1 resolves

> "That the refugees wishing to return to their homes and live at peace with their neighbours should be permitted to do so at the earliest practicable date, and that compensation should be paid for the property of those choosing not to return and for loss of or damage to property which, under principles of international law or in equity, should be made good by the Governments or authorities responsible.[6]

The Jewish scholar, William Zukerman, commented in the *Newsletter* of September 1950:

"The fact that the Arab refugees fled in panic because of real or imaginary danger is no excuse for depriving them of their homes, fields and livelihood. No people is exempt from panic in war time; least of all the Jews. In their long wanderings, Jews have often fled from real and imaginary threats of pogroms and wars. To deprive the Arabs of their homes and property because they, like most humans, sought safety for themselves and their children, is a grave act of injustice."

Because of the urgency of the matter, the Security Council took a decision asking the Israelis to permit those who fled as a result of the 1967 war to return home. The Israeli answer was to disregard the Council's resolution completely. The United Nations, in fact, got the same answer it had received from Israel every year since it was admitted to the main body in 1949 when the General Assembly called on the Israeli authorities to repatriate the Palestinians who chose to go home.

On 14th June 1967 the Security Council passed the resolution, calling on the Government of Israel to ensure the safety, welfare and security of the inhabitants of the areas where military operations have taken place and to facilitate the return of those inhabitants who have fled the areas since the outbreak of hostilities.[7]

---

6. General Assembly Resolution No. 194, dated 11th December 1948.
7. Security Council Resolution No.237, dated 14th June 1967.

Three days earlier, on 11th June 1967, General Moshe Dayan said on the American weekly TV programme "Face the Nation", in reference to the Arabs of Palestine:

"We can absorb them but then it [Israel] won't be the same country."

When asked "And is it necessary in your opinion to maintain this as a Jewish State?" he replied: "Absolutely, absolutely, we want a Jewish state like the French want a French state."

This is the heart of Zionist philosophy. Israeli leaders do not seem to want gentiles in Israel. They want it to be Jewish — purely Jewish, with no room for gentiles. That is why the refugee problem continues and why the Arab-Israeli conflict goes on, the root cause of instability in the Middle East.

Chapter 5

The U.S. *Liberty* and the Strategic Co-operation Agreement

"Unless the United States wished the Russians and Arabs to learn of joint C.I.A.-Mossad covert operations in the Middle East and of Angleton's discussion before the 1967 fighting started, the questions of the lost American Ship and how the war originated should be dropped."

Israeli Defence Minister Dayan

My experience with American Ambassadors at the United Nations deliberations in the Security Council in 1967 and 1968 left me in no doubt that the U.S. was a strategic partner of Israel. It was clear to me that the constructive policy of President Eisenhower had been changed completely by succeeding presidents. The U.S. was now deeply and heavily involved.

This awareness — call it conviction — helped me in my dealings with the U.S. representatives on the Security Council.

The case of the U.S. ship *Liberty* has now confirmed much of what I suspected, and it is now also clear why the murderous Israeli attack on the *Liberty* was not given adequate consideration in either the United Nations or the United States Congress.

In the introduction to his book on the *Liberty*, Anthony Pearson explained clearly what occurred, obtaining his information on the attack from members of the U.S. Navy, many of them survivors of the *Liberty's* crew.[1] He also interviewed senior officers in the Pentagon, friends and interested parties in the C.I.A., together with important former members of the Johnson administration. He described *Liberty* in the following terms:

"When the Arab-Israeli war began the listening devices on *Liberty* had been tuned to transmissions from both sides. With radar monitoring it had been possible to carefully map the movements and positions of troops, armour and aircraft showing the true progress of battle. This information was being transmitted in full to the NSA at Fort Meade and selected parts were being passed to the U.N. Security Council in New York,"[2] namely to the U.S. side in the Security Council.

Thus, at the outbreak of the 1967 war Ambassador Arthur Goldberg, U.S. representative on the Security Council, was among the first American officials to know about the "progress of troops".

This explains why he was instrumental in delaying any action by the Security Council. The records of the Council's fifth of June meeting reflect the unusual practice adopted by Ambassador Tabor of Denmark who was our misfortune its president for that month. The President convened the meeting in New York on Monday 5th June 1967 at 9.30 a.m. He stated that he had received two complaints, from the Israeli and the U.A.R. (Egypt) representatives. He claimed that the Israeli representative had informed him officially at 3.10 a.m. that the Egyptian land and air forces had moved against Israel and the Israeli forces were engaged in repelling the Egyptians. He had requested an urgent meeting of the Security Council. The President said further that the Egyptian representative had informed him twenty minutes later, i.e. at 3.30 a.m., that Israel had committed a "treacherous premeditated aggression against the Gaza Strip, Sinai and airports in Cairo, in the Suez canal and several other airports within the U.A.R."

After hearing the statement of the Secretary General on the question followed by that of the Representative of India who condemned Israeli attacks against Indian soldiers in the UNEF, the President suggested: "that the best course . . . could be for the

1. Anthony Pearson, *Conspiracy of Silence,* Quartet Books, London, Melbourne, New York, 1978.
2. (Ibid, p.30)

Council to hear the two parties and then to have a short recess for urgent consultation among the members as to the course of action to be taken by the Council in this emergency situation. If there is no objection," he said, "I shall take it that the Council agrees to follow this procedure." Then he rather hastily declared: "It is so decided."

Unfortunately, no Arab State was represented on the Council that year and this being a procedural matter and since the President emphasised that it would be "a short recess" and "for urgent consultation", no Arab representative asked any of his friends on the Council to object to the President's move. The two speakers were heard and the meeting was "suspended" at 11.15 a.m. The few minutes expected for the "recess" lasted until 10.20 p.m., i.e. about eleven hours, when the President appeared before the members of the Council to apologise "to members of the Council for having kept them waiting for most of the day". He added:

"I had hoped indeed that the recess would be considerably shorter. However, consultations are still going on; they have been going on the whole day without any recess. They are still going on, as I have said, and will continue tomorrow morning. I understand that it is the wish of members of the Council that we should adjourn now until tomorrow morning, at 11.30 a.m. I would ask members of the Council to make themselves available for consultation about an hour before the scheduled time of the meeting tomorrow morning. If there is no objection, I shall take it that it is so decided." After a short pause he said: "It is so decided."[3] The meeting rose at 10.25 p.m.

Meanwhile, the *Liberty* was busy sending messages on the war development to its headquarters which forwarded them to various branches of the U.S. Government; they were immediately received by Ambassador Goldberg at the United Nations.

The *Liberty* reported that Israeli troops were advancing and that the Egyptian planes and airports had been completely destroyed. Of course, to finish the job the Israelis needed more time and both the Security Council President and the United States Ambassador were there to secure the necessary delay through "the recess for consultation". It was consultation with the unknown because Mr Tabor let the cat out of the bag when he asked "members of the Council to hold themselves available for consultations about an hour before the scheduled time of the meeting."

General Dayan confirmed that consultations on different levels

---

3. Security Council Meeting, no. 1347, 5th June 1967.

were going on between the Israeli secret service, Mossad, and its counterpart, the American C.I.A.

The meeting suggested by the President, however, was not convened at 11.30 a.m. as decided. Security Council members were kept waiting from 11.30 a.m. until 6.30 p.m. of the following day when the President "called the meeting to order". He did not even bother to explain the delay or apologise to the members of the Council for it. This happened while the whole world was witnessing the war and looking to the Security Council for immediate action.

After this very long delay "an immediate cease fire and cessation of all military activities in the area was ordered by the unanimous vote of the Council." It was however defied by Israel, who continued the war which was reported by the *Liberty*. The *Liberty* had acquired much confidential information which the Israelis had never wanted any "eavesdropper" to know.

Mr Pearson stated:

"It had quickly become clear to the observers on *Liberty* that the strength of the Israeli offensive lay in a superb intelligence capability. The Israelis had broken the Arab codes from the moment the fighting began and were tuned to every Arab communication. The importance of this became evident when the *Liberty* began monitoring exchanges of war information between Nasser and King Hussein of Jordan concerning the strategy and progress of the Arab allies. Somewhere between Cairo and Amman, in a field relay station hastily constructed in Sinai, the messages were being blocked by the Israelis, reconstructed and passed on so swiftly and effectively that there was no apparent break. The outgoing transmissions from Egypt did not appear in the same form as incoming transmission to Jordan. In the language of electronic intelligence this type of interference is called "cooking".[4]

Mr Pearson referred to one specific case showing how the U.S. *Liberty* discovered Israeli interference or "cooking":

"The first batch of these messages transmitted from Cairo advised King Hussein of the bad military situation in Sinai, that the Egyptian army was hard pressed and was unable to give him tactical support to hold his position on the West Bank. The

---

4.   A. Pearson, op.cit., p.31

message also told Hussein that the Israelis now had total air superiority and that he could expect heavy air strikes against his ground troops with no chance for the Arab armies to throw any opposition against them. The Israelis blocked these transmissions and re-worded them to misinform Hussein that three-quarters of the Israeli Air Force had been destroyed over Cairo and the three hundred plus aircraft he was now picking up on radar approaching Jordan were Egyptian jets sent to raid targets in Israel. They were in fact Israeli aircraft returning from the destruction of Egyptian airfields."[5]

2

It was this kind of "cooking" during the first days of the war that created the impression in Arab minds that the war was going progressively in their favour. The *Liberty,* according to Anthony Pearson, took up a new position and "as dawn broke on 8th June *Liberty* stood thirteen miles off the coast of Gaza directly out from the town of Al Arish."[6]

The Israeli claim that the ship was the victim of mistaken identity was a lie. The officer of the watch, Lieutenant Stephen Toth, reported that the light and visibility were so good that he was able to see the outline of the Sinai coast and all relevant details. He could also see the minaret of the mosque at Al Arish in Sinai.

He noted in the log that "the day was still, the sea calm and the sky clear."

Pearson continued: "When Armstrong of the U.S. Navy saw the Israeli planes coming in fast and low he said 'By God, these guys look as though they mean business.' Then the first battery of cannon and rockets hit the ship, 'shaking and rolling her like a tiny dinghy in white water'. Armstrong could see 'three jets in triangular attack formation.' Armstrong said 'My God they are Mirages. Can't they see our Flag?' "[7]

A few minutes later Armstrong was among the unfortunate victims.

Pearson added:

"The Mirages were banking for another run. The decks were

---

5. Ibid, p.31

6. Ibid, p.32

7. Ibid, p.40

covered with bodies, some moving, some still. Men were crawling, crying, bleeding. The decking and the wheelhouse superstructure forward was ripped to shreds by cannon and machine-gun fire. A plume of black smoke was swirling from a blazing rubber liferaft."

"The Mirages came streaking back, still in their deadly battle triangle. The Putt! Putt! Putt! rattle of the twelve wing-mounted heavy machine guns drowned out the cries of the wounded. Bullets tore into the bodies forward and aft. They cut up the dead, the dying and the frightened, hurling them about like rag dolls. The strafing fire ran the length of the ship in straight following lines."[8]

Three runs were made by the Israeli Mirages. As a result, the Israeli airforce completely destroyed the *Liberty's* equipment and disabled her, causing the death of thirty-four and the injury of one hundred and seventy-one American seamen.

In the beginning the American media attacked the perpetrators of this crime. A short time later it became clear to the whole world that Israel was responsible for the attack.

The tragic news of the attack on the *Liberty* reached us in the U.N. Security Council. I asked why this serious incident was being treated so lightly. Both Abba Eban of Israel and Arthur Goldberg of the United States made only low-key statements.

The Israeli representative wanted the Security Council to believe that the attack was a result of mistaken identity. He apologised on behalf of his government to the government of the United States. Both parties let the matter rest there, but it was perfectly clear to everybody that the ship had been spying on military operations.

This is what that week's issue of *Newsweek* had to say:

> "First of all, the *Liberty* was no ordinary vessel, but an intelligence-gathering ship on a "ferret" mission. It carried elaborate gear to locate both Israeli and Egyptian radio and radar and to monitor and tap all military messages sent from command posts to the battlefield."

It continued:

> "Although Israel's apologies were officially accepted some high Washington officials believe the Israelis knew the *Liberty's* capabilities, and suspect that the attack might not have been accidental".

---

8. Ibid, p.41

> "One top-level theory holds that someone in the Israeli
> armed forces ordered the *Liberty* sunk because he suspected it
> had taken down messages showing that Israel started the
> fighting. (A Pentagon official has already tried to shoot down
> the Israel claim of 'pilot error'.)"

The article went on:

> "Not everyone in Washington is buying this theory, but some
> top Administration officials will not be satisfied until fuller and
> more convincing explanations of the attack on a clearly marked
> ship in international waters are forthcoming."

Many Security Council members wondered why Israel should attempt to sink the *Liberty* and to kill all its fifteen officers, two hundred and seventy-nine men and three listed Department of Defense technicians. Even if it was spying, it was a ship of a friendly country. The information gathered was being used to help Israel. Ambassador Goldberg, thanks to the U.S. *Liberty,* had more information about the war than all the other Security Council members put together. He chose, however, not to present the details of the attack to the Security Council, nor did he want it debated. Thus, the attack was never seriously discussed.

Outside the United Nations it was different. Israel insisted that the U.S. *Liberty* had been mistaken for an Egyptian warship. The Pentagon rejected that; the matter was raised in Congress, then closed. Wilbur Crane Eveland wrote:

> "A United States naval board of inquiry found that the
> daylight attack had been unprovoked and deliberate. Then the
> United States government shrouded the entire *Liberty* matter
> in secrecy under a cloak of 'national security' considerations,
> where it remains even now. Individual claims of compensation
> for the ship's dead and wounded were paid by the U.S.
> government, supposedly on behalf of Israel. Even moves by
> Congress to stop all aid to Israel until seven million U.S.
> dollars in compensation for the *Liberty* was paid succumbed to
> White House and Department of State pressure. Why?
> Defence Minister Dayan had stated his government's position
> bluntly: Unless the United States wished the Russians and
> Arabs to learn of joint CIA-Mossad covert operations in the
> Middle East and of Angleton's discussions before the 1967
> fighting started, the questions of the lost American ship and

how the war originated should be dropped. That ended the
U.S. protestations!"[9]

Moshe Dayan was appointed Israeli Minister of Defence on 1st June
1967 i.e. four days before the Israeli jets swept down on Egyptian,
Syrian, and Jordanian airfields destroying over four hundred
aircraft on the ground, giving Israel air superiority and thus
facilitating the taking of Sinai, the West Bank and the Syrian Golan
Heights.
Eveland went on:

> "Message intercepts by the *Liberty* made it clear that Israel had
> never intended to limit its attack to Egypt. Furthermore, we
> learned that the Israelis were themselves intercepting
> communications among the Arab leaders. The Israelis then
> retransmitted "doctored" texts to encourage Jordan and Syria
> to commit their armies in the erroneous belief that Nasser's
> army had repelled the Israeli invaders. To destroy this
> incriminating evidence Moshe Dayan ordered his jets and
> torpedo boats to destroy the *Liberty* immediately."[10]

3

In a meeting between the Jordanian Foreign Minister and Arthur
Goldberg, which I attended, details of which follow, the U.S.
representative claimed that the United States had advised Jordan
not to enter the war. This was only half the truth, because to my
knowledge the United States never gave Jordan, or any Arab State,
a true picture of what was going on.
The facts revealed later, together with those above, show that the
war was the result of joint Israeli-American planning. The *Liberty's*
function was to keep the United States informed of every
development. The U.S.A. wanted to destroy Arab leadership and
undermine any possibility of Arab unity. It wanted a weak Arab
world so that the Eisenhower Doctrine, rejected by Arab leaders in
1957, would be accepted in 1967. It wanted Israel to be its strategic
partner so that both could be joint masters of the area, with Israel as
a watch dog for the United States.

---

9. W.C.Eveland, *Ropes of Sand*, Norton and Co., London, New York, 1980,
   p.325.

10. Ibid. p.325.

This became yet more obvious after the Israeli invasion of Lebanon in 1982 when the United States did not play an effective role in stopping the war against a friendly country — Lebanon. It can be argued that the United States felt that the war would serve its interests. Later developments admitted openly by both the United States and Israel leave no room for doubt about the special relationship exisiting between the two countries.

On 29th November, 1983 the U.S.A. and Israel announced the signing of a new agreement. It called, inter-alia, for the establishment of a joint political and military committee to discuss military planning, air and naval exercises and for the positioning of American weapons, medical facilities and other material in Israel. The agreement was strongly criticised by Mr Chadli Klibi, the Secretary General of the League of Arab States, and by all Members of the League.

On 5th December 1983 I told the United Nations General Assembly, on behalf of the League of Arab States, that the new strategic agreement with Israel represented a serious turn in American policy in the Middle East, because it ensured unlimited American support for Israel in all its acts of aggression against the Arabs. It was bound to make the U.S. lose the last shreds of the credibility that had formerly enabled it to take peace initiatives in the region.

These developments, I said, necessitated a reconsideration of the Arab position.

The strategic agreement also created a special relationship between the U.S. and Israel, which embodied discrimination between Arab and Israeli. It offended the Arab States and created bitterness among the Arab peoples, causing a situation which would directly affect the vital interests of the United States. It would feed Israeli plans for further expansion on Arab land which would result in the expulsion of more Palestinian people. The agreement thus represented U.S. protection for Israel's conquests in contravention of one of the basic principles of the United Nations, the inadmissibility of the acquisition of territory by force.

On 20th December 1983 I was in Los Angeles, visiting relatives and friends, when it was announced that President Reagan would appear on television to speak on the Middle East. I cancelled my appointments, and waited for the President's Press conference.

The President was happy and smiling. He was asked about the American-Israeli co-operation agreement, and commented "we made no new pact with Israel. It was a reaffirmation of a past relationship." He emphasised "we signed no agreement . . . We reaffirmed our relationship with Israel which has been in existence since 1948."

A few hours later it was reported in Washington that "Defense Department officials confirmed that General John W. Vessey Jr., Chairman of the Joint of Chief of Staff, will visit Israel early next month (January 1984) and begin a discussion of details of the new United States/Israeli agreement on strategic co-operation."[11]

In the space of a few hours, we heard two contradictory versions. The President said that no agreement had been signed on strategic co-operation. The Department of Defense, one hour later, announced that a high-ranking officer would be visiting Israel to work out a plan for the implementation of the Agreement in particular the formation of the Joint American-Israeli Committee to work on political and military planning in the area and the detailed arrangements for the storage of military and medical equipment in Israel.

All subsequent official statements and practices show that an agreement was, in fact, entered into between President Reagan and the Israeli Premier, Yitzhak Shamir, former Stern Gang leader. The agreement was referred to in the statement issued by the White House after Shamir's departure and the subsequent double-talk was intended to confuse the issue and mislead both the Arab States and U.S. public opinion.

This American attitude created a dilemma for those Arab States which had been trying hard to convince their people that there were new developments in Arab-American relations; and that the United States was determined to bring peace with justice to the area.

For a while, the trend of moderation, even amongst the Palestinian resistance organisations, had gained ground. Now it became clear that the whole thing was a mirage. How could any Arab Government continue to tell the same story to its people? How could they expect the U.S. to follow the steps of Washington, Lincoln, Jefferson and Eisenhower? Indeed, how could anyone like Yasser Arafat, Chairman of the Palestine Liberation Organisation, continue to lead his people towards whole hearted support for the spirit of moderation championed by some Arab States, when the promises by successive American administrations had turned out to

---

11. *Los Angeles Times* 21.12.1983 p.11.

nothing but a kind of sedative for Arab opinion. An apple skin with no apple inside.

The Arab States now witnessed the complete disregard of the United States as well as of Israel for United Nations resolutions. There was a similar disregard for earlier American commitments, and for the promises given to various Arab leaders. This complete indifference to United Nations resolutions, and to America's own promises and commitments, heralded the new Israeli-American relationship finally crowned by the new strategic co-operation agreement.

The whole attempt by Arab states to improve Arab-American relations, in the hope that the U.S.A. could be persuaded to work for a just settlement in the Middle East, had been shown to be useless. The entire concept behind Arab foreign policy was false. What both the United States and Israel wanted was the complete disintegration of the region, a kind of Balkanisation, with more conflicts and with many mini-states, not realising that neither this nor an imposed peace would bring stability to the region. Such was the policy behind Israeli backing for sectarian forces in Lebanon before and after the 1982 invasion.

In his television appearance of December 1983, President Reagan had assured his audience that the new relationship was nothing but a re-affirmation of the relations already existing between the two countries and that the U.S. was simply institutionalising that policy. But in this way he revealed the existence of the secret Israeli-American strategic agreement.

Chapter 6

The Tragic Consequences of General Dayan — and Robert Kennedy

"The Israelis know very well when to start, but to their misfortune they do not know where to stop. This has been the cause of their tragedy throughout history."

Dr Ralph Bunche
Acting U.N. Mediator 1948-49,
later U.N. Under-Secretary for
Political Affairs

General Moshe Dayan who died in 1982 had an impressive record in serving Zionism. He used every trick in the book to acquire more Palestinian land and to displace yet more Palestinian people. He was known for contradictory utterances before and after every war. Palestinian farmers remember the various unethical ways in which he deprived them of their lands. Early in 1949 he and his aides were attending a meeting of the Mixed Armistice Commission with Jordan. The issue was how to apply the Armistice Agreement. Suddenly Dayan came up with what appeared to be a generous offer. He declared to his Jordanian counterpart: "Why not include the Israeli occupied part of this village of Bartaa on your side of the line? That is, let us agree that Jordan incorporates all the village of Bartaa within the area allotted to it under the Armistice Agreement."

A farmer who happened to be present from the village jumped up and whispered to the Jordanian officer: "Dayan wants to give you the village and its people so that he can separate the lands from the village and thus keep the land for himself! Please leave us on the occupied side so we can still keep our land. It will be difficult for us to be separated from our own people but it would be still more tragic to lose our land to General Dayan!"

The Jordanians rejected the offer. Dayan realised however, that the Palestinian farmer had been the one to enlighten the Jordanian officer of the consequences. He turned to one of his aides and said in Hebrew: "See to it that this farmer is liquidated immediately."

A member of the Jordanian team who knew Hebrew informed his superior that the unfortunate villager would be murdered, and he was smuggled by car to the town of Irbid. Thus the Arab inhabitants of Bartaa, except one, remained in their village enjoying the fruits of their land. This one villager, the man who dared to speak out, is now living in Kuwait. In this case General Dayan's trick did not succeed. Later Israelis, however, declared all that part of Palestine to be a closed military area and confiscated tens of thousands of acres belonging to the people of the villages of Beir Essikka, Jat, Baka, Kufr Karei, Araara, Aara, Muawiyah and others. Many Jewish settlements were built on the land and the Palestinian owners could do nothing to recover their farms, for many their sole source of income.

Through similar actions, Israel had taken the land of many villages in the Gaza Strip. Today the original owners are neither refugees nor non-refugees. They do not qualify for help under any United Nations definition because they remain in their homes. Yet they have lost their lands, property, and livelihood. They are, in fact, worse off than refugees.

2

In December 1972 a farmer from Palestine visited me in Cairo, and explained to me one of the many methods the Israelis used to dispossess Palestinians of their land.

In order to tempt the farmer the Israelis offered him what amounts to five pounds sterling a day if he will work as a labourer in their factories instead of on his farm. He could not earn that much in agriculture, because the Israeli government controls all farming, production and marketing.

Not only do inflation and the high Israeli standard of living demand an increase in income to meet daily needs, but since the occupation in 1967 of the remaining part of Palestine taxes have risen. To cope with this the farmers find themselves obliged to shift from cultivating the land into working in a factory, without the slightest suspicion of course, of the hidden design that lies in store. Three years later Israel enforces its rigid regulations and seizes the land from the farmer, either for "public use" or by claiming that it has been "abandoned" by its legitimate owner. A Jewish settlement is then built on the land. A year or two later the factory sacks its now landless employee. Israel has special offices in every area ready to offer free transport, with pocket money, to any Palestinian who wants to emigrate to any corner of the earth. This is only one of several ways used to take the land, dispossess its owner, and then displace him. By such means is the Zionist slogan satisfied: "We want a land without people for a people without land."

Those Palestinians who refuse to accept emigration can settle for a three-year permit in virtue of which they can travel anywhere in the Arab world and beyond. They can then reside abroad for three years. The Israelis hope during this period that the Palestinian will find a permanent job and new home so that he will not return to his native land.

3

While these practices continue, Israel assures the United Nations and indeed, the world at large, that it recognises its responsibility for the welfare of all the inhabitants in the occupied territories. These assurances have always proved to be nothing but a cover-up or smoke screen to conceal Israel's repeated defiance of its obligations under UN resolutions, international agreements and commitments. Israel's obligation towards the welfare of the people in the West Bank and the Gaza Strip became mandatory after it signed the Geneva Convention. That Convention expressly states that in occupied territories no coercion "physical or moral" will be exercised against the inhabitants for any reason, including the procuring of information (Article 31). Acts of brutality are forbidden (Article 52). No protected person may be punished for an offence he or she has not personally committed. Pillage and reprisals against persons and property are prohibited (Article 33).

How has Israel carried out these obligations?

In 1977, in an Administrative Order the Israeli Minister of the

Interior stated that the West Bank had been given the names "Judea" and "Samaria" and that these areas were not legally "enemy territory". This was a clear attempt to free Israel from its obligations under the Geneva Conventions and enable Israeli leaders to resort to this simple way of quiet annexation. The Israeli Foreign Ministry denied any political significance to these measures, but this statement has been belied by Israeli practice. It was clear that both Ministries and the Israeli Government as a whole were co-ordinating efforts for the complete annexation of the territories, by stages. They started with Jerusalem within a month of the 1967 war.

Israeli violations of the Geneva Convention are daily occurrences. Among the alarming number of violations are confinement orders, limitation of free movement, arrests without trial and the imposition of collective punishment such as curfews and the dynamiting of houses. Obstructing the work of the International Red Cross has also become a frequent practice. This has resulted in an unprecedented movement of refugees and escapees leaving the West Bank and the Gaza Strip and crossing the River Jordan looking for shelter, precisely what the occupiers wanted.

Many other violations are committed for the alleged purpose of military security. The destruction in June and July 1967 of the villages of Yalu, Beit Nuba and Imwas, accompanied by the summary removal of their inhabitants and the resultant economic dislocation, is a shameful example. In the Security Council I referred in detail to the systematic destruction of dozens of villages in the West Bank.

Israel refuses to abide by the will of the Security Council. It has also made every attempt to frustrate Security Council efforts to put an end to these acts of ruthlessness. After the adoption of the Security Council Resolution 237 on 14th June 1967, I contacted my Government to suggest that all new refugees should proceed the following day to the Jordan Bridge to cross to the Israeli occupied West Bank to implement the Security Council Resolution. That cable never reached my Government. Why? How was it that almost all cables I sent immediately prior to and during the June War never reached their destination, either never arriving at all or arriving when it was too late; they included a cable dealing with the cease-fire, which was never received. The action suggested by me to my Government on Resolution 237 would have exposed Israel to world public opinion because Israel would never implement that resolution. It was, to say the least, helpful to the Zionists that that cable should "disappear".

The Tragic Consequences of General Dayan and Robert Kennedy

The sad fact is that there is no limit to Zionist ambitions. In 1967 Dr Ralph Bunche, Under Secretary for Political Affairs in the United Nations, said to me: "You Arabs do not know how to start, but once you start you know where to stop. The Israelis, on the other hand, know very well when to start, but to their misfortune they do not know where to stop. This has been the cause of their tragedy throughout history."

Dr Bunche had acted as a mediator between the Arabs and the Israelis and had first-hand experience of Israeli lust for power and land which, he came to realise, knew no end. Dr Bunche blamed the Israelis for what he called the "evasive peace"; he, as a good Christian, wanted to see peace in Palestine. Alas, Dr Bunche failed to accomplish his mission. He received the Nobel Prize and many other awards but peace, the genuine and real prize he sought, he never won. He described his achievement to me, sadly: "Armistice, yes. But peace, no."

Israeli behaviour now is in utter contradiction of the assurances given in the thirties by the Zionist leader who later became the first President of Israel, Dr Chaim Weizmann. In an extraordinary issue of the *Official Gazette* of the Government of Palestine, dated 24th October 1930, there is a "Statement of Policy" by the British Government. In it, the United Kingdom explained its policy in detail and emphasised its intention to conduct that policy in conformity with the Mandate. It declared it wished to promote the essential interests of both "races" in Palestine, and that it would also work consistently for the "development in Palestine of a prosperous community, living in peace under an impartial and progressive Administration."

The statement refers to a resolution passed by the Executive of the Zionist Organisation, which assured Britain that the activities of that organisation would be conducted in conformity with the policy of the United Kingdom.

In a letter conveying the text of the Resolution, Dr. Weizmann wrote:

> "The Zionist Organisation has, at all times, been sincerely desirous of proceeding in harmonious co-operation with all sections of the people of Palestine. It has repeatedly made it clear, both in word and deed, that nothing is further from its purpose than to prejudice in the smallest degree the civil or religious rights, or the material interest of the non-Jewish population."[1]

---

1. *Official Gazette of the Government of Palestine*, 24th October 1930, p.858.

What has happened to all these commitments and pledges? Why are Palestinians homeless today? Why are they left deprived of their inalienable rights? Why do the Israelis adopt an extremist policy, saying "no" to repatriation and "no" to civil and religious rights of the people of Palestine? Have they forgotten that in a formal document addressed to the Mandatory Power the first President of Israel, as head of the Zionist movement, gave an undertaking that the Zionist Organisation would not "prejudice in the smallest degree the civil or religious rights or the material interest of the non-Jewish population" in Palestine? Or is it that the Zionist Organisation never considered the resolution as anything more than a form of words designed to fool the British mandatory power, while they themselves continued their plans to rob a people of its homeland? Today, Israel resorts to various forms of violence to achieve its goals. The examples cited earlier show the extent of violence in the Holy Land.

4

Of course, violence breeds violence. The leaders of Super-Powers, who have a special responsibility for world peace and security, can themselves become the target of such violence. It was while we were debating an aspect of the Palestine problem in the Security Council, that we received the report of the assassination of Senator Robert Kennedy in California on 4th June 1968.

A Palestinian called Sirhan Sirhan, who carried a Jordanian passport, was arrested and charged with committing this murder. Immediately Ambassador Goldberg of America came to see me. He said: "You know, being the Ambassador of Jordan, you need protection. I would like to contact the competent authorities to arrange some protection for you and for Ambassador El-Kony of the United Arab Republic (Egypt). I want to know whether either you or Ambassador El-Kony has any objection."

I replied that the man charged with the murder of the senator was now under arrest. He was either a U.S. citizen or about to be one. Why should I and El-Kony be the two Goldberg thought needed protection? And why should we be asked whether we wanted it? I finally said: "You are the host country and it is up to you to do what you feel necessary and proper." Ambassador El-Kony said the same thing, and we both went home.

In less than an hour, at around 8 p.m., a policeman in his navy-blue uniform knocked at my door. I was alone and opened it. He said he had instructions to protect me and my residence and wanted to inspect the main door entrance and the back (delivery) entrance. I showed my "protector" what he wanted to see. He sat for a while and later went downstairs to the lobby.

I was furious about the assassination, and watched television to see how the murder had been committed. It showed the carrying of the body of the Senator to hospital, then to Washington for burial. Why, I wondered, should people die like this, in a murder senseless as the many we were witnessing in the occupied territories. Why should Sirhan Sirhan, who came from a good Christian Arab family, have killed the Senator? Had he been provoked because the Senator made some sarcastic remarks about Arabs at a Jewish function at which he was the main speaker? I remember hearing Robert Kennedy speaking with a hoarse voice. He had apologised to his audience, saying: "Please excuse my voice. I just drank some Arab coffee!" The Zionists present received this remark with much applause. Is this what provoked Sirhan? Or was it the many other remarks the Senator made during the election campaign? I myself was unhappy about many of the Senator's unfair jibes. I once answered him in the Security Council, saying: "Here is a man who does not have the courage to speak the truth nor the dignity to keep silent."

Senator Kennedy was killed, but he was, too only a victim of the bigger crime committed in the Holy Land. Sirhan was a Christian Palestinian, displaced by the Israelis, who had been expelled from his home, finally finding shelter in the United States. In Court psychiatrists explained his state of mind and it is not appropriate here to discuss the circumstances that led to the murder. All of us in the Security Council regretted the Senator's death, offering our condolences to the family of the victim, to our host government and to the American people on this national tragedy.

That night, in spite of the fears for my safety which had been expressed, I decided to go to Washington and attend the funeral of the Senator. I called my Deputy, Dr. Anton El-Naber, who was not only a colleague but a friend and a good nationalist, who worked hard to promote human rights. I had the highest regard for his ability, dignity and integrity. I asked whether he would care to go with me to Washington. He pondered for a minute then said: "Do you think this is alright?" I replied, "Sure, why not?" He said without hesitation "O.K."

The funeral was very impressive, with everything efficiently, magnificently and immediately arranged. It was also sad. Anton and I were touched to see the tragically orphaned children, the widow and the members of the Kennedy family. Nevertheless I could not help thinking of the senseless wars that had left so many Palestinian orphans, widows and others without shelter or any means of living, all caused by the cupidity of man, by the selfishness of human beings and by the lust for power. Anton shared my feelings. At the same time we both felt sorry for Sirhan Sirhan, the assassin, twenty years old or less. We were sure that that boy had not really known what he was doing. He too was a victim.

We arrived back in New York the same day at around ten in the evening. I walked into my home and the same "security" policeman was still there. He was having a nap when I left my house and was similarly engaged when I returned. He did not see me going out, nor did he see me coming back. This was on Sunday. When I appeared the next morning to go to my office, the policeman saw me and said: "You were very wise. It is good that you did not leave your home yesterday. You knew it was the funeral. On such a day there was much emotion and the best thing for one like you was to stay home."

Another "security" man, in civilian clothes sat on the front seat, next to the driver of my car. I sat in the back. He told me that he was there to be with me while I was in the United Nations or at my office, but he also informed me that he could not enter the United Nations headquarters building. His authority only held good outside U.N. premises. The U.N. has its own protection for delegates within its headquarters. In the evening he turned over the "protection" to the regular police. The same routine applied to Ambassador El-Kony.

Every day early in the evening Ambassador El-Kony and I used to walk all the way from 80th Street on Park Avenue to Times Square and then back. Two tall policemen would walk behind us all the way. They never complained or showed any sign of disagreement. One evening, on one of our walks, Ambassador El-Kony said to me: "What is the use of those policemen?" I smiled and answered: "You don't know? They walk behind us in their navy-blue American uniforms. To me they look like two arrows pointing at us and saying to any murderer: 'Here are the two Ambassadors!' "

The following day we asked the U.S. mission to the United Nations to relieve the two policemen of their assignment. We explained that we felt there was no further need for them. They were withdrawn and our lives returned to normal. In fact, we felt more secure when we were able again to walk like any other human being in the big city.

Chapter 7

The Massacre of Karameh and U.S. Diplomacy

*"When we condemn resistance movements we actually would be con-
demning ourselves after six years of our independence. This is because our independence was the result of bitter struggle and resistance
to foreign occupation."*

Tewfic Bouattoura
Algeria's Ambassador to the U.N.

On 21st March 1968, I had the duty of presenting another Jordanian
complaint to the Security Council about the Israeli invasion of
Karameh, a village of the East Bank of the Jordan.

The Israelis invaded the village with three brigades, backed up by
jet-fighters and helicopters. They destroyed, plundered, bombed
and murdered at will. Karameh was a village which provided shelter
to those Palestinians whom the Irgun, Haganah and other Jewish
terrorist organisations had expelled in 1948, taking over their homes
and lands and forcibly seizing all their property. Those expelled
then built their village on a piece of land on the east side of the
Jordan river. The late King Abdullah of Jordan gave this new village
its name, Karameh, which means "dignity".

Today it is completely in ruins. It is true that its inhabitants,
together with the Jordanian army and Palestinian Fedayeen resisted
the Israeli invasion, but by the time the Israelis were forced to
retreat Karameh had been reduced to little more than a mountain of

rubble. Casualties were high on both sides and those who survived were mostly women and children.

While Moshe Dayan was carrying out his ruthless campaign against the innocent Palestinians of Karameh, I was asked by my Government to convene the Security Council "in order to take necessary measures against Israel".

The Council met, and U.S. Ambassador Arthur Goldberg also met with the Israeli Ambassador to draw up a joint strategy, although I did not realise that until later. I was in contact with my own Government and immediately passed all news from Karameh to the Big Powers and to all other members of the Council.

The President of the Council, at the time the representative of Senegal, realising the seriousness of the matter, did not even consult members of the Council about the timing of the meeting as had been the earlier practice, but called an immediate meeting, within an hour and a half of my request.

I asked for the Council to be kept in session until a decision was taken because constructive debate had so often in the past been interrupted by a decision to turn to some other problem. Because the matter was serious, the President agreed.

The U.S. Delegation then asked for a postponement, which the President refused. Arthur Goldberg then asked me to approve an adjournment to give the State Department time to see "what was going on". I too declined. We knew from past experience that any delay by the Council would adversely reflect on our claim that the matter threatened international peace and security and required urgent attention.

In the field, the situation had already deteriorated. The Jordanian Army and the Palestinian resistance worked together to repel the Israeli aggression, showing both heroism and determination because this time they had expected the attack and were ready to repel it. Reports of the fighting kept coming to the Council on news agency wires and through UN reports. The reports were very encouraging and were received by my Arab colleagues with pride and happiness. We needed such encouragement after the 1967 war.

The U.S. pressure for an "adjournment" grew. Since I expected the U.S. to work for a "mild" resolution, I decided to devise my own strategy to counter the U.S. and Israeli strategy. I agreed with Ambassador Tewfic Bouattoura, Algeria's Ambassador and the only Arab on the Security Council, that he should negotiate with Arthur Goldberg of the U.S. on the draft resolution in order to relieve me of direct American pressure. I said that if they disagreed I would step in to help. He readily assented.

A few minutes before the convening of the Security Council Arthur Goldberg, who had arrived earlier from Washington, asked to see me. When we met he repeated the same request made earlier by his Deputy for the adjournment of the debate. He said, in support of his request, that the matter was very serious and that his government was deeply concerned and would take a strong stand in favour of Jordan.

I thanked the Ambassador for his government's sentiments, adding that I looked forward to hearing this stand reflected in his speech during the coming meeting. Adjournment, I added, was however out of the question.

Meanwhile Washington was in touch with Amman for the same purpose. Mr. Goldberg then asked me whether it would be acceptable to me and to the Arab group in the United Nations if the U.S. presented its own strong draft resolution, "because we are deeply concerned about what is going on".

I said "by all means, please do". He then asked: "Is this not embarrassing to you back home and towards your Arab colleagues over here?"

I answered: "It is just the opposite. What you would do would show that you are a 'friend in need'. It would show that you have taken an even-handed policy, which you mention to me all the time without practising it. This, Mr Ambassador, will also serve your interests in the Arab countries. I urge you to do it. But will you?"

"Of course, I have just arrived from Washington," Goldberg replied, adding: "But tell me, are you contemplating presenting a draft during this coming meeting of the Council?"

I answered: "The Algerian Ambassador is now working with the Asian and African members of the Security Council on a draft resolution. Being the Arab member in the Security Council he is the one authorised to negotiate the draft resolution on behalf of Jordan."

He asked me to delay the presentation to give him time to contact the State Department.

I wondered about his motives, but it made no difference whether we submitted the draft immediately or on the following day. We still had to hear all the members of the Council before we proceeded to the vote. Meanwhile, it was worth testing U.S. credibility.

I promised that the draft would not be presented that day and that a U.S. draft, if presented and acceptable, would have priority. Goldberg was very happy. He walked with me to the Council smiling broadly and, before departing, he whispered in my ear: "I hope you will not say anything in your speech against the U.S. You know, President Johnson is very sensitive to public opinion at this time. Please don't say anything that may complicate matters."

I answered: "How can I attack a friendly state that has assured me that it would put its political weight in our favour and would take the initiative for us?"

I then made my first intervention in the Security Council debate saying nothing against the United States and also halting the tabling of the Asian-African draft for twenty-four hours.

I was almost sure from past experience that nothing that Ambassador Goldberg had promised would come through. I felt that what he had offered me earlier about an American draft resolution was put up for me to reject, so that my rejection could be reported to Amman. On the other hand, if I accepted the offer, as I did, then it would gain the American side a certain delay. Of course, he was not expecting merely a few hours, but much more.

I listened carefully to the statement that Ambassador Goldberg made in the second Council session. He tried openly to establish a relationship between the Israeli aggression and what he called "infiltration and terrorism" by the Arab side. He did not condemn or censure Israel nor the Israeli action, but simply deplored it, and, of course, did not offer to present a draft resolution as he had promised.

After the meeting Arthur Goldberg came to see me. He tried to demonstrate that his stand in the Security Council was stronger than that of his government, by asking me to compare the statement issued by the State Department with the one he had made in the Council. I could not help asking with a smile: "Don't you represent your government?" He had often accused me of not carrying out the specific instructions of *my* government.

On the question of submitting an American draft resolution, he told me that his government had reconsidered its stand, and had decided not to present its own draft. He added: "But we have certain ideas and we would like some members to sponsor them."

He gave me a copy of those ideas, which I, on behalf of my government, immediately rejected.

Having heard the U.S. statement in the Security Council and because of the atmosphere the statement had created, I felt it necessary to reply to it. I suggested this to my government but never received an answer. I later discovered that they answered in the affirmative the same day, but the cable never reached me. Why? How? I often wonder!

2

The following day I received a telephone call from Arthur Goldberg, asking to see me before the Council's next meeting. He said he was happy because I had made no reference to his government in my two speeches, but had attacked Zionism in the U.S.A. It was unfortunate he added, that he had been compelled to answer me, because I had attacked American Zionists who played a role in the United States. He hoped, however, that I now considered the matter closed.

I responded that I had not answered the points made in his speech because I was waiting for my own government's guidance, but that this did not mean that we did not want or intend to keep the record straight. As to his defending Zionism in the U.S. this led me to wonder who he was representing — Zionism or the interests of the United States.

Goldberg replied: "Don't you think that it is better to let this matter rest?"

I disagreed. "You accuse Jordan of intervening in American domestic affairs. I will prove this afternoon that it was the pressure group in the U.S. who intervened in the matter of Jordan's security. This is clear. It is accomplished through collecting American funds and using these funds for buying military equipment to be used for massacres similar to the one of Karameh now before the Security Council. U.S. tax-exempt donations are used in order to enable Israel to cultivate our Arab soil and expand into our lands."

I told him that while Israeli fighters were bombing the refugee camps and dwellings, in contempt of every human value, and while I was alerting the Security Council to what was happening, not far from the United Nations building, the United Jewish Appeal was organising a dinner for the opening of a campaign to collect tax-exempt donations to Israel, sponsored by Zionist leaders in the big city of New York. I was later told that over 16 million American dollars were collected that night, but I never heard of any allusion or any reference to the Israeli acts of lawlessness and banditry against my people in Karameh. Instead, the competition to praise Israel continued, as American politicians called Israel a sister democracy. This answered those of us on the Security Council who knew the truth.

"Honestly, Mr Ambassador," I said, "to call Israel a sister democracy at a time when the Security Council is about to condemn its naked act of aggression, invites contempt and disgust. The fathers of the United States who built this great democracy on the basis of American values, which are rooted in our own values, had a different definition of what a sister democracy is. You have also made your contribution to this campaign by defending Zionism and its pressure groups in America. And you are, with all due respect Mr Ambassador, making a contribution now by asking me not to answer your statement on this matter."

I went on: "You heard how the Ambassador of Israel was on the offensive. He went to the extent of calling me, together with those colleagues who could not condone Israeli crimes, 'the messengers of hate, murder and terror". He cited the ancient Hebrew saying: 'On three things stands the world: truth, justice and peace.' I wonder: Is Israel part of the world? And with all this background, is it fair to accept your advice 'to let this matter rest'?"

"Please don't say anything which will create more complications for us in Congress," Goldberg replied. "As you know, the President will send you some arms as a gift."!

At this stage, I told Goldberg that he had his own convictions. I had mine. My principles were never subject to compromise, especially when Jordan was the victim. I would, I said, explain our position a few hours later in the Security Council.

He said that it was his government's view that there should be a paragraph in the resolution calling for observation on the cease-fire lines, and another emphasising support for the UN peace mission led by Gunnar Jarring.

I said to him firmly that any question of drafting should now be discussed with the Algerian delegate. At the same time I made it clear that any attempt to inject foreign substance into the resolution would be unacceptable to Jordan. "We want a very short clear-cut resolution, not going beyond the four corners of our complaint, namely, the Karameh invasion."

Ambassador Goldberg then asked me once again for an adjournment, arguing that the weekend was starting and he had to get some instructions. I again refused.

As I said: "How many times have you convened the Council on a Sunday on a question less important and serious than this? What is more, members who came from distant continents have received their instructions. You Mr Ambassador, keep telling me, maybe to impress me, that you have a direct line with 'Lyndon', the President. Why don't you use it now?"

When our meeting was over, Ambassador Goldberg again sought the support of the Asian-African members of the Council on the vexed question of an adjournment. They stood firm against any postponement which greatly upset the U.S. representative.

The Algerian, together with his Asian and African colleagues on the Council, met and prepared their draft. They, as a courtesy, gave Goldberg a copy of it. He apparently discussed the contents with the Algerian and tried to make some changes, but got nowhere.

Goldberg then asked to see me to discuss what he called "an urgent development". I agreed to meet him immediately and we met in the small Security Council chamber within ten minutes.

I informed the heads of the Arab delegations of this meeting. Since the Council would convene its own meeting immediately after we finished, Arab Ambassadors, in the adjacent lounge, were to be informed of the result of our talks, because they had a role to play, whether in the debate, or in the contacts needed. Ambassador El-Kony of Egypt, Ambassador Tomeh of Syria, Ambassador Benhima of Morocco, together with the Algerian Ambassador, were involved.

Ambassador Goldberg arrived with three aides, Joe Sisco, Bill Buffum and Dick Pedersen. He looked very tired and exhausted. He said: "I am glad we are having this important meeting, Mr Ambassador." He usually addressed me in the American way, "Muhammad". I normally called him "Arthur". This time, however, he started out being very formal.

He continued:"The case we are dealing with is a Jordanian, not an Algerian case. The initiative should therefore remain with Jordan. When we agree on something, then you can notify your brothers and friends. I do not like it for Jordan to have other colleagues handle its case. This is bad, Mr Ambassador. I don't know why you insist that I should negotiate with the Algerian and the Indian and the Pakistani, not with you. You do not want even to attend those informal meetings except when we reach a dealock." He then added: "Don't forget that Algeria is a country that is different from you completely. It has different rules and a different political line and it is difficult for us to agree with the Algerian."

I answered: "My dear Ambassador, the Algerian Ambassador represents the Arab seat in the Security Council. Algeria, therefore, represents Jordan. I am ready to discuss any problem that arises as a result of your negotiations with Ambassador Bouattoura of Algeria. I refuse to ask the Algerian, the Indian, the Senegali or the Pakistani to stop helping Jordan until I agree with the American Ambassador! This is bad diplomacy. I am sure you know this. As to the Algerian political line and the Jordanian political line, this is irrelevant. We are seeking the help of the Soviet Union too. You yourself negotiate with them on many vital issues because you have to. We know what we want from the Council. I assure you that the

Algerian representative reflects our desire and interest and represents the Arab members on the Council."

3

The meeting ended here. On the afternoon of Friday, 22nd March 1968 I met Ambassador Bouattoura of Algeria to exchange notes and I also met the Senegalese President, as well as the Indian, Pakistani and other members, of the Security Council. The co-ordination between the Algerian, Indian and Pakistani representatives helped Jordan a great deal. We agreed on what we wanted and on the way to attain it.

Ambassador Goldberg called on Tewfic Bouattoura of Algeria the same evening. He said he had noticed the Arabs were pressing for a vote in the Security Council and he wanted to "relax the matter" a little bit.

Meanwhile, the battle itself was going well. Reports were arriving at the United Nations which stressed the close co-ordination between the Jordanian soldiers and the Palestinian Fedayeen, who were defending their own soil. Ambassadors of friendly countries kept coming to me with big smiles on their faces. They conveyed to me the information they received and showed their pleasure at our ability to stand up and repel the aggressors. The Ambassador of the Soviet Union was the happiest. He said to me: "You have proved that you are good fighters. You have given Dayan a lesson." He went on: "Dayan had invited members of the press and TV for a press conference to be held a few hours after the invasion, announcing victory. The press people are still waiting and no victory has been announced. The press reports are coming out, but they are not what poor Dayan wanted!"

The Goldberg-Bouattoura meeting was not a pleasant one. Harsh words were exchanged about "resistance" and "terrorism". Goldberg wanted what he called a "balanced" resolution which would make specific reference to "acts of terrorism" against Israel. Bouattoura of Algeria was not happy at all about what Goldberg requested. With a frown on his face he said to Goldberg: "No Sir" and added the following points:

1. "If we condemn resistance movements we actually would be condemning ourselves, only six years after our independence. Our independence was the result of bitter struggle and resistance to foreign occupation. You call the Palestinian resistance "terrorism". This is exactly what we

in Algeria were called by the French occupiers. Do you want our men in Algeria, through accepting your suggestion, to condemn themselves? This applies to most members of the United Nations.

2.   "You want through the resolution on the Jordanian complaint to resist and undermine all liberation movements in Angola, Vietnam, Mozambique, Rhodesia and elsewhere. This, I admit, is a smart try but we will not let you get away with it."

No state friendly to us including France and other Council members supported Goldberg. Only the acceptance of the U.S. resolution by Jordan could help America. Goldberg refused to admit defeat and still hoped that Washington would "convince" Amman to accept this so-called "balanced resolution", but Jordan stood firm.

Meanwhile Bouattoura, at the end of his meeting with Goldberg, insisted that their draft "would be put to the vote tonight", immediately after my speech. He proclaimed the matter important and urgent and said that a decision had to be taken that night without any further delay.

After that, U.S. Ambassador Goldberg rushed to see me, in a state of high tension, tired, upset and frustrated. "The Algerian representative and your other friends in the Council insist on a vote tonight," he told me. "I cannot work in this atmosphere of threats and pressure. You are the only speaker tonight and Bouattoura intends to put the draft to the vote after you finish your speech. This means not having a resolution at all because the U.S. will not accept the present draft resolution. Not having a resolution is not in the interest of Jordan. On the other hand, you refuse to have the negotiations on a resolution take place with you or in your presence. And this adds to the complications."

I answered: "You mention that you are facing threats and pressure. Now you speak about having no resolution from the Council. You mean you will use the veto. Will you tell me who is intimidating who now? As to the negotiations, I am not creating a new procedure. It has been the practice that some members of the Security Council work on a draft resolution, sometimes in consultation with the complainant. I am available for consultation when you face difficulties."

I emphasised: "You, Mr Ambassador, have announced from the very beginning the desire of the U.S. to support Jordan. You went to the extent of offering to sponsor a strong draft resolution. Was it all a manoeuvre? Was it one of your delaying tactics? Not only did you not fulfill your promise, but you made a very disappointing speech. Now you come with the threat of a U.S. veto. We know that we cannot take a decision in the Security Council without your consent, but we regret the idea of tabling a resolution condemning the resistance as well as Israel. We would rather have no resolution than be guilty of sacrificing that principle. We will not accept this, Mr Ambassador. We also reject any attempt to inject foreign material in the draft resolution. It should be confined to our complaint — namely the Israeli aggression against Karameh. If you really can offer anything new I shall postpone my speech and also the voting."

Ambassador Goldberg replied: "I assure you that postponement will be in the interest of Jordan. And I hope it will be adjourned until Monday."

I said: "I am sorry, this is impossible. I can only agree to have it adjourned till tomorrow, Saturday."

He accepted and the meeting was postponed for twelve hours.

The next morning, Saturday 23rd November 1968, Lord Caradon asked that I, Goldberg and he should get together. We met and Goldberg gave me a new text which I read, rejected forthwith, and handed back. He was angry and wanted me to keep the draft. I refused to do so knowing that if I did he would turn around and tell every member of the Council that we were negotiating a new draft.

Lord Caradon saw through Goldberg's ploy and commented: "I quite understand your position." The meeting was over in less than two minutes. I then informed all the members of the Council of what had happened and emphasised that the Asian-African draft was the one on the table and that there was no other draft acceptable to, or under consideration by, the Jordan Government.

I also informed my Government, which urged me to press for a vote on the Asian-African draft resolution. I felt it necessary to expose all attempts to equate between the aggressor and the victim, and showed the Council how Israel finds support in the United States, which has always been accommodating to Israeli aggression. This, we felt, was the reason for Israel's arrogance and for the continued tension in our area.

On Saturday new efforts were made to adjourn the meeting until Monday. I refused saying that the United States should take an "either/or" stand. I refused to put Jordan's complaint on ice while our people were being killed and their village demolished.

Under this pressure, the Indian representative put forward an amendment which he said was acceptable to the U.S. Ambassador.

It read as follows:

"The Security Council deplores all violent incidents that violate the cease-fire, and declares that such acts of military reprisal and grave violations of the cease-fire cannot be tolerated and that the Security Council would have to consider further and more effective steps as envisaged in the Charter to ensure against repetition of such acts."

This new text was communicated to and accepted by the Jordanian Government. I contacted the U.S. Ambassador who then surprised me with a "no acceptance" answer, saying that the acceptance given to the Indian representative was his personal view, but his government had not yet taken a stand. He would inform me later of their official stand. Ten minutes later, Mr Pedersen from the U.S. Delegation asked to compare the texts and put forward a new text, pretending that it was the original one. I said that the one I used was the Indian Ambassador's text. "The man is honest and very particular and you know it. This is the text he gave me. It is the text I cabled to Amman and it is the text Amman accepted."

Ambassador Goldberg called me a few minutes later still hoping to make some changes. I said I was not in a position to agree to any change in the new text, which had been accepted by my Government.

Fifteen minutes before the Security Council convened its last meeting on Karameh, Ambassador Goldberg again asked to see me for "a most urgent and important development." He suggested his office as a place for the meeting, but since I had other meetings in the UN lounge before the vote, I suggested the Security Council Chamber.

He then informed the Security Council president that a last attempt was now being made with me to reach an agreement and asked that the Security Council should give this attempt a chance, going into a recess until the meeting was over. I assented.

4

Goldberg and I met, for our ninth and last meeting on this matter. He looked even more tired and exhausted. He expressed his regret for the "mis-understanding with Pedersen" and said that he had brought all the texts and cable with him. The U.S. Ambassador in Amman he claimed had informed the State Department that the Jordanian Foreign Minister had accepted the Indian text as conveyed to the American Ambassador in Amman, "not what you sent."

This, to me, seemed merely another attempt to delay the vote, and I answered sharply: "Your ambassador in Amman can write what he wants. I do not take my instructions from him. I have a specific message stating that my people in the Foreign Ministry accept the text I sent them, namely the Indian text which I was told you accepted."

Goldberg adopted a variety of tactics, at one moment an extremist, rigid and harsh line, and at another a soft and humble one but he failed to convince me or achieve what he wanted. He and his colleagues, kept insisting "Amman accepted this" or "Amman accepted that."

"I am the one who speaks for Amman," I insisted. "I know what Amman has accepted and what it has not."

Finally Goldberg turned to me and declared: If this is your position, then you do not want a resolution."

I said; "I shall tell the Security Council what I want, and what you want. I shall expose all the tactics of a Big Power as represented by you. I shall leave it to the Council and to the whole world to decide who is responsible for the failure of the Council. Let me emphasise now that to the resolution you have in mind I say: NO."

At this point Goldberg said that we should compare the texts all over again. He accepted the original Indian text and asked me if everything was now satisfactory.

"No," I said, "It still isn't Okay. We should now go to the preamble to fit it in together with the new Indian amendment. Something should be mentioned in the preamble."

At this point he lost his temper and said "This is not being serious!"

I stood up. So did he, then his deputies, Sisco, Buffum and Pedersen. I said to him: "I cannot work in this kind of atmosphere, and I reject the statement you just made. It is unbecoming. I represent a sovereign state and I consider our meeting over. Let us go to the Security Council. There is nothing to discuss."

For the first time Ambassador Goldberg looked very embarrassed. He looked at his three deputies and asked them to leave the room. They left. The two of us remained, still standing and looking at each other. Arab Ambassadors waiting outside saw the three American aides leave and started wondering why we were left alone.

Goldberg said: "It takes a man to admit his mistake when he makes it. Please accept my apology. I never meant you. I am tired and exhausted. Your colleagues whom you asked me to negotiate with gave me a hard time. I have nothing but appreciation for you. I appreciate your feelings as an Arab of conviction. I have on another occasion said to President Johnson that if I were an Arab I would do what Ambassador El-Farra is doing. He is defending a cause."

He then clasped my shoulder and said: "Let us sit and try again. Tell me, what else do you want in the draft resolution?"

I said "since I was not the one meant in your statement, I wish you had made it in the presence of those you had in mind. However, I will forget it."

We then proceeded to reconsider what changes I wanted. He accepted every one of them, but asked for time to consult with Washington.

A few minutes later he came to inform me that everything was agreed. Thus the draft contained nothing to justify the Israeli attack. It made no reference to "terrorism", to Fateh or to infiltration. It simply referred to cease-fire violation and this was a governmental violation, not that of individuals.

I met my Arab colleagues who were waiting impatiently outside, much worried about the outcome. They could not believe that the Americans had given all those concessions. "I asked for less, without success," said Ambassador Bouattoura. "What happened?"

"Let us go to the Council and have the draft adopted first," I said. "We will discuss what happened later. It is a long story."

The revised draft was eventually adopted unanimously at the 1407th meeting.[1]

---

1. Security Council Resolution no.248, dated 24th March 1968.

    "The Security Council,
    Having heard the statements of the representatives of Jordan and Israel,
    Having noted the contents of the letters of the Permanent Representatives of Jordan and Israel in documents S/8470, S/8475, S/8478, S/8483, S/8484 and S/8486.
    Having noted further the supplementary information provided by the Chief of Staff of UNTSO as contained in documents S/7930, Add. 64 and Add.65,
    Recalling resolution 236 (1967) by which the Security Council condemned any and all violations of the cease-fire,
    Observing that the military action by the armed forces of Israel on the territory of Jordan was of a large-scale and carefully planned nature,
    Considering that all violent incidents and other violations of the cease-fire should be prevented and not overlooking past incidents of this nature,
    Recalling further resolution 237 (1967) which called upon the Government of Israel to ensure the safety, welfare and security of the inhabitants of the areas where military operations have taken place,

CONTINUED

This was the seventh time that Israel had been condemned by the Security Council. This time it committed itself to "consider further and more effective steps as envisaged in the Charter to ensure against repetition of such acts," representing an indirect reference to Chapter VII of the Charter, relating to sanctions. Many more violations have been perpetrated by Israel but because of the U.S. commitment to Israel, the Council has not been able to take more effective steps as envisaged in the Charter to ensure against their repetition.

5

I have dwelt at length on the American role in the Security Council debate and on the other forms of U.S. pressure in order to show the new style of diplomacy of my American colleague, Ambassador Goldberg. In the U.S. attempt to prevent condemnation of the Israeli attack on Karameh the Americans tried hard to achieve the adoption of what they called a "balanced" resolution by the Council. By "balanced" they meant a wording which condemns both the invader and the victim. They had to freeze the complaint until the invasion was over, time and again, but unlike other similar attempts during the 1967 war, they failed. Another attempt to make the complaint part of the whole Arab-Israeli conflict, or better still, of the Middle East crisis, also failed. A third objective, to put observers on the so-called cease-fire line, so that it would permanently separate the West Bank from the East Bank of Jordan and thus nullify the armistice agreement and facilitate the incorporation of the West Bank into Israel, also failed. Their fourth goal was to make special reference to terrorism or Fateh or infiltration. This too was not reached. We resisted all these attempts, despite the

---

CONTINUED
1. Deplores the loss of life and heavy damage to property;
2. Condemns the military action launched by Israel in flagrant violation of the United Nations Charter and the cease-fire resolution:
3. Deplores all violent incidents in violation of the cease-fire and declares that such actions of military reprisal and other grave violations of the cease-fire cannot be tolerated and that the Security Council would have to consider further and more effective steps as envisaged in the Charter to ensure against repetition of such acts;
4. Calls upon Israel to desist from acts or activities in contravention of resolution 237(1967);
5. Requests the Secretary-General to keep the situation under review and to report to the Security Council as appropriate."

weight of American pressure.

No reference whatsoever was made to Fateh, infiltration or terrorism in the Karameh resolution.

The Israeli representative played no role in this affair, apart from delivering violent speeches. Lobbying, manoeuvres, pressure, intimidation and contacts with Security Council members were all left to Israel's strategic partner, the United States, which used its entire diplomatic weight as a Big Power for this purpose. Not only did the U.S. give Israel this diplomatic support, but all the weapons used in Karameh including communications systems, artillery, jets, rifles, ammunition, tanks and their cannons, were generously provided by the U.S.

Members of the Security Council avidly watched the continuous U.S. pressure on a small country, Jordan, and Jordan's strong resistance to such pressure was obvious to all Council members and earned her much sympathy and respect, giving our case wider support. One member of the Security Council who watched every U.S. move closely came to me at the end of the debate and said: "The way the U.S. has behaved towards its friend, Jordan, reflects one thing — the bankruptcy of American diplomacy."

6

I will conclude this chapter with an incident which indicates the difference between promises and commitments given to Israel and those given to an Arab state at the highest level. In autumn 1969 President Nixon visited the United Nations and made a major speech to the General Assembly. Later he and Secretary-General U Thant greeted all the Ministers and Ambassadors accredited to the U.N. The same day the President asked to meet a few delegations from friendly countries, Jordan amongst them. We went to the Waldorf Astoria Hotel to meet him, at around four o'clock. He was apparently briefed by the State Department about our delegation and he was very cordial.

Our delegation consisted of Jordanian Foreign Minister Abdul Monem Rifai and the late Prime Minister Abdul Hamid Sharaf, who was then the Jordanian Ambassador in Washington, together with myself as the Permanent Representative of Jordan to the United Nations.

Mr Rifai thanked Mr Nixon for receiving us in spite of the pressure of work in New York and then turned to discussing the Israeli occupation of the West Bank and other Arab territories: "No progress whatsoever has been made to bring about the withdrawal of Israeli troops from that part of Jordan," he said. "I do not want to go back home empty-handed. You know, Mr President, we are counting a great deal on your support and help. His Majesty King Hussein has been expecting stronger American assistance."

President Nixon answered: "Please Mr Minister convey to His Majesty the King my highest consideration. You are right about the need for more progress on your problem with Israel. I do not want you this time to go back empty-handed. We are concerned about Jordan. We want to change our image among the one hundred and fifty million Arabs. This takes time. I assure you we are not concerned about our American politics. Our politics should be even-handed. We want to be the friend of the Arabs and Israel."

Then the President turned to his Secretary of State, William Rogers, while Henry Kissinger of the National Security Council and Joseph Sisco of the State Department were watching and listening, and said: "Listen Bill, I do not want the Minister to go back empty-handed. Otherwise, the position of Jordan will be undermined before the revolutionary forces. Discuss the matter in detail and make sure the Minister does not go back empty-handed." William Rogers replied: "Fine. I'll do that."

To the late Minister Abdul Monem Rifai and his assistants the meeting was fruitful. Mr Nixon walked with us to the elevator, shook hands with everyone and assured us again that he would see to it that Minister Rifai would not go home empty-handed.

The following day Joe Sisco arranged for a meeting for the Foreign Minister and myself with Secretary Rogers, which Sisco attended. William Rogers, who was known for his honesty and straight-forwardness, spoke to Foreign Minister Rifai very openly and frankly. He said: "Mr Minister, let us be frank and honest about it. There is nothing we can do for you other than arranging for you to meet Golda Meir."

The Foreign Minister could not believe what he heard. It was a shock to us both. We had expected President Nixon's promise to mean anything but this. The American Minister, however, did not want to beat around the bush and to mislead us.

The day before, immediately after our meeting with the President, we had met Mahmoud Riad the Foreign Minister of Egypt, since in accordance with the instructions of our Heads of State, we were co-ordinating our work in the United Nations. He was happy to hear what my Minister had to say about President Nixon's promises, but he expressed his doubts about them. For him, American policy-makers had lost credibility a long time before.

"Don't be too optimistic," he told Rifai. "You might be very much disappointed. I have been dealing with the Americans for almost two years on this very issue. They are evasive. They are not very honest in their promises. Their diplomacy is not like that of other countries. Don't take what you hear literally." We had, however, remained more optimistic than our Egyptian colleague.

William Rogers had proved Riad right. Rifai was greatly shocked, and disappointed. "Is the whole thing a joke?" he asked Rogers. "I cannot understand it. You tell me there is nothing you can do other than arranging a meeting between me and Golda Meir. But this, Mr Secretary, does not need your good offices. I can go and meet Golda Meir right now without your help if I want to. She stays downstairs in this hotel."

Secretary Rogers said: "I am sorry. There is nothing else I can do for you. You have to help us so we can help you." Minister Rifai said: "Is this all you have to say, Mr Secretary?" William Rogers replied: "Yes Sir."

At this stage Minister Rifai said: "In that case I shall have to leave for Jordan today. I shall put before His Majesty the King all that has happened. I shall let everyone know how a Big Power treats a friend, the small country of Jordan."

He then stood up. So did I, together with Secretary Rogers and Joseph Sisco.

We excused ourselves and left. Mahmoud Riad was waiting downstairs and could see the irritation on Rifai's face. He said: "I see you are not happy. I told you not to rely on the Americans. Israel is their favourite baby. You have to understand that. They want to pull us to the negotiating table. This we know. And until you are strong, you will get nothing out of any negotiations."

That same evening both Rifai and Riad left New York for home to report to King Hussein and President Nasser.

Chapter 8

Resistance versus Terrorism: Zionism and the Policy of Expansion

"A third conflict is inevitable and the most important thing is that in this third conflict we must fight in the entire area. This conflict must be a new war of independence."

Yitzhak Shalov
(prior to the 1967 war)

While I was at the United Nations the representative of Israel consistently called the Palestine resistance "terrorism". Ambassador Goldberg of the United States and Lord Caradon of the United Kingdom often supported this Israeli contention, agreeing with the Israeli definition during such UN debates as that on the Israeli invasion of Karameh in Jordan in 1968.

I, of course, called the Palestinian actions "legitimate resistance".

When the people of Europe formed themselves into resistance groups to oppose the Nazi forces during the Second World War, they were rightly hailed as heroes, not as terrorists. When Charles de Gaulle, the hero of the French resistance, went to London to make it his headquarters from which to conduct his resistance, Winston Churchill, then British Prime Minister, hailed him at the airport saying: "Here is the man who is carrying the honour of France," and offered him all facilities.

I always tried to explain, in the Security Council and elsewhere, that Israeli acts of repression against our people naturally stimulated acts of resistance in return. No matter how one looked at the problem it was clear:

1. That there was Palestinian territory occupied by Israeli forces.
2. That there was a decision by the Security Council calling for Israeli withdrawal.
3. That the Israelis had not only refused to withdraw, but had established, and kept on establishing, Jewish settlements on these Palestinian lands.
4. That the Israeli authorities had illegally annexed parts of the occupied territory, thus violating Security Council decisions requesting Israel to rescind all these measures.
5. That the Israelis had resorted to all forms of oppression to perpetuate their illegal occupation.
6. That in the United Nations no effective measures, namely sanctions, could be taken in accordance with Chapter VII of the United Nations Charter to remedy the situation because of the attitude of the United States.
7. That these factors — the occupation, the inaction of the United Nations, the arbitrary measures of repression and political expediency — all led to one conclusion, Resistance.

On another occasion I reminded Security Council members of Europe's resistance to the Nazis. Many members had themselves been anti-Nazi freedom fighters. I showed the Council a book with the names and pictures of some of those European freedom fighters, who eventually became high responsible officials of the United Nations. They had much sympathy for the Palestinians, and rejected the Israeli claim that resistance in Europe was different from resistance in Palestine or the Lebanon. Occupation, whether in Asia, Africa or Europe, is the same.

Israel has thus left the Palestinians no other choice but to resist. What else is left for a man who lost everything? Is he to surrender his values and heritage? Should he and his accept being a people without a country, without a future? This would mean their complete destruction, and this is why they have resisted occupation.

The Israeli representative once complained that Palestinian and other Arab leaders had urged the Palestinians to resist occupation. I reminded him that such encouragement was by no means unique, quoting part of an appeal broadcast to Europe, inviting the people to resist Hitler and Nazism:

"Dear brothers, dear sisters!
We remember you,
We think of you.
We are with you with our hearts.
In this serious hour, do not despair,
We are coming soon.

We shall return to you under the banners of victory,
Await each day the victory,
Do not spend the time idly
Suffering quietly and asleep
Holy hatred and pure reason will show you the right way.

Strike, strike the enemy in the rear without pity.
Destroy the houses, trains, stations and trucks!
Burn the grain, the forests and the warehouses,
Blow up the tanks. Tear down the wires!

We shall overcome all difficulties,
The hour of revenge is coming.
Dear brothers! Dear sisters!
We remember you. We think of you."

When the United Nations General Assembly recommended the establishment of a Jewish state, it was the conviction of those who supported the resolution that Israel would be peace-loving; that its people would benefit from their past tragic experience and champion human rights, and help in putting an end to lawlessness in world affairs. They could never expect that a new and aggressive Israel would itself defy the United Nations. Indeed, Israel was only admitted to membership of the United Nations after Abba Eban came before the United Nations and declared that his government unreservedly accepted the obligations of the United Nations Charter and undertook to honour them from the day when it became a member of the United Nations. He expressly undertook, on behalf of his government, to implement the U.N. partition plan and the protocol of Lausanne, and thus undertook to ensure the repatriation of over two million refugees expelled by Israeli forces from their homes and homelands, and to pay adequate compensation to those who chose not to return.

In practice, however, Israel had defied all U.N. resolutions, and has shown no respect for the sanctity of international agreements. The flouting of U.N. resolutions for over thirty-seven years indicates how much respect the Israelis have for the family of nations and world public opinion. The whole policy of piecemeal expansion and annexation was part of the original plan. Theodor Herzl, the founder of Zionism, declared openly that when the Zionists occupied the land they would spirit the population across the frontiers. A later affirmation of this same view can be found in the Report of the King-Crane Commission in 1919 that "all the Zionists who testified before us spoke of the eventual dispossession of non-Jewish communities in Palestine, who then constituted more than 90 per cent of the population".

The facts, of course, tell the real story. In 1947 the Zionists accepted the United Nations partition boundary; in 1948 the Israelis advanced further into Palestine land, then claimed the new Armistice Agreement and its demarcation line as the border. As a result of the 1967 invasion and occupation of all Palestine, they called the whole occupied area *Eretz Israel,* and claimed that the Jordan River was the border. Now they are occupying more Arab lands still in line with their *"fait accompli"* policy.

It is since the occupation by Israel of yet more Arab territory in 1967 that the United States has made it a condition that the PLO should first recognise the legitimacy of Israel before it could itself be granted recognition. Israel was established by the same U.N. partition resolution which also recommended the establishment of an Arab State of Palestine. Following the 1948 War, however, Israel enacted legislation by virtue of which much of the territory set aside for the Arab State of Palestine was incorporated into Israel. By virtue of that legislation 94.4 per cent of Arab territory is now considered by virtue of this legislation Israeli property.

On the other hand would not Palestinian recognition of the legitimacy of Israel amount to acceptance of its illegal legislation and admission of the impossibility of achieving the Palestine state, prescribed by the United Nations? Does it not mean waiving all Palestinian rights, property and statehood? Would it not, indeed, violate the partition resolution itself, which has been regularly re-affirmed ever since it was first passed?

Does it make sense, moreover, that the victim of aggression should be the first to recognise the other side? How can the Palestinians give Israel documents that would ensure its right to live, the right to peace and the right to security, before Israel has even recognised the existence of the legitimate rights of the people of Palestine, which have been recognised by the United Nations and which Israel itself accepted as a basis for settlement when it signed the Protocol of Lausanne on 12th May 1949? To do this is for the Palestinians to surrender to Israel before it withdraws from Palestinian and other Arab territories, and before it recognises that the people of Palestine have more legitimate rights in Palestine.

I once had occasion to remind the Special Representative of the Secretary-General of the United Nations, Gunnar Jarring, that the United Nations Palestine Conciliation Commission consisting of France, the United States and Turkey, had reached in Lausanne on 12th May 1949, an agreement called the Protocol of Lausanne, which was signed by Israel and all parties concerned. The agreement stated clearly that the partition line, as fixed by the partition resolution of 29th November 1947, would be the basis for any settlement and reiterated the international commitment to establish a Palestinian Arab State. The Protocol was later unilaterally revoked by Israel in defiance of the Commission. No action was taken either by the United States or by any other permanent member of the Security Council to remedy the situation, although the Charter gave them a special responsibility for world peace and security. This encouraged Israel to continue its defiance. Prior to the 1967 war, Israel used to claim that the Armistice lines were her borders, while we used to answer that the Armistice Agreement did not fix boundaries but simply fixed Armistice demarcation lines pending a final settlement of the problem on the basis of the partition resolution.

I explained to Ambassador Jarring that the Arabs had always sought peace but that it had not been achieved because Israel's leaders lived in the colonial era of the last century. They feel at home not with the spirit of today, but with a vicious ideology of domination and expansion — an ideology of the past. Their behaviour revealed their hidden intentions. It showed that their acceptance of the United Nations resolution and the partition line as the boundary was meaningless and that their undertaking to abide by the terms of the partition resolution was also meaningless, although they owe their very existence as a state to this Partition resolution.

2

The obdurate Israelis today should also consider the last words of

Chaim Weizmann, the first President of Israel, words which I cited time and again in the Security Council. The last occasion was while dealing with the Jerusalem Question on 2nd July 1969:

> "We are a small people but a great people, an ugly and yet a
> beautiful people; a creative and a destructive people — a
> people in whom genius and folly are equally co-mingled. We
> are an impetuous people who have time and again repudiated
> and wrecked what our ancestors built. For God's sake let us
> not allow the breach in the wall to swallow us."

Israel's representatives at the United Nations have resorted to all kinds of tricks to defend their expansionism, showing the impetuosity and folly to which President Weizmann referred.

On 21st March 1968 Joseph Tekoah, the Israeli permanent representative to the United Nations, said to the Security Council:

> "I am, however, surprised by the sudden affection he
> (referring to me) has displayed for the Armistice Agreement
> and the Armistice Lines because it was he who, on 31st May
> 1967, before this body, declared:
> "Mr President, to my knowledge the question of Palestine is
> still before the Security Council. The problem is not solved.
> There is an Armistice Agreement. The Agreement did not fix
> boundaries; it fixed a demarcation line. The Agreement did
> not pass judgement on rights — political, military or otherwise.
> Thus I know of no territory;" I repeat "I know of no territory";
> I know of no boundary; I know of a situation frozen by an
> Armistice Agreement.[1]

When in 1978 the Egyptian Delegation visited Israel in order to prepare for the Camp David Accords, they found in their hotel rooms Israeli propaganda material containing the above quotation. Naturally the Israelis did not mention my reply.

> "I continue to maintain that the Armistice Agreement did not
> fix boundaries; it did not fix borders, it only froze the situation.
> The line which is recognised by this body is the partition line of
> 29th November 1947. It was never the intention — and what I
> am saying is taken from the Armistice Agreement — to fix

---

1. Security Council Meeting no. 1401, 21st March 1968.

borders. It did not fix boundaries. It simply froze the situation pending a final settlement. On 12th May 1949 the Israelis signed the Protocol of Lausanne, by virtue of which they accepted the Partition as the basis for the settlement. Therefore, when this representative comes and says that I said this, I reply: Yes, I said it and I maintain it. The Armistice Agreement did not give you a border or a boundary. It simply froze the situation. And by might you cannot acquire right. This is a well-known principle which is our jurisprudence. Article 17 of the Charter of the Organisation of American States, of which the United States is a member, is very clear on this."[2]

This was my answer to Israeli distortion.

In August 1963, a "Round Table" forum was held in Israel, reported in the newspaper *Ma'ariv*.[3] This meeting was attended by Eliahu Sassoon, Yigael Yadin, Yitzhak Shalev, Geula Cohen and others, all of whom were recognized Zionist leaders in Israel. Yitzhak Shalev told his colleagues:

"What are we doing today? We are planning for a third conflict with the Arabs, and at the same time we do not believe in this third conflict and are waiting for peace. In my opinion, the person who proves that peace will not come until after this third conflict will do a great thing, because a third conflict is inevitable and the most important thing is that in this third conflict we must fight in the entire area. This conflict must be a new war of independence, but not independence of some additional "triangle" — independence of the Promised Land within her geo-political borders."[4]

He also said:

"The borders of the Armistice Agreement are by no means the borders which were created to feed the Jewish people"[5]

---

2. Ibid.

3. It was later reproduced in English in the *Middle East Journal,* vol.18, Spring 1964 under the title "How to speak to the Arabs", pp. 143-162.

4. Ibid. p.159

5. Ibid, p.162, quoted in my speech before the Security Council meeting no. 1401, 21st March 1968.

"Chapter 15 of the Book of Genesis is the only document on which one can base his stand in peace negotiations . . . Fruitful and forthright negotiations on a peace pact will come to the region only after the armies of the area are finally defeated and Israel's borders are fixed according to the Biblical vision. Until this final fall of the enemy we cannot pray for peace because peace such as this will be based on compromises and we have nothing on which to compromise. On the contrary, we must make clear to the world the nature of our requirements which are as yet unfulfilled."[6]

Yigael Yadin spoke about education in Israel. He wanted every child to know the "history of his ancestors". He added: "We will tell our children the truth. Hebron is not ours today, but it was ours in the past, and King David ruled over it. The fact that we were forced to give up Hebron today does not mean that we must eradicate it from Jewish history."[7]

Thus, long before 1967, Israel was turning her eyes to yet more war and expansion.

This arrogance explains the Israeli performance in the United Nations, and is a reflection of the beliefs of the present Israeli leadership, all of whom are adamant about continuing their extreme expansionist line. As a result, a new generation of Israelis is growing up with similar views. A large majority today favour continued Jewish settlements, colonisation as Toynbee calls it, on the West Bank, the Gaza Strip and the Syrian Heights — the Golan, the Arab area they occupied in 1967. According to reports carried by various international news agencies on 9th May 1981 just under 74 per cent of those polled favoured continued Jewish settlements on the occupied West Bank. The report said that Prime Minister Begin had demonstrated his determination to retain perpetual "Israeli domination over the West Bank", when he marked Israel's independence day by visiting Ariel settlement, one of the biggest in the occupied territories. To a crowd of settlers chanting "Begin, Begin" he swore the following oath:

"I Menachem, the son of Ze'ev and Hasia Begin, do solemnly swear that as long as I serve the nation as Prime Minister we

---

6.   Ibid, p.161

7.   Ibid, p.151

> will not leave any part of Judea, Samaria, the Gaza Strip and
> the Golan Heights."[8]

Judea and Samaria are the Zionist terms for the West Bank. Begin
and his colleagues of the same generation would like Jewish history
to record that they died leaving behind them a greater Israel and
that, despite all world pressure, they did not abandon a single inch
of the Holy Land. It is for this reason that the Israeli leadership is
creating a new generation, full of bitterness, and is making Israel an
island of hatred in the occupied Palestinian territories although
hatred was never part of their tradition or heritage.

The former Israeli Minister of Finance has maintained that Israel
should annex the uninhabited areas and abandon the inhabited
areas. Former Israeli Foreign Minister Abba Eban, however, took a
different view, supporting the establishment of a Palestinian State in
the inhabited areas on the West Bank only on condition that the
state should form together with Israel and Jordan a kind of
commonwealth or confederation. According to Eban the state of
Palestine should not have any army of its own, nor act as a member
of the Arab family.[9] This idea of depriving an Arab state from acting
as a member of the Arab family is exactly what the Israeli leadership
has tried to achieve at Camp David. Menachem Begin, former Irgun
terrorist leader, was yet more frank. In a statement he made to the
Israeli Knesset on 28th December 1977 he presented his plan for
peace in the Middle East, which was accepted by sixty-four votes in
favour with eight votes against and forty abstentions. The plan
would enable the Palestinians within the occupied territory to have
their own administrative council, provided Israel "retained"
sovereignty over these territories. All twenty-six Articles of the plan
revolved around the same idea of keeping the territory, permitting
the people to manage their own affairs while living within territory
over which Israel had complete sovereignty. Furthermore, article 20
enabled the Israelis to own property in the West Bank and the Gaza
Strip and gave "equal rights" to those who could obtain Israeli
citizenship to have the same privileges in the other part of Palestine.
But who can obtain such citizenship in an area intended to be a
purely Jewish State? Gentiles can hardly be encouraged to have
Israeli citizenship, because the land is intended by Begin and his ilk
to be purely Jewish. This therefore was no more than yet another

---

8. *Jordan Times,* 9th May 1981

9. *Davar,* 11 December 1979.

method confiscating Arab property, through pressure and intimidation.

On 14th October 1966 a few months before Israeli occupation of the remaining parts of Palestine together with the Syrian Heights — the Golan — and Sinai in Egypt, Abba Eban appeared before the Security Council to sing the song of peace. He emphasized:

> "We do not covet an inch of Syrian territory or of the territory of any other state."

Yet, after the 1967 war and the occupation of that territory, Moshe Dayan told the youth of the United Labour Party in Israel:

> "Our fathers made the borders of 1947; we made the border of 1967; another generation will take our frontiers to where they belong."

The then Defence Minister had stated on 5th June 1967, i.e. after the Six Day War had begun:

> "We have no invasion plan. Our only target is to foil the Arab armies' aim of invading our country."[10]

Only two months later, after Israel's armed forces had completed occupation of Palestinian territories, the very same Moshe Dayan had the following to say:

> "People abroad must realise that with all the strategic importance to Israel of Sinai, the Golan Heights and the Tiran Straits — the mountain range west of the Jordan lies at the heart of Jewish history. If we have the Book of the Bible, and the people of the Book, then you also have the Land of the Bible — of the Judges and of the Patriarchs in Jerusalem, Hebron, Jericho, and thereabouts . . . On no account will we force ourselves to leave (the Hebron) . . . This may not be a political program, but it is more important — it is the fulfilment of a people's ancestral dreams."[11]

---

10. Jerusalem Israel Domestic Service (in Hebrew), 0837 hours GMT, 5th June 1967.

11. As summarised in the *Jerusalem Post* of 10th August 1967.

Begin himself wanted then, as he always wanted, Israel to retain sovereignty over all the lands of Palestine, be it those occupied in 1948, those annexed after that occupation, or those occupied in 1967 — indeed he even felt that it should expand over the river to the other side of Jordan.

Golda Meir, when Prime Minister of Israel, was one of the first to go as far as ignoring the very existence of the people of Palestine, telling the London *Sunday Times* on 15th June 1969:

> "It was not as though there was a Palestinian people and we came and threw them out and took their country away from them. They did not exist."

Later she told one of the American TV networks:

> "Where are the Palestinians? They simply do not exist."

These statements reflect a state of mind which developed after the Israelis had accomplished the second stage of their expansion and began to question the very existence of the people of Palestine. They reached the extent of challenging the legitimacy of the State of Jordan. In a speech to his party, the Mapai, on 8th September 1967 Abba Eban declared:

> "The problem is not any longer whether Jordan recognises the existence of Israel, but whether Israel recognises the existence of Jordan."[12]

The Israeli leadership has always strongly opposed the establishment of a Palestinian state in Palestine, or in any part of Palestine. Both the United States and Israel would even prefer to see the West Bank and the Gaza Strip annexed by Jordan, Syria, Egypt or any Arab state, rather than become an independent *Palestinian* state. To the Israelis, any arrangement of this sort would be regarded as temporary and would be revoked when Israel seized those territories. Then Israel would argue that those territories were parts of *Eretz Israel* and that, this being the case, Israel had a better claim than any of the Arab States. The creation of a Palestinian state in Palestine however would stand in the way of any attempt at Israeli annexation. This is simply because the world would not permit

---

12. *L'Orient*, 9th September 1967.

Israel to annex another state. What is more, the people of Palestine have a stronger claim to the land than the Israelis just as they have better claims on Haifa, Lydda, Jaffa, Ramleh, Acre, Gaza, Khan-Yunis and elsewhere.

If the state of Palestine were to be created, one other matter would worry every Zionist: Israel has occupied part of the Palestinian homeland by force. It has no right to it. That territory, part of the Palestinian homeland, would always be looked at as a usurped territory by the rest of the world. But denial of the national rights of the people of Palestine is no answer. The only way out is for the Israelis to recognise Palestinian rights. Attempts to impose an unjust solution by force or with the aid of outside powers, will eventually fail, for they do not remove the injustice done to the Palestinians and to their homeland. Only thus can the region live in peace.

But this seems to be a vain hope. Israeli wars of expansion do not decrease, indeed it seems as though they will never cease. The *International Herald Tribune* of Friday 16th May 1980 reported that Israelis were preparing terrorist attacks against the Palestinians of the occupied territories. This, the paper said, was the first time this had happened since the formation of the Israeli State. United States-born Rabbi Meir Kahane headed this militant terrorist group and the Jewish Defense League, the same man who once threatened my life.[13]

According to the *Herald Tribune,* Kahane told a news conference that the Israeli Government should support a "Jewish terror group"; that, he hoped, "would through bombs and grenades kill Arabs to drive them out of Israel and the occupied territories." Kahane confirmed in this news conference that "there are Jews in this country (Israel) at the moment who are planning things . . . and will do terrorist acts".

Sure enough, fifteen days later, on 2nd June 1980, Israeli terrorists used bombs and grenades to attack the Mayors of Nablus, Ramallah, and Bireh, in the occupied West Bank. The two former Mayors of Ramallah and Nablus, were seriously injured. A doctor had to amputate both legs of Bassam El-Shakaa, the mayor of Nablus, and Kareem Khalef, the Mayor of Ramallah lost a foot. In March 1985 Khalef died of a heart attack. The Zionists cannot, however, sustain a state through such acts of terror and violence.

---

13. Kahane cabled the author at the U.N. and the cable was handed to the Security Council.

According to press reports from Tel-Aviv on the 7th of May 1980, General Rafael Eitan, who was Chief of Staff of Israeli armed forces during the invasion of Lebanon and who was elected to the Knesset as a "Tehiya Party Knesset Member in 1984"[14] said openly that acceptance of the rule of International Law vis-à-vis the Palestine question would cause "our loss of cities such as Jaffa, Beersheba, Nahariya and others. These, according to the partition resolution, were allocated to the Arab State of Palestine.

Eitan, like most other Zionist leaders, knows that Israel owes its very existence to the United Nations but has no wish for the United Nations jurisprudence to prevail. He has therefore said "No" to International Law, "No" to the family of Nations and its resolutions, and "No" to peace. Eitan supported Kahane's terrorist organisation called "Terror Against Terror". It is little wonder that his behaviour as Chief of Staff was characterised by the infliction of terror upon the Palestinian people.

The Israeli invasion of Lebanon in 1982 was yet another of those futile wars which haunt the Middle East, more destructive and brutal than all previous wars. Compared with the massacres I have mentioned earlier, the murders of Ein El-Hilweh, Sabra and Shatila in Lebanon were still more savage and brutal, and this was in addition to the indiscriminate Israeli bombing of Beirut and its heavy shelling by the Israeli and the American navies. The Israeli artillery fired indiscriminately at all civilian areas but this has not brought an end to Palestinian resistance. Israeli might and superiority could intoxicate the Israeli Government just as it thrilled their speakers at the United Nations, but it did not bring security to Galilee, the purported objective of the invasion.

During their speeches at the UN Israel's leaders seemed thrilled by their successes against the Arabs and by their expansion into extra territories which they considered part of their little empire. Their actions, however, have not brought peace to the Holy Land any more than American bombing of Vietnam brought peace there.

3

Indeed, the consequences of these continuing actions are serious not just for the Arabs but also for the world, and there are many who have dwelt on this point. Thus Arnold Toynbee, in his book *Experiences,* commented on the similarity between Israeli wars in

---

14. Tehiya means "Revival"

the Holy Land and the American war in Vietnam:

> "The military might of the United States was being frustrated
> in Vietnam in 1968 because Nationalism is a cause for which
> present-day human beings are willing to sacrifice their lives![15]

He added that the Palestinians have a "still greater incentive to
resist than the Vietnamese had."

This last work of the British historian emphasised the fact that so
long as a subject people survived physically, it could eventually look
forward to recovering its political independence. And as Israelis
certainly know, neither the Palestinians nor the Vietnamese can be
exterminated. The Palestinians will continue to resist Israeli
occupation not because they like to see people die, houses
destroyed or human beings disfigured, but because the Israelis have
left them no other alternative.

I have used the word "colonialism" but it is not mine; it was given
to Israeli practices by Toynbee. In the same book he said:

> "Israeli colonialism since the establishment of the state of
> Israel is one of the two blackest cases in the whole history of
> colonialism in the modern age; and its blackness is thrown into
> relief by its date. The East European Zionists have been
> practising colonialism in Palestine in the extreme form of
> evicting and robbing the native Arab inhabitants at the very
> time when the West European peoples have been renouncing
> their temporary rule over non-European peoples."[16]

The other "black case" mentioned in Toynbee's book is that of the
Red Indians of the United States, who were evicted from their
ancestral homes in what are now the States of Georgia, Alabama,
Mississippi and Tennessee and placed on 'reservations' in what is
now the state of Oklahoma. The British historian said about these
two cases of colonialism:

> "This nineteenth-century American colonialism was a crime;
> the Israeli colonialism, which was being carried on at the time
> when I was writing, was a crime that was also a moral
> anachronism."[17]

---

15. A. Toynbee, *Experiences,* OUP, London 1969, p.263.
16. Ibid p.266.
17. Ibid, pp 266-267

Toynbee drew an interesting parallel between Israel's continued wars against the Palestinians and the American wars in Asia:

"In November 1968 Israel in South-West Asia and the United States in South-East Asia were each in the awkward position in which Japan found herself in China before the end of the Sino-Japanese war of 1931-45.

It is the position that has frustrated, and has eventually defeated, a number of successive invaders of Russia: the Poles in the seventeenth century, the Swedes in the eighteenth, the French in 1812, and, most recently, the Germans in the Second World War (in contrast to the Germans' ephemeral success in imposing a peace settlement on Russia before the end of the First World War). Like Hitler and Napoleon and Charles XII in Russia and like the Japanese in China, the Americans in South-East Asia and the Israelis in South-West Asia had challenged infinity. They could win battle after battle and occupy territory after territory, but their opponents would still stay in the field, because, though these opponents could not hold their ground, they had at their disposal a virtually endless space into which they could continue to retreat till their pursuers had extended themselves over more territory than they could effectively control.

"Beyond the River Jordan the Arab World stretches away eastward to the Zagros Mountains and the Persian Gulf; beyond the Suez Canal it stretches away westward to the Atlantic; beyond the Sinai Peninsula it stretches away southward to Aden and to the Sudanese Jazirah; beyond Qunaitreh it stretches away northward to the Syrian Jazirah. In South-East Asia the Americans were confronted with the problem that confronted the Israelis in the Arab World. Behind the Vietcong stood North Vietnam; behind North Vietnam lies China; and, though the population of the United States is today about twice as big as Japan's, Japan's experience in her invasion of China in 1931-45 indicates that even the United States' manpower and industrial power and economic resources would be unequal to the task of bringing a war with China to a victorious conclusion. She would have to conquer and occupy North Vietnam before she could begin to invade China; and here she had to reckon not only with China but with the Soviet Union. The two major communist powers were at loggerheads by now over most of the issues between them but they still saw eye to eye in their common determination to make it impossible for the United States to win her war in Vietnam.

"In this frustrating strategic situation the United States and Israel have both been handicapped by the inhibiting psychological effect of their past unbroken series of victories...

"The Israelis have been the victorious party in three successive Arab-Israeli wars; their victory in the third of these wars has been the most swift and the most sensational of the three; and victors are seldom in a mood for making concessions; a dazzling series of victories is apt to blind the victors to the truth that military victory is a wasting asset. Thus the very brilliance of Israel's military performance hitherto has become a serious psychological obstacle to her attainment of her objective. This sounds paradoxical, but it is the truth."[18]

Toynbee's theory proved to be correct as far as Vietnam was concerned. The war came to an end, and American troops withdrew. It cost the United States a great deal to learn this lesson. Will the Israelis pay the same price before they too learn or will they benefit from American experience?

Isaac Deutscher, a political commentator, critic and economist, himself a Jew, said that after the Israeli victory in 1967, they now appeared as the Prussians of the Middle East, having won three wars against their Arab neighbours. He added that the Prussians also, a century ago, defeated all their neighbours within a few years; the Danes, the Austrians and the French.[19]

Deutscher did not live to witness the fourth war, dying in Rome in August 1967. He predicted, however, that "next time the Egyptian Air Force may strike the pre-emptive blow."[20] In October 1973, it was Egypt and Syria who struck first.

Pre-emptive strikes, however, are not the answer. They do not solve disputes, neither do they bring peace. Israeli military aggression has the support of the United States, military and political. This support is not given for nothing. There is a price to be paid.

"The succession of victories bred in them an absolute confidence in their own efficiency; a blind reliance on the force

---

18.   Ibid, pp. 234-235

19.   Isaac Deutscher *The Non-Jewish Jew*, O.U.P. London, 1968, p.141.

20.   Ibid, p.144.

of their arms; chauvinistic arrogance and contempt for other peoples. I fear that a similar degeneration — for degeneration it is — may be taking place in the political character of Israel. Yet as the Prussia of the Middle East, Israel can be only a feeble parody of the original. The Prussians were at least able to use their victories for uniting in their Reich all German-speaking peoples living outside the Austro-Hungarian Empire. Germany's neighbours were divided among themselves by interests, history, religion and language. Bismarck, Wilhelm II and Hitler could play them off against one another. The Israelis are surrounded by Arabs only. Attempts to play off the Arab states against one another are bound to fail in the end. The Arabs were at loggerheads with one another in 1948, when Israel waged its first war; they were far less divided in 1956 during Israel's second war; and they formed a common front in 1967. They may prove far more firmly united in any future confrontation with Israel.

The Germans have summed up their own experience in the bitter phrase; 'Man kann sich totsiegen!' 'You can drive yourself victoriously into your grave.' This is what the Israelis have been doing.

World public opinion forgets that what applied to Europe during World War II applies to all areas where there is foreign occupation and domination. A people's desire to liberate itself from foreign occupation is a sacred cause. Zionist leaders reject the application of this logic to the Palestinian people, but not all Jews are in agreement with this view. Mr Moshe Menuhin, the 78 year-old Jewish author and father of the famous concert violinist Yehudi Menuhin, asked, after long experience with Zionism:

"How can a...Jew imagine that Zionist Israel...after twenty-five years of expanding...be allowed...to expand still further in search of still safer "secure boundaries"? How can wise Jews allow themselves to be used by superpowers and constantly treat with contempt the United Nations which gave birth to Zionist Israel?"[21]

Another musician, Joseph Elgar, who at the time of writing his article in *Newsweek* on 15th September 1980, was music director of

---

21. Moshe Menuhin, *Jewish Critics of Zionism*, Detroit 1976

the Symphony Orchestra for the United Nations, warned that the policy of Begin would lead to the 'growth of anti-Semitism.' He wrote: "The fires are stoked when a Geula Cohen makes the preposterous statement (in the Knesset) that 'the Jews did not come back to Israel to be safe, but to build a nation on the lands given to us by the Bible', and forces Knesset support for a new law that unnecessarily antagonises most of the world."

Mr Elgar referred here to the illegal annexation of Jerusalem. From his personal experience he emphasised that the "Arabs want peace as much as we Jews do. The concept of winner and loser is obsolete in the nuclear era. Either we will all win or we all lose. The solution for us Jews lies in our real strength which is not in force or arms but in the morality, fairness and justice we learned as children in our chaders (schools). We must stop seizing the lands of people who have lived on them for centuries, biblical-geographical names notwithstanding."

The writings of many other Jewish scholars and philosophers stress the point that expelling the Palestinians and taking their homes and lands will always be considered an unforgiveable crime. Scholars such as Rabbi Elmer Berger, Judah Magnus and Martin Buber condemned Zionist behaviour for this reason. Dag Hammarskjöld, the Swedish United Nations Secretary-General, once told me that "if B.G. (referring to Ben Gurion, who was then Israeli Prime Minister) would follow Buber's wisdom and philosophy there would be lasting peace in the Middle East."

4

Now Ben Gurion is dead. So is Golda Meir. So are Allon and Dayan. The former Irgun terrorist leader, Begin, during his term of office as prime minister which expired in 1983, merely continued with his old habits. The younger generation in Israel and its present leadership have been brought up to follow in the steps of Dayan, Meir, Ben Gurion, Shamir, Sharon and Begin. Many Israelis have rejected Zionism and formed some organisations to oppose it such as the "Peace Now" movement. Some of those Israelis who could not see eye to eye with Zionism have been disillusioned and many have left Israel to reside either in the United States or in Europe.

Take the case of an American Jew, I. F. Stone, a writer and scholar, who at one time was a member of one of the Zionist terrorist organisations. In his publication *I. F. Stone's Weekly* of 13th January 1969 he wrote:

"We made the Palestinian Arabs homeless to make a home for
our people. That is the simple truth as history will see it, and
until we make amends and resettle the refugees and create a
new political framework in which Jew and Arab can live
together in a new and greater Palestine there will be no peace."

He expressed the views of those Israelis who got sick and tired of
Zionist ruthlessness. But Israel's leaders are still adamant about
their dream of expansion. They adopt savage methods to achieve
this purpose. The parties in power and the major parties in the
opposition agree, with some exception, over substance even if they
seem to disagree over form. They all wanted to annex the territory
acquired by force in 1967 and to work for further expansion. They
merely disagreed over whether the annexation of Palestine territories should take place through special legislation or through actual
practice, quiet annexation; whether it should be by stages or at
once. Zionism and annexationism are two sides of the same coin.

With this background I found Zionists who said that they were
victims of "dislike" because they were "unlike" others are now
practising worse violence against those whom they call "unlike", i.e.
the Palestinians. They have waged their wars because of their lust
for more territories, dictated by cupidity and prejudice. They are
practising prejudice against the Palestinians, and as a cover-up for
that, they keep complaining of anti-semitism. The Israeli leadership
is unable to learn from its own tragic experience. This cruelty, which
spreads like fire and ends up in destruction and mass killings, cannot
but breed counter-violence.

Chapter 9

Ambassador Jarring, the Big Four and Resolution 242

"As I review the march of world events in recent years I am ever more deeply convinced that the processes of the United Nations represent the soundest hope for peace in the world."

Dwight D. Eisenhower
President of the United States

When the text of Security Council Resolution 242 was discussed with the leading UN official, Gunnar Jarring, as well as in the United Nations Security Council, the question of Israeli withdrawal was raised.[1] The Israelis maintained that Resolution 242 in fact

---

1. Resolution No. 242 (1967) dated 22nd November 1967:

    STATING THE PRINCIPLES OF A JUST AND LASTING PEACE IN THE MIDDLE EAST

    The Security Council,
    Expressing its continuing concern with the grave situation in the Middle East,
    Emphasizing the inadmissibility of the acquisition of territory by war and the need to work for a just and lasting peace in which every State in the area can live in security
    Emphasizing further that all Member States in their acceptance of the Charter of the United Nations have undertaken a commitment to act in accordance
    CONTINUED

meant withdrawal to *secure* borders. They claimed, therefore, that the security of Israel was a basic element in that resolution. How the Israeli Ambassador arrived at that contention I did not know. I only knew that the Security Council unanimously adopted the resolution on 22nd November 1967, and the expression "secure borders" was mentioned in the resolution. It never stated, however, that the withdrawal should be "*to* secure and recognised borders". The resolution spoke about the right of every state "to *live* in peace within secure and recognised boundaries," something quite different.

The emphasis here is on living, which does not involve any physical changes in the border to meet the shrill demands for Israel's so-called security. The right to *live* is a mental, not a physical, situation. It is a state of mind. The idea was that every state, including the state of Palestine, had the right to live within secure borders undisturbed by any acts of violence or resistance by either side which might affect that security. What would secure such security? The answer is clearly a just solution to the Palestinian problem following whose adoption there would be no need for

---

CONTINUED

with Article 2 of the Charter,

1. *Affirms* that the fulfilment of Charter principles requires the establishment of a just and lasting peace in the Middle East which should include the application of both the following principles:

(i) Withdrawal of Israeli armed forces from territories occupied in the recent conflict;

(ii) Termination of all claims or states of belligerency and respect for and acknowledgement of the sovereignty, territorial integrity and political independence of every State in the area and their right to live in peace within secure and recognized boundaries free from threats or acts of force;

2. *Affirms* further the necessity

(a) For guaranteeing freedom of navigation through international waterways in the area;

(b) For achieving a just settlement of the refugee problem;

(c) For guaranteeing the territorial inviolability and political independence of every State in the area, through measures including the establishment of demilitarized zones;

3. *Requests* the Secretary-General to designate a Special Representative to proceed to the Middle East to establish and maintain contacts with the States concerned in order to promote agreement and assist efforts to achieve a peaceful and accepted settlement in accordance with the provisions and principles in this resolution.

4. *Requests* the Secretary-General to report to the Security Council on the progress of the efforts of the Special Representative as soon as possible.

Adopted unanimously at the 1382nd meeting.

either Israeli terrorism on the one hand or Palestinian resistance on the other.

The Arab side actually had this interpretation explained to them before they accepted the draft. Both the United States and Britain affirmed that withdrawal under the resolution should be total. It was meant to be complete. It was intended to be a withdrawal from *all* occupied territories. Otherwise the major principle of international law that considers as invalid the acquisition of territory by force or war would be violated.

I need not reiterate the fact that all the talks and contacts between the U.S. and all the Arab governments concerned concentrated on the situation that had arisen as a result of the so-called Six Day War. It was never the intention of the Americans or of the Arabs to draft a resolution containing a recipe for the solution of the Palestinian problem. The intention was to return to the *status quo* — i.e. withdrawal and the other points in 242, to be followed by the opening of the Palestine File. This was affirmed by Ambassador Goldberg in his talks with Mahmoud Riad, was affirmed to me by the American Ambassador and it was only later that matters started taking a different shape as a result of the American-Israeli common stand.

In Ambassador Goldberg's negotiations with Mahmoud Riad, Egypt's Foreign Minister, that preceded resolution 242, it was agreed that the resolution would be confined to the 1967 war; it would not deal with the Palestine problem which had been on the agenda of the General Assembly since 1947.

This agreement was made clear when Mahmoud Riad asked Goldberg to clarify on what basis we should carry out our consultations. Riad said that Ambassador Goldberg "could not give me an answer before referring to Washington. A few days later, he informed me that his government was of the view that consultations on a draft resolution to the Security Council should be confined to the consequences of the June war, and not extend to the Palestine issue."[2]

Prior to the adoption of Resolution 242, Mahmoud Riad came to my office accompanied by Lord Caradon to discuss the draft resolution with the heads of some Arab delegations including my Minister, Abdul Monem Rifai. Riad asked Lord Caradon, the author of 242, the following questions in order to clarify some points

---

2. Mahmoud Riad *The Struggle for Peace in the Middle East,* Quartet Books, London, 1981, p.61

raised earlier by Arab representatives:

> *"Riad:* according to your consultations with the Americans, and according to the meaning of the draft-resolution, [242] does it mean the withdrawal of Israel from all the West Bank?
> *Caradon:* Yes
> *Riad:* Sinai and the Gaza Sector also?
> *Caradon:* Yes
> *Riad:* The Golan Heights?
> *Caradon:* Yes. In brief, the Resolution means the return of Israel to the 4th June position."[3]

Riad also met Kuznetsov, the Deputy Foreign Minister of the U.S.S.R., and asked him the following:

> We have understood from the British and the Americans that the draft presented by Lord Caradon means total Israeli withdrawal from all Arab territories . . . do you have the same understanding?
> Kuznetsov replied: Yes.[4]

What is more, the so called vagueness in the resolution does not appear in the other four official languages of the Security Council, namely the French, Russian, Spanish and Chinese. In all four languages the question of Israeli withdrawal from the occupied territories was clearly stated.

Although Ambassador Arthur Goldberg committed America's moral and political weight to the implementation of the resolution, nothing was done. This lapse of time gave the Israelis the opportunity to start "reading" their own interpretations into Resolution 242.

When Resolution 242 spoke about the right of every state to live within secure and recognised borders, the Arab state of Palestine was one of those states. This is all the more so since the states of both Palestine and Israel were intended to be established by virtue of the same UN partition resolution in 1947. The fact that one was in fact established while the establishment of the other was delayed did not deprive the other of its equal right.

To live "within secure and recognized borders", therefore, never

---

3. Ibid, p.70

4. Ibid, p.70.

1. *The author delivering a speech to the members of Al-Najjadeh organisation at El-Bassa field, Jaffa 1947.*

2. *Alia between her real and her adopted father with the author.*

3. *Khan Yunis refugee camp.*

4. *The author with Dr Ralph Bunche.*

5. *The author with Arthur Goldberg (right) and Bill Buffum (left), both ambassadors of the American delegation to the United Nations.*

6. *The author presiding over the Security Council, talking to the Secretary-General, U Thant. Behind him stand America's ambassadors Richard Pedersen (left) and Theodore Roosevelt Jr (right); 15 March 1966.*

7. On the right Abba Eban, Israel's Foreign Minister, is making a statement to
the Security Council. Behind sits the Permanent Representative, Joseph Tekoah.
On their left is the Jordanian delegation headed by the author. 14th October 1966.

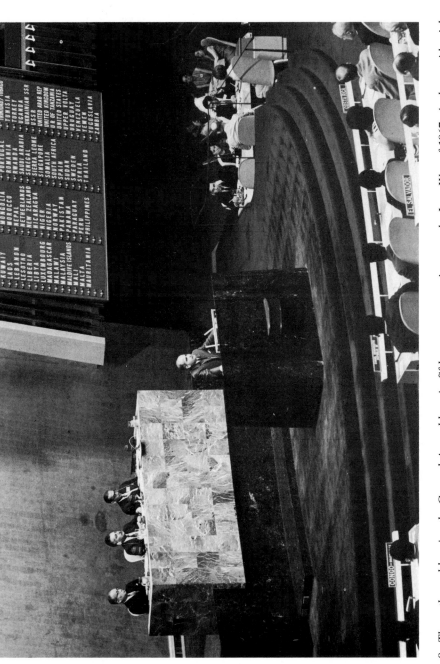

8. *The author addressing the General Assembly at its fifth emergency session over the June War of 1967. At the presidential rostrum behind the speaker sit, left to right, Secretary General U Thant, the President of the Assembly, Abdul Rahman Pazh-wak (Afghanistan) and C. V. Narasiman, Under Secretary for General Assembly Affairs.*

meant that either state could annex the land of the other. The intention was that the Israelis should show by acts and behaviour that they were determined, once and for all, to abandon their dream of expansion so they could *live* in peace within the area allotted to them by the 1947 partition resolution. They should show that they were determined to cultivate a peaceful atmosphere and to prepare the ground for peaceful co-existence. Equally, the other side should demonstrate the same spirit. This would change the nature of the relationship between the parties. When this was done any border would be secure for both parties to live "within". The expansion of and the building of more Jewish colonies on Palestinian lands, almost on a daily basis, would not cultivate the ideal of "living within secure borders", no matter where that border might be.

This background to Resolution 242 is absolutely essential for understanding the point stated above, and equally so really to comprehend the intention of those who unanimously adopted it. In the first place, it was the result of many attempts to reach agreement on an acceptable text that did not compromise the rule of law. It was the result of six months of negotiations, deliberations and diplomatic efforts.

Israel opposed any unconditional withdrawal and insisted on including withdrawal as part of an overall settlement of all issues. The Arab side, on the other hand, insisted that there should be no fruits of aggression and that no conditions should be attached to withdrawal. They asked that withdrawal should precede any other discussion of a solution. The stand of President Eisenhower during the 1956 Tripartite Aggression of France, Britain and Israel against Sinai and the Gaza Strip was cited as an example. During that invasion of Egypt firm and strict adherence to the rules of the Charter was championed by the overwhelming majority of members of the United Nations, with the United States playing a leading role. The American President Dwight D. Eisenhower told his people:

> "As I review the march of world events in recent years, I am ever more deeply convinced that the processes of the United Nations represent the soundest hope for peace in the world."[5]

In 1967, by contrast, Israel used all its diplomatic efforts and all its pressure groups in the United States to ensure that no action would

---

5. See Public Papers of the Presidents of the United States: Dwight D. Eisenhower; 1956 at 1065.

be taken to bring about her complete withdrawal before peace was achieved.

In an article about the Israeli diplomatic campaign during the 1967 war,[6] Gideon Rafael, who was then Permanent Representative of Israel to the United Nations, said that prior to the 1967 invasion Israel felt it necessary to ensure that there would be co-operation between Israel and the United States, in order to avoid what happened in 1956, when both the United States and the Soviet Union took similar stands in the United Nations and, through their combined efforts, enforced complete withdrawal.

The thinking of the American administration in 1956 was based on the theory that Israel could not dictate its conditions for withdrawal and that military conquest could not be the framework within which peace terms might be negotiated. At the time the United States told the General Assembly that the Israeli request implied recognition of the rights of conquest, but that conquest conveys no right. Mr Herbert Hoover, then Under Secretary of State, reminded the Assembly that:

> "The basic purpose of the Charter is peace with justice. The United States is convinced that the United Nations is the best instrument for achieving this end. Peace alone is not enough, for without justice, peace is illusory and temporary. On the other hand, without peace, justice would be submerged by the limitless injustices of war."[7]

2

On the 1967 war, President Lyndon Johnson adopted a different policy. Ambassador Goldberg told the Security Council:

> "What the Near East needs today are new steps towards real peace, not just a cease-fire, which is what we have had for eighteen years; not just withdrawal which is necessary but insufficient."[8]

The question of Israel's occupation of Arab territories and the need

---

6. *Ma'ariv* Magazine 25th January 1972.

7. 11 U.N. GAOR 91 (1956).

8. Security Council Meeting, No.1358, June 13th 1967.

for immediate withdrawal was first discussed in the Security Council. When no agreement could be reached among Security Council members, it was taken to a special session of the UN General Assembly. A summary of the important developments in both organs of the UN may be in order.

On 6th June 1967 the Security Council adopted Resolution No. 233 (1967) which read as follows:

> "The Security Council
> *Noting* the oral report of the Secretary General in this situation, having heard the statements made in the Council, concerned at the outbreak of fighting and with the menacing situation in the Near East:
> 1. *Calls upon* the Government concerned as a *first step* to take forthwith all measures for an immediate cease-fire and for a cessation of all military activities in the area:
> 2. *Requests* the Secretary General to keep the Council promptly and currently informed on the situation."

It was clear that a cease-fire was meant to be the first step. Withdrawal was the next, and this was understood by all members of the Security Council. Indeed, it was the understanding of the overwhelming majority of the members of the United Nations.

Eighteen Latin American states submitted a draft resolution to the Special Session of the General Assembly on 30th June, 1967.[9] Emphasising that the cease-fire ordered by the Security Council was "a first step" towards the achievement of a just peace in the Middle East, "a step which must be reinforced by other measures to be adopted by the Organisation and complied with by the parties", the draft resolution urgently requested:

> 1. "Israel to withdraw all its forces from all the territories occupied by it as a result of recent conflicts,
> 2. The parties in conflict to end the state of belligerency, to establish conditions of co-existence based on good neighbourliness and to have recourse in all cases to the procedure for peaceful settlement indicated in the Charter of the United Nations."

It follows, therefore, that complete withdrawal was not negotiable.

---

9. General Assembly Document No. A/L 523.

It was the second step, after the cease-fire. The parties in conflict were then requested urgently to end the state of belligerency and endeavour to establish conditions of co-existence based on good neighbourliness, and to have recourse in all cases to the procedure for peaceful settlement indicated in the Charter of the United Nations. Thus the Latin American draft resolution was, on this, basically the same as Security Council Resolution 242 and reflected the intention of U.N. members on the question of withdrawal as well as the interpretation to be given to Resolution 242. It also stressed the need for Israeli withdrawal from "all the territories occupied by it as a result of the recent conflict."

The draft was submitted by Argentina, Brazil, Chile, Colombia, Costa Rica, Ecuador, El Salvador, Guatemala, Guyana, Honduras, Jamaica, Mexico, Nicaragua, Panama, Paraguay, Trinidad and Tobago, and Venezuela.

Another draft resolution of the United Nations A/L 522 Rev. 2, dated 3rd July 1967 and submitted to the General Assembly by Afghanistan, Burundi, Cambodia, Ceylon, Congo (Brazzaville), Cyprus, Guinea, India, Indonesia, Kenya, Malaysia, Mali, Pakistan, Senegal, Somalia, United Republic of Tanzania, Yugoslavia and Zambia, read as follows:

"The General Assembly
1. *Calls upon* Israel to withdraw immediately all its forces to the positions they held prior to 5th June, 1967." (paragraph 1)

India, Mali and Nigeria submitted to the Security Council on 7th November 1967 draft resolution No. S/8227 affirming that:

"(i) Occupation or acquisition of territory by military conquest is inadmissable under the Charter of the United Nations and consequently Israel's armed forces should withdraw from all the territories occupied as a result of the recent conflict."

On 10th November 1967 the U.S.S.R. submitted draft resolution No. S/8228 to the Security Council. Paragraph 2(a) reads as follows:

"The Security Council
2. *Urges that* the following steps should be taken:
(a) The parties to the conflict should immediately withdraw their forces to the positions they held before 5th June 1967 in accordance with the principle that the seizure of territories as a result of war is inadmissable."

The United States, on the other hand, tried to make an Israeli withdrawal conditional on the achievement of a state of just and lasting peace in the Middle East. Article 1 of the draft Resolution tabled by the United States No. S/8229 dated 7th November 1967, read as follows:

"The Security Council:
1. *Affirms that* the fulfilment of the above Charter principles requires the achievement of a state of just and lasting peace in the Middle East embracing withdrawal of armed forces from occupied territories, termination of claims of belligerence, and mutual recognition and respect for the rights of every state in the area to sovereign existence, territorial integrity, political independence, secure and recognized boundaries and freedom from the threat or use of force."

The American attempt to make peace negotiations precede the withdrawal of Israeli forces from occupied territories was rejected by the Arab States, who reiterated their support for the principle that withdrawal should be unconditional. It was this Arab objection, supported by the majority of the members of the Security Council, that led to the passing of Resolution 242.

However, when the Secretary-General, through his Special Representative, Gunnar Jarring, started to work for the implementation of Resolution 242, he faced the same American stand. Neither the principles of international law nor United Nations jurisprudence could persuade either the United States or Israel to change their positions on the question of withdrawal. On the contrary, the United States played an effective role to make it possible for the Israeli occupation to continue.

Annexation of some parts, such as the Holy City of Jerusalem, as well as the establishment of Zionist settlements also met with American inaction. This United States stand became more rigid as time passed.

In July 1967, however, the United States had supported the principle of a prior Israeli withdrawal. The operative paragraph of the tentative American-Soviet draft, dated 19th July 1967, which was not introduced to the General Assembly, stated the following:

"The General Assembly:
Affirms that the principle that conquest of territory by war is inadmissable under the United Nations Charter and calls upon all parties to the conflict to withdraw without delay their forces

from the territories occupied by them after June 4, 1967.

"Affirms likewise the principle of acknowledgement without delay by all member states in the area that each of them enjoys the right to maintain an independent national state of its own and live in peace and security, as well as the renunciation of all claims and acts inconsistent therewith are expected."[10]

3

This was the situation prior to the adoption of Security Council Resolution 242 of 22nd November 1967. Against this background Lord Caradon presented the draft resolution 242 to the Security Council following lengthy discussions between the United Kingdom (Lord Caradon) and the United States (Ambassador Goldberg) and between the foreign ministers of the Soviet Union and USA and after consultations with all parties concerned and other members of the Security Council. The Soviet Deputy Foreign Minister Kuznetsov asked for more time to contact Moscow.

Lord Caradon agreed, hoping that the Soviet Union would lend its support to the British draft, which it did on the following day.

In presenting his draft Lord Caradon emphasised that the intention was to achieve a balanced resolution. Therefore, the first part called for withdrawal and the ending of the state of war while the second part embodied what was needed to ensure peace. It was the understanding of the Arab States that the implementation of the first part would come first, because it cleared the ground for the implementation of the second.

In order to convince the Arab states to accept the resolution and to show the seriousness of the U.S. wish to achieve its rapid implementation, the United States assured us that it would use its weight in order to implement the Security Council resolution. It was agreed that the United States would make this stand clear in the Security Council. On the same day that the resolution was adopted, the American representative pledged to the Security Council and to the parties concerned that his government "would exert its diplomatic and political influence in support of the efforts of the UN Special Representative to achieve a fair, equitable and dignified

---

10. Appendix 25, *The UN and the Middle East crisis, 1967,* Arthur Lall, Colombia University Press, 1968.

settlement so that all parties in the area can live in peace, security and tranquility."

To implement the resolution, the Secretary-General of the United Nations, U Thant, appointed the Swedish Ambassador Gunnar Jarring as his special representative. Jarring immediately ran up against evasiveness from the Israelis. They refused to withdraw, calling for an overall solution before any kind of withdrawal. The United States backed their suggestion that both parts of the resolution be treated as a unit, and that it should be implemented as a "package deal". After consultations among the Arab states which had earlier accepted Resolution 242, they agreed to accept the American suggestion.

Mahmoud Riad, Egypt's Deputy Prime Minister and Foreign Minister, announced on behalf of those Arab states who accepted the Resolution that they welcomed the submission by Ambassador Jarring of a programme for the implementation of all parts of the resolution. This was also rejected by Israel, which now wished for the second part to be implemented first, thus turning the resolution upside down!

Israel then pretended that the Resolution had called for the establishing of secure and agreed boundaries through direct negotiations between the parties.

Many such fraudulent ideas, suggestions and proposals were submitted by the Israelis as a basis for negotiations and many different interpretations were presented by the various Israeli officials. In the United Nations, however, both U Thant and Jarring refused to agree to such an approach which was neither in accordance with the resolution nor in accordance with the jurisprudence of the United Nations on the matter.

Whilst the efforts for peace were obstructed by these Israeli tactics, the Palestine Revolution grew stronger. It became clear to the United Nations that a just solution and permanent peace required the acceptance of the people of Palestine as the party most immediately involved. Ambassador Jarring rapidly realised that there was a basic defect in Resolution 242 because it ignored the people of Palestine, who were represented by the Palestine Liberation Organisation, as a party to the dispute and made no reference to the question of Palestine which was the main cause of all past and present conflicts.

4

France then suggested that the Big Four (the U.S.S.R., U.S.A.,

Britain and France) play a role in order to help Ambassador Jarring. The four agreed to meet and consult over what to do in this connection. They hoped to reach a united stand that could be presented as their contribution to the parties involved, through Ambassador Jarring, but their efforts soon failed and were discontinued.

The reasons for the failure of the "Big Four" meeting are worth detailing.

They started in the Spring of 1969. The first meeting was held at the residence of the French Ambassador, Bérard, and he presided because the whole idea was a French initiative. The second was held at the residence of the Soviet Ambassador, Jacob Malik, the third at that of the British Ambassador Lord Caradon and the fourth was at the residence of America's Ambassador Yost.

Each host ambassador presided over the meeting accompanied by his deputy and one adviser. Their meetings were secret, with English the accepted language and with two interpreters available in case the French or the Soviets asked for their services.

A sub-committee called "the working group" consisting of the deputies was entrusted with drafting and preparing the working papers. This group met only once a week, which led the Egyptian Ambassador and myself to believe that its work was not serious. The unrest and complications in the area necessitated urgent action. We both raised this point with the four ambassadors. The U.S. and U.K. answer was very clear: "We need time for instructions from our governments on every question raised and particularly those on which there is no agreement." That failed to convince us, and Ambassador El-Kony and I came to the conclusion that some big powers wanted all this work to soothe the area and prevent further complications and threats to peace.

The committee of four agreed at an early stage of their deliberations on six points as general guidelines to help Ambassador Jarring.

1. That Resolution 242 would be implemented in all its parts as a "package settlement."
2. That the elements of the settlement will be agreed upon as a package settlement.
3. There will be no territorial gains through war.
4. There will be no imposed solution. Suggestions regarding the settlement will be submitted to the parties for agreement.
5. The ultimate goal is to reach a permanent peace based on justice whereby every state will live in peace and that the

relationship will not be based — as in the past — on cease-fire or armistice agreement.

6. The member states by accepting the Charter had committed themselves to abide by Article 2 thereof which emphasised the equality of all states and the settlement of their problems by peaceful means and would not resort to force or the threat of force or intervene in the domestic affairs of other states.

These six points were considered the framework for the settlement. They embodied an attempt to clarify any vagueness in the 242 Resolution.

Lord Caradon, who presided over the third meeting opened it saying: "We work within the framework of the November Resolution, all of the Resolution, and nothing but the November Resolution." When Ambassador Malik of the U.S.S.R. conveyed this information to me I suggested that he, the Russian Ambassador, should have added the phrase "So help me Lord." It was an amusing start to the meeting.

Ambassador Charles Yost of the United States explained that the policy of his government stands on "three no's — *no* sweeping changes, *no* Allon plan and *no* weight of conquest."

Ambassador Malik replied that "on the basis of those two statements, a statement clarifying the paragraph in the Resolution on "withdrawal" should be the first priority in our work."

He added: "Let us say withdrawal from Sinai, the Gaza Strip, Jerusalem, the West Bank and the Golan Heights."

Yost: "We should say withdrawal to secure borders."

Malik: "This is not included in Resolution 242. The Resolution speaks about withdrawal from the occupied territories. Secure borders comes in the second stage and it means secure for both parties."

To have a clearer picture of what was going on, I visited Ambassador Bill Buffum of the United States mission on 18th April 1969. Bill is now Under-Secretary of the U.N. and is known for his integrity. He said that so far they had had four meetings. In the first meeting discussion had concentrated on the Resolution. It was agreed that it would be the basis for discussion and that a statement to the press would be issued to emphasise this. The statement would be helpful to avoid any misinterpretation of what was going on in that meeting.

At the second meeting the Ambassador of the United States presented the American working paper and the Soviet Ambassador presented the Russian paper. It was agreed to consider both together.

The American paper consisted of "headlines" such as "peace" "Withdrawal to secure borders", etc; no agreement was reached on those headlines nor on the Soviet paper. The four then agreed that the Resolution should be discussed paragraph by paragraph.

The French position was always clear. Lacking neither clarity or precision, because the French text of the Resolution was clear, it needed no interpretation.

The members started discussing paragraph 1 of the Resolution, namely: Withdrawal. They could not agree on one specific point: should withdrawal be *from* the occupied territories or *to* secure borders? That is: Should the matter be handled in one stage or two?

The Soviet Ambassador asserted that the Resolution called for two stages, starting with complete withdrawal and then secure borders for all parties as the second stage. The meeting was adjourned to await instructions from the four governments.

In the third and fourth meetings the discussion continued on the same paragraph (1). No agreement was reached. It was suggested by the French however, that a "Declaration of Intent" should be drafted to reassure the peoples of the area and thus ease tension. It was not accepted; some felt that it would have the opposite effect which might create obstacles for Jarring's mission. It might be a disappointment to the peoples there, while Israel, which kept obstructing all efforts aimed at securing a withdrawal, might come up with its own counter draft or an amendment in order to obstruct the work of the four. For all those reasons the idea of issuing a "Declaration of Intent" was dropped.

During the third meeting members also turned to substantive matters. A formula was suggested whereby Israel would offer "withdrawal" and the Arabs would offer "contractual peace" or a "peace contract". No one proposed a "peace treaty" since all four agreed that that was impossible.

When the four convened their fourth meeting they reverted to consideration of Article 1 paras 1 and 2. The American delegation re-emphasised what the Secretary of State had said, that withdrawal should be "to secure borders". The Soviets, on the other hand, insisted that withdrawal should be from the occupied territories, and that "secure borders" should come in the second stage.

U.S. Ambassador Yost said that both went together. "There can be no secure and recognised boundaries without withdrawal from occupied territories. Boundaries," he said "are connected with the security of all parties." He added: "Location of boundaries is related to security for both sides."

He emphasised that changes of the Armistice demarcation lines of

1949 depended on the need for the security of both sides, adding: "Changes from pre-existing lines should be confined to those required for mutual security. It should not reflect the weight of conquest."

All parties recognised, he said, that some areas on the 1949 Armistice demarcation lines needed rectification. This however, "cannot be imposed." He added: "The United States cannot support territorial change of a sweeping character, such as the so-called Allon Plan. Equity and justice require that changes must be with the consent of the parties concerned. The Arab states have every reason to think of their security. Therefore, agreement is needed."

In meetings with the U.S. Ambassador I raised this issue:

"You maintain that withdrawal is tied up with secure borders and this, you insist, needs the consent of Israel. Israel will never agree and will continue to change the character of the occupied territories, and will then face you four with yet another *fait accompli*."

The American ambassador answered that world public opinion, the Security Council and the Big Four would not permit this to happen.

In the fourth meeting, Ambassador Yost said: "We do not see withdrawal unless Israel gets assurances of binding and permanent peace. Actual attainment of binding contractual commitment to peace is essential and vital to both parties."

He added that the form should embody the following:

1. The commitment should be comprehensive.
2. It should be contractual and reciprocally binding i.e.: the state of peace must be juridically defined and contractually binding.
3. The contents should be arrived at by agreement among the parties through Ambassador Jarring, although a meeting could be convened to work out the final details.

On the question of a peace treaty the Americans felt that since a peace treaty was difficult to achieve, it might be possible, if the idea of an agreement were accepted, to make use of the formula employed after World War II by the Soviet Japanese bilateral arrangement. This did not have the force of a peace treaty but was a binding agreement between the parties.

Ambassador Malik maintained that the nature of the document would come later, though Ambassador Yost felt that the form was a substantive question, and that an agreement should be permanent.

It was clear that the four completely disagreed on the interpretation of Resolution 242. Ambassador Yost said: "We all agree about withdrawal from occupied territories. But the Resolution did not say to where. We are not a border commission. Parties have to agree themselves about what brings mutual security."

When I discussed this matter with him, he continued to insist that any agreement must be permanent adding that we had to be ready to sign a document, not a peace treaty. As to withdrawal, he said that occupation was Israel's trump card, and that they would not leave unless they knew what the stakes were. "The concession to be given by the Arab side is a formal declaration of peace. This will not be effective, however, until withdrawal. Therefore, this is part of a package deal. There must also be a binding contract to bring about withdrawal."

During my visit with Ambassador Buffum in April 1969 I asked him to explain the Israeli stand. The Americans, he said, had told the Israelis that there would be a four power meeting and that no Allon Plan could be accepted. There would be *no* Peace Treaty and *no* major acquisition of territory by Israel. Moreover, there was no question of dealing simply with security for Israel but rather mutual security for all.

He reassured me: "We are subjected to pressure from Tel Aviv, but no pressure will stand in the way of us having evenhanded policy."

I learned that at the end of the fourth meeting there had been no agreement on the summary of statements, but that the United States felt that the issues could be summed up as follows:

1. Just and lasting peace is essential and an agreement to this effect is needed.
2. There should be a mutually binding commitment which should be comprehensive.
3. There should be a commitment by agreement of the parties under the auspices of Ambassador Jarring and with Four Power assistance.
4. Commitment must be irrevocable and there should be a role for the United Nations to play.

At a later stage the four disagreed on further steps to be taken. The United States did not want genuine progress to take place since this would reflect favourably on the role of all Big Powers and the United States, and Henry Kissinger in particular, wanted himself and the United States to be the sole beneficiaries. So while the U.S.S.R. and France wanted to have clear and specific suggestions for the implementation of Resolution 242 the United States and the United Kingdom did not share this view. Thus there was a stalemate. The United States also felt that neither Britain nor France could play any genuine role in the Middle East and wished, also, to prevent any Soviet involvement in securing a settlement. Jacob Malik in an attempt to push for serious discussions, announced his intention of leaving by sea for the Soviet Union in the middle of June. This did not help, and the stalemate continued until late in the year.

These consultations and contacts brought home to me that only one of two things would bring about Israeli withdrawal from Arab lands: American pressure or Arab strength. But since neither was available, there would be more trouble ahead.

On 2nd December 1969 the four met at the American residence under the presidency of Charles Yost. They agreed that they would start developing the six points so that they could be presented to Jarring as guidelines in order to help him in his mission. Through Jarring they wanted to help the parties to reach a "just and durable" peace. They agreed that their role was "to advise and assist Jarring during negotiations."

In that meeting the main focus was Jordan and all agreed that the question before Jarring in connection with Resolution 242 was not "a territorial question but a security question."

Once again no material progress was made, and I felt I had to reveal what was happening to the United Nations General Assembly. I said that the Resolution carried the number 242, and that the four powers could not reach an agreement because they stood two-for-two! The United States and the United Kingdom were in one corner and U.S.S.R. and France stood in the other, yet another stalemate!

5

Meanwhile Palestinian resistance to Israeli occupation grew stronger. More commandos, with better training and better know-how, appeared in the field. The Israelis resorted to more acts of revenge against neighbouring Arab states, attacking Jordan, Syria and Egypt. Many complaints were presented to the Security Council for action, some of which have been cited earlier. But against U.S. opposition the Security Council was unable to agree on sanctions against Israel.

During this time the United States did not want the Soviet Union to get any credit for any peace efforts. Later, after the 1973 war,

Henry Kissinger, then U.S. Secretary of State, did not want *any* member of the United Nations to get any credit for achieving peace in the Middle East. He wanted everything to be American and he wanted to be the shining star of American diplomacy. By early 1971, lack of U.S. cooperation brought about the freezing of Ambassador Jarring's activities, Kissinger started his own step-by-step diplomacy. Later the American administration changed and Kissinger was out of office. Reagan's election brought a new approach, the President's own "Reagan Plan", dated September 1982.

Throughout Israel aimed at gaining more time so that it could change the character of the occupied territories. Many Jewish colonies were built in the West Bank, on the Gaza Strip and on the Golan Heights. Step by step the Israelis annexed parts of the occupied territories and created more colonies in Jerusalem, the Gaza Strip and the West Bank in order to face the world with another *fait accompli*. The United Nations resolutions stood in Israel's way, while the United Nations Secretary-General stood for the implementation of those resolutions. Israel therefore, wanted to have nothing to do with the U.N. or its executive branch.

Part of that Israeli evasiveness was the interpretation that Israel gave to the question of withdrawal embodied in Resolution 242. The question of withdrawal was never a matter for compromise. Not a single member of the United Nations raised an objection to complete withdrawal. Even the United States, which has given Israel much support on many aspects of the Palestine question, did not at that early stage oppose the principle. All that President Johnson wanted was a minor adjustment which should be on both sides, the word "minor" being continually stressed. Lord Caradon, who negotiated the text of Resolution 242, never intended to exclude any part of the occupied territories. It was for this reason that he embodied in his draft the principle of international law that prohibits acquisition of territory by war. The same principle was embodied in Article 17 of the Bogota Convention which fixed the relationships among the various American states. The United States played a leading role in drafting Article 17 of the Convention and naturally in this particular matter the United States could not stand against a principle which affected its own interest. The United Nations General Assembly has reaffirmed this same principle time and again, and it continues to be part of international law today.

In an unpublished article written by Lord Caradon about his Middle East impressions and reflections when he returned to Jerusalem in 1975, he referred to a report he had seen just before he set out for his visit.

"Some Israelis," the report said, "doubt whether a narrow coastal strip would be defensible and would like to draw a line from El-Arish on the Mediterranean to a point west of Sharm El-Sheikh dividing the peninsula into two."

Lord Caradon commented that:

"What is disturbing about such reports is the spirit they display, the spirit of take what you like, do as you please; a disregard, a contempt for the rights of others; that was the influence which dominated Israeli actions between the two wars of 1967 and 1973."

Lord Caradon referred to a conversation he had had with an Israeli General who had taken part in a joint radio discussion with him in Jerusalem:-

"Surely you realise," Lord Caradon had said, "that forts in hostile territory are not an insurance of peace but a guarantee of continuing enmity."

Speaking about Resolution 242 Lord Caradon emphasised two "essential principles": first "the inadmissibility of the acquisition of territory by war" and second "the sovereignty, territorial integrity and political independence of every state in the area and their right to live in peace within secure and recognised boundaries free from threats and acts of force."

He raised the question "if Israel were to live in peace free from threats and acts of force what was to happen to territories occupied in the 1967 war from which, under Resolution 242, Israel must withdraw?" He added:-

"At first it was assumed that the regained territories would revert to Jordan but this was questioned by the leaders of the Palestine Liberation Organisation. So if the PLO contention that all Palestine should one day become a single Arab-Israeli state was not to succeed (the contention has been backed by no major power and is specifically rejected by both the United States and the Soviet Union) and if the reversion to Jordanian rule was to be questioned, then clearly the remaining possibility was the establishment of a separate Palestinian State."

The Palestinians, Lord Caradon wrote, "are a gifted, virile and highly-educated people. They need to have recognition and a homeland to make and preserve their distinct identity, and an opportunity to put their remarkable gifts to constructive use."

The London *Times* of 28th August 1975 reported that "Dr. Kissinger told Israeli leaders that the United States will not exert pressure on them to disband any of the Golan settlements in an interim agreement. The Israelis are also confident that no pressure will be exerted to prevent continued building of settlements in the West Bank, Gaza Strip and Northern Sinai."

Complete withdrawal as a condition prior to permanent peace is the only logical interpretation of Resolution 242. Genuine peace requires that all forces of occupation should first withdraw. Furthermore, any agreement on a solution while the occupation continues will be made under duress and will therefore be null and void, as no doubt, the Security Council was aware when Resolution 242 was adopted.

When on 6th June 1967 the United States delegation suggested drafting a cease-fire between the parties, the Arab side insisted that, together with the cease-fire, there should be a call on the Israelis to withdraw all armed forces from the occupied territories immediately. "They go together" said the Arab side, reminding the Security Council that this had occurred in the 1956 war against Egypt.

Because of the urgency of the matter, the continuing fighting and in order to stop bloodshed and to avoid any further delay that might be caused by the consultations among the members of the Security Council and the parties involved, it was finally agreed that the Security Council should adopt a cease-fire resolution as a "first step". This was done with the understanding that the second step would be withdrawal and the third step would be genuine efforts for peaceful settlement.

Mahmoud Riad, the Deputy Prime Minister of Egypt, Abdul Monem Rifai, the Prime Minister of Jordan and Anton Attallah, the Foreign Minister of Jordan, all agreed that withdrawal should be complete. In fact when Gunnar Jarring asked the two countries about their understanding of the term "secure borders", they said that they knew of nothing that had been recognised other than the partition line embodied in the General Assembly resolution of 29th November 1947. Their identical answers were published at my request in an official document of the United Nations. Here are Gunnar Jarrings two questions to the parties and their answers:

Question (1)   Does Israel (Jordan, United Arab Republic) accept the right of Jordan Lebanon and the United Arab Republic (Israel) to live in peace within secure and recognized boundaries free from threats or acts of force?

Jordan answered thus:-

> Jordan accepts the right of every state in the area to live in peace within secure and recognized boundaries free from threats or acts of force, provided that Israel withdraws its forces from all Arab territories it occupied since June 5th 1967 and implements the Security Council Resolution of November 22nd, 1967.

The Egyptian answer was identical.

The Israelis answered, however:

> Israel accepts the right of Jordan, Lebanon, the United Arab Republic and other neighbouring states to live in peace within secure and recognized boundaries, free from threats or acts of force. Explicit and unequivocal reciprocity is Israel's only condition for this acceptance. "Acts of force" include all preparations, actions or expeditions by irregular or para-military groups or by individuals directed against the life, security or property of Israel in any part of the world.

Question (2)   If so, what is the conception of secure and recognized boundaries held by Israel, (Jordan, the United Arab Republic)?

Jordan and Egypt replied:

> When the question of Palestine was brought before the United Nations in 1947, the General Assembly adopted its Resolution 181 part II of November 29th, 1947 for the partition of Palestine and defined Israel's boundaries.

The Israelis, however, refused to define their border claims:

> Secure and recognized boundaries have never yet existed between Israel and the Arab states; accordingly they should now be established as part of the peace-making process. The cease-fire should be replaced by peace treaties establishing permanent, secure and recognized boundaries as agreed upon through negotiation between the governments concerned.

On 25th January 1971 the government of Jordan presented its official position through me to Ambassador Gunnar Jarring upon resumption of his mission as follows:[11]

1. Withdrawal of the Israeli armed forces from all occupied territories without exception in conformity with Resolution 242 (1967), which emphasized "the inadmissibility of the acquisition of territory by war". Israel must accept and put into effect this concept which governs relations amongst nations.

2. Peace is indivisible. Every State in the area is entitled to live in peace within secure and recognized boundaries free from threats or acts of force.
   Israel should unequivocally repudiate its policy of territorial expansion.

3. The Government of Jordan recognizes the religious and cultural importance of the Arab City of Jerusalem to all faiths. It will, therefore guarantee free access to all religious and historical places to all concerned as well as freedom of worship. Jordan stands ready to make all necessary arrangements to this effect.

4. A just settlement of the Palestine refugees must be reached. This can only be realized through Israel's respect for the rights of the Palestinian people in accordance with the United Nations Resolutions.

5. The termination of all claims or states of belligerency and

---

11. Security Council Document No. S/10089, dated 26th January 1971, p.2-3.

guaranteeing freedom of navigation in international water-ways.

6. Guaranteeing the territorial inviolability and political independence of every State in the area.
   The four permanent members may, through the Security Council, obtain adequate arrangements to provide security to all States in the area. Such arrangements may include United Nations Observation Force in which the permanent members may participate.
   Arrangements for ensuring security of the States in the area might also include the establishment of demilitarized zones on a reciprocal basis.

7. With the implementation of the above steps the elements of conflict and dissension will disappear and a just and durable peace will ensue. There will be respect for and acknowledgement of the sovereignty, territorial integrity and political independence of every State in the area and their right to live in peace within secure and recognized boundaries free from threats or acts of force as envisaged in Resolution 242 (1947).

To conclude this chapter it is clear that Resolution 242 re-emphasised the right of every state to live within secure and recognised borders. Here I must again reiterate that the emphasis was on the right of every state "to live" within secure borders, that is, every state is entitled not to have any military act or resistance to it which would disturb its life or make its living within its borders insecure. Those who negotiated the draft resolution had in mind both Israeli trespasses and attacks on its neighbours and the Commando operations carried out by the people of the Palestine Liberation Organisation. They knew that once there was a just peace there would be secure borders, within which every state could live. It was never the intention to change borders. The emphasis on the word "live" was meant to rule out any possibility of any claim to extra territory to make the border secure.

I argued these points with all permanent members of the Security Council and in all my meetings with Ambassador Jarring. Ambassador El-Kony of Egypt had been succeeded in the United Nations by Ambassador Mohammed El-Zayyat. Jarring was continuing to contact the parties to seek the implementation of United Nations Security Council Resolution 242 and used to meet every representative separately. El-Zayyat and I were requested by our governments to co-ordinate before meeting Jarring, and after to exchange notes in order to communicate the results to our authorities back home. El-Zayyat, a distinguished diplomat, used to spend a short time answering Jarring's questions, then come out and turn to me to inform me of what had happened. Then he had to wait until I finished my meeting with Jarring. I used to spend double or treble the time El-Zayyat spent with Jarring. And when I came out I found El-Zayyat, who was a heavy smoker, had smoked almost a packet of cigarettes. One day he looked at me with surprise on his face and said: "What makes you stay that long. Jarring had four simple questions which require four short answers. I am curious to know what do you both say all that time" I could not help telling my friend: "You have nothing to worry about. Israel will abandon Sinai for a price but will never voluntarily leave the West Bank or the Gaza Strip, at any price. When the Israelis leave Sinai the Egyptian people will call you a hero because they would say that you had liberated what the Egyptian armed forces had lost in the field. You will be recorded in Egyptian history as a hero. In my case the opposite is true. I know that Israel is not sincere with Jarring and without Arab strength or American pressure will never abandon any Palestinian territory. Today neither Arab strength nor American pressure exists. Therefore, knowing the record of Israel vis-à-vis all instruments and agreements of the past, I have to be very careful about every paper presented or every question adduced or problem raised, to make sure that our position does not lack clarity."

Jarring's efforts failed to achieve anything.

Ambassador El-Zayyat's assignment ended and he became a member of the Egyptian cabinet. In 1971 I was transferred to Amman and then appointed Ambassador to Spain. Earlier Lord Caradon retired and returned to British politics. In 1968 Ambassador Goldberg resigned. Later Jarring went home. Today Resolution 242 rests in the Archives of the United Nations.

Chapter 10

Jerusalem the Magnificent and U.S. Pressure

"The commission found that the ownership of the Wailing Wall, as well as the possession of it and parts of its surroundings, accrues to the Moslems. The Wall itself, as an integral part of the Haram-Al-Sharif area, is Moslem property."

The International Commission of Jurists, 1929.

What of Jerusalem, the Holy City? Jerusalem the Magnificent, the City of Peace? Why should Israel alter its character when in the first place their occupation of it is illegal, gained by force in 1967?

In 1968 the Jordan Government asked me to bring to the attention of the Security Council the question of Jerusalem and the serious and grave Israeli violations of UN agreements and international law relating to the city. I requested an urgent meeting of the Security Council to consider steps to be taken to remedy the situation. Before this meeting, the U.S. representative, Arthur Goldberg, said to me that we should not have 'rushed' to the Council, claiming "Quiet diplomacy would have been the answer. The U.S. could do this for Jordan." He added: "A quiet attitude would create an atmosphere which would affect the mission of Ambassador Jarring in the area. We should give him every opportunity to make progress."

This was his first approach to me on the subject of Jordan's complaint. I responded: "My God! Is it we who obstruct the mission of Jarring, or is it the one who is changing the character of the City? Am I to blame if I try to prevent steps which may make peace impossible?"

He replied: "No, I don't mean that. But I hope we will have a quiet debate", — with which I concurred.

In that debate I reminded the Council that East Jerusalem, like the rest of the West Bank and Gaza had been seized in war, and that acquiring territory by force gives no right to the occupier. It is, in fact, the duty of the people under occupation to resist the occupier. I added that it is axiomatic that by an illegal act no legal result can be produced, no right acquired, so that no legal fruits could be harvested from aggression. I went on to cite the two resolutions adopted by the United Nations General Assembly in July 1967; the first called on Israel to rescind and desist from measures to change the status of Jerusalem, the second deplored not only the measures but also Israel's failure to comply with the earlier resolution.[1] Both had received overwhelming majorities, nobody voting against them.

The Israeli representative could not justify the changes made to the City, but he insisted that Jerusalem was their eternal capital.

Another point was raised on the Jerusalem issue. The Israelis claimed that they owned the Wailing Wall, part of the Holy (Moslem) Haram Al-Sharif sanctuary, and, that therefore, no-one should deprive them of their so-called rights in the Holy City. The Israeli Ambassador became emotional on this, citing the phrase: "If I forget thee, oh Jerusalem..." He kept repeating *"our* Jerusalem" and *"our"* city", part of a conscious campaign to emphasise that Jerusalem is "Jewish". He spoke about the city as if it belonged to the Jewish people only, and as if all Gentiles, Christians and Moslems, were strangers to the City.

In a speech on 27th April 1968 to the Security Council, during the Council's second debate on Israeli violations of international law in Jerusalem, I reminded him that the Israelis had no valid claim to the Wailing Wall and the adjacent area.[2] I presented to the Council an impartial report by the International Commission of Jurists of 1929, requested by the United Kingdom of Great Britain and Northern Ireland, with the approval of the Council of the League of Nations, to determine the rights and claims of both Moslems and Jews in

---

1. General Assembly Resolutions No.2253 (ES-V) of 4th July 1967 and No.2254 (ES-V) of 14th July 1967.

2. Security Council Meeting, No.1416, 27th April 1968.

connection with the Wailing Wall and the adjacent area in Jerusalem.

The Commission consisted of three learned jurists from Sweden, Switzerland and the Netherlands. Eliel Löfgren, formerly Swedish Minister for Foreign Affairs, who also sat in the upper Chamber of the Swedish Riksdag, acted as Chairman. Charles Barde, Vice-President of the Court of Justice at Geneva and President of the Austro-Romanian Mixed Arbitration Tribunal, and C. J. Van Kempen, formerly Governor of the East Coast of Sumatra, a member of the States-General of the Netherlands, were the other members.

The Commission, which was approved by the League of Nations, held twenty-three meetings during which it listened to evidence from fifty-three witnesses, twenty-two from the Jewish side, thirty from the Moslem side, and one British officer.

It examined all reports, dispatches, memoranda and minutes relative to matters connected with the Wailing Wall and heard the arguments and counter-arguments of Palestinian lawyers, together with eleven other lawyers, Moslem and Christian, defending the Moslem case, who came from India, Morocco, Algeria, Tripoli, Egypt, Syria, Trans-Jordan — as it was called at that time — Iraq, Iran, the Dutch East Indies and parts of Africa.

The Commission found *first* that the ownership of the wall as well as the possession of it and parts of its surroundings, accrues to the Moslems. The Wall itself, as an integral part of the Haram-Al-Sharif area, is Moslem property.

Second, the Commission found that in no stage of the investigation did the Jewish side make any claim of ownership, whether to the Wailing Wall or to the Magharba Quarter, or to any part of the surrounding areas, (the areas now subjected to illegal Israeli demolition, construction and acts of aggression.) The Commission stated that the Jewish side, when making its claim, had expressly stated:

"The Jewish side do not claim any proprietary right to the wall."[3]

Third, the Commission found that no matter how one looks at the Jewish claim, it cannot go beyond a simple privilege to visit the

---

3. Security Council Document No. S/8427/Add. 1 and also as General Assembly Document No.A/7057 Add.1.

Wall. Even this privilege, as I submitted to the U.N., was a result of Moslem tolerance.

Fourth, the Commission found that even the pavement and the area coincident with it were Moslem property and constituted Moslem Waqf, or Moslem religious endowments, originally made by Afdal, the son of Saladin, in 1193 A.D.

Fifth, the Commission found that the Magharba Quarter buildings (bulldozed in 1967 and 1968 by the Israeli authorities) had been put up in 1320 A.D. "to serve as lodgings to Moroccan pilgrims" and had been made a Moslem Waqf — religious endowment — by Abu Madian.

Sixth, the Commission found (and this shows that the Moslem pilgrims and Arab inhabitants of Jerusalem were always aware of the danger that Moslem tolerance would be exploited at a later stage to claim Jewish ownership) that in 1911 the guardian of the Abu Madian Waqf complained that "the Jews, contrary to usage, had placed chairs on the pavement and he requested that 'in order to avoid a future claim of ownership' the present state of affairs should be stopped".

In his complaint to the Jerusalem Administrative Council the Guardian argues that after stools would come benches, which could then be fixed and before long the Jews would have established a claim to the site. Seventy years ago — and nearly sixty years before the Israeli occupation of Jerusalem — the Palestinians were aware of Zionist designs.

The Jerusalem Administrative Council decided that it was not permissible to place any article on the Waqf property that 'could be considered as indication of ownership', a finding which coincided with the findings of the Commission of Jurists nineteen years later.

Seventh, the Commission found that the British Government had stated to Parliament in the White Paper of November 1928 that the Western or Wailing Wall "is legally the absolute property of the Moslem community and the strip of pavement facing it is Waqf property as shown by documents preserved by the Guardian of the Waqf".

2

In addition to the findings and decision of the Commission of Jurists we have as evidence the minutes of the hearings. Dr Eliash, a leading Jewish lawyer, presented the case for the Jewish people aided by many other Zionist leaders. In the minutes we find that Dr Eliash was careful not to claim any title to any stone in the Wailing

Wall. As a lawyer who had spent all his life dealing with land disputes he realised that all the evidence supported the Arab claim and therefore confined his case to a request that a privilege be given to his people; that they be allowed to visit the Wailing Wall. He said that the Arabs in Jerusalem had tolerated this in the past and requested that this be endorsed by the Commission.

Most Zionist leaders agreed with his plea. How today do the Israelis have the nerve to ignore this completely, and pretend that all Jerusalem belongs to the Jewish people? How can they say that the Jewish people have an historic title to it, and that Moslems and Christians are foreigners?

Such were the findings of an impartial tribunal — the Commission of Jurists — presented by me to the United Nations Security Council on 23rd February 1968. The situation has not changed since. The facts about the legal situation in Jerusalem make it unmistakably clear that all recent Israeli measures — including forcible occupation — are no more than naked acts of aggression. They make nonsense of the cynical Israeli claim that Jerusalem is a Jewish city and should be the "eternal capital" of the Israeli state. The occupation, the annexation, the bulldozing of Arab property in the Magharba quarter and other adjacent areas together with other changes defy Arab rights adjudicated on and affirmed by a competent body constituted with the approval of the League of Nations. These Israeli practices also made a mockery of the earlier U.N. General Assembly and Security Council resolutions on the question of Jerusalem. The bulldozing in the Magharba Quarter as well as the burning of the Al-Aqsa Mosque was also an encroachment on the second holiest place in Islam, the Aqsa Mosque and the Haram-Al-Sharif. The Al-Aqsa burning was stated at the U.N. Security Council to have been encouraged by the authorities. At least, they made no attempt to prevent it. It was a violation of the Geneva Convention of 12th August 1949, article 53, which prohibits any destruction by an occupying power of real or personal property belonging individually or collectively to private persons, to the State, to other public authorities or to social or co-operative organisations.

Israel's policy of distortion and misrepresentation showed no bounds as far as Jerusalem was concerned. On 30th June 1969 the Israeli Ambassador told the Security Council that the majority of the city's population were Jews when the British mandate was established. This was not of course true, as I showed by quoting statistics from a survey by the Government of Palestine during the British Mandate prepared by the Secretary of Information for

Palestine of the Anglo-American Committee of Enquiry, a British-American body. They spoke about the census of 1922 and 1931 when there were 56,346 Arabs and 34,431 Jews in Jerusalem. At the same time they gave the figures for the total settled population in Jerusalem for the end of 1944 when there were 140,532 Arabs and 100,200 Jews. Those were figures of the Palestine Anglo-American Committee. The figures above were printed in the *Palestine Yearbook 1947-1948*. So it was not true that the majority in Jerusalem consisted of Jews. The Israeli Ambassador had no answer. This was unfortunate for him in the Council. He did not realise that "falsehood flies on very short wings". It soon falls on the rock of truth.

After Israel's illegal occupation of East Jerusalem, many changes were made to the nature of the city. These acts were condemned by the Security Council. They amounted to usurpation and therefore conveyed no rights on the Israelis who have no legal basis on which to speak about the unity of the city. The Israeli Ambassador cannot camouflage its illegal annexation as "unity". This is exactly what Hitler said when his Nazi forces occupied Czechoslovakia and Poland. Hitler's exact words were, "Now our unity has been accomplished."

Despite all the legal evidence, and the firm opposition of the international community, the Israelis continued to claim that Jerusalem is their "eternal capital", and therefore that it was excluded from "the November 242 Resolution".

This reminded me of Zionist practices in the past vis-à-vis all international documents on Palestine to which the Zionists give different interpretations, at different times, to fit their own designs. I thought they would come up with this point on Jerusalem in the 1968 debate in order to obstruct all efforts for peace based on Resolution 242. I therefore wanted the Security Council to incorporate the same international legal principle of the inadmissibility of acquisition of territory by war in the new draft resolution on Jerusalem, thinking that this would prevent any possible future allegation of vagueness in Resolution 242 regarding the Holy City. With the approval of my government, a draft resolution was therefore submitted to the Council it reads:

CALLING ON ISRAEL TO RESCIND ALL MEASURES TO CHANGE THE STATUS OF JERUSALEM

The Security Council
Recalling General Assembly resolutions 2253 (ES-V) and 2254

(ES-V) of 4 and 14 July 1967,
Having considered the letter of the Permanent Representative
of Jordan on the situation in Jerusalem (S/8560) and the report
of the Secretary-General (S8146),
Having heard the statements made before the Council,
Noting that since the adoption of the above-mentioned
resolutions, Israel has taken further measures and actions in
contravention of those resolutions,
Bearing in mind the need to work for a just and lasting peace,
Reaffirming that acquisition of territory by military conquest is
inadmissible,
1. Deplores the failure of Israel to comply with the General
Assembly resolutions mentioned above;
2. Considers that all legislative and administrative measures
and actions taken by Israel, including expropriation of land and
properties thereon, which tend to change the legal status of
Jerusalem are invalid and cannot change that status;
3. Urgently calls upon Israel to rescind all such measures
already taken and to desist forthwith from taking any further
action which tends to change the status of Jerusalem;
4. Requests the Secretary-General to report to the Security
Council on the implementation of the present resolution.
(The italics are those of the author)

The United States Government was very angry, not wishing such
a resolution to be passed, and protested to my Government.
Realising the seriousness of the matter, I was in contact on every
little development with my Government to avoid any possible
misunderstanding of what was going on in the United Nations.
In an attempt to put an end to this controversy the United States
tabled its own draft resolution. It reads:

"The Security Council,
Having heard statements made before the Council,
Recalling pertinent resolutions with respect to the situation in
Jerusalem.
Reaffirming resolution 242 of November 22, 1967,
Declares that unilateral actions and measures by Israel cannot
be accepted and are not recognised as altering or prejudging
the status of Jerusalem,
Calls upon Israel to refrain from such actions and measures,
Calls upon all parties to avoid all acts that might prejudice
efforts to achieve a "just and lasting peace" in the area,

> *Affirms* its intention to keep this matter under continuing review,
> *Reaffirms* its support for the efforts now proceeding under the auspices to the Secretary-General's Special Representative Ambassador Jarring to achieve a peaceful and accepted settlement in accordance with Security Council Resolution 242".

The American draft made no reference to the principle of inadmissibility mentioned above. Contacts amongst Security Council members began. The Americans wanted the Council to endorse their resolution, while I, with strong backing from Jordan's Prime Minister, Mr. Bahjat Talhouni, and Foreign Minister, Abdul Monem Rifai, insisted that our draft, sponsored and presented very ably by the representative of Pakistan, Agha Shahi, be put to the vote first. More consultations between Ambassador Goldberg and myself commenced. He said that he would not accept our draft and that if put to the vote it would be defeated, although he avoided direct reference to a veto. This meant defeating the draft either through putting pressure on member states in the Council not to vote for it, or through the use of the American veto.

I was shocked to hear this from him, and asked him what was his main objection. He said it was simple: "You want to dynamite all our work for peace based on Resolution 242".

I asked: "But how?"

He said: "You know how."

I said: "No I don't. Tell me."

He explained that Resolution 242 was the result of months of negotiations. "Our whole idea is to keep it balanced in the form in which it was presented and adopted. You want in two minutes to change the whole idea and thus rewrite the resolution."

Here I asked for his indulgence. I asked: "Is Jerusalem covered by Resolution 242? In other words, is the principle of withdrawal intended to apply to Jersualem?" He said: "Yes, but this will come up during the negotiations." I said: "O.K. If this is covered by the call for withdrawal in 242, what is wrong with incorporating the same principle of non-acquisition of territories through war in our present resolution on Jerusalem?" He replied: "No. This is not acceptable to the United States Government. I advise you not to insist on it. It is not in the interest of Jordan, my friend."

I could not help telling him: "I know the interest of Jordan. Its interest is to have a clear and straight-forward resolution, as I am sure you know".

He then said that the State Department was in contact with the Jordanian Government and we agreed to meet the following day.

I communicated what had happened in this meeting to Amman. While contacting my Government on this matter, and before reaching their own definite and final stand, the United States delegation got the impression that a final stand had been taken and that specific instructions had reached me, so they decided to push for a quick meeting of the Council so that they could put their draft to a vote.

In my report to my Government, I recommended the rejection of the American draft resolution because it did not, in any way remedy the situation created by Israel which was the subject before the Security Council. Not only did it ignore completely the established principle under international law that acquisition of territory by military conquest was inadmissible, but it did not — even — deplore the failure of Israel to comply with the General Assembly Resolutions Nos. 2253 (ES-V) and 2254 (ES-V) of 4th and 14th July 1967.

It also, in an attempt to confuse the issue, called upon all the parties to avoid all acts that might prejudice efforts to achieve a 'just and lasting' peace in the area. Moreover, the American draft reaffirmed its support for the efforts proceeding under the auspices of the Secretary-General's Special Representative Ambassador Jarring to achieve a peaceful and accepted settlement in accordance with Resolution 242, which bore no relationship to Jordan's complaint. The draft merely gave routine treatment to the serious developments in Jerusalem while reinforcing the so-called vagueness in the Resolution 242 with regard to the city.

If the Security Council rejected the incorporation of the relevant principle of international law I mentioned earlier, then our historic rights would be in doubt and the only result from our complaint to the Security Council would be a victory by Ambassador Goldberg in favour of Israel. The matter was most serious.

Mr Rouhi El-Khatib, the Mayor of Jerusalem, was with me when we debated the question of Jerusalem in the Security Council in 1968 and presented his views. When U.S. pressure mounted on my government, as happens to every small country, I sensed that the State Department was resorting to other ways and means in order to get Jordan to accept the American draft resolution. At this stage of the deliberations Mr Rouhi El-Khatib, offered to go to Amman and put the Government in the true picture. I welcomed the idea. Before the Mayor arrived in Amman, Ambassador Goldberg came to see me. He wanted to ask the Security Council to convene the meeting immediately and have the American draft resolution put to the vote. He said that I had already, according to their information, received my instructions so that there was no need for any further delay. I explained to him that his information was inaccurate and that I was still in contact with my government, so it remained too soon to convene the Council.

The following day I received new instructions from my government reiterating their fear that an American veto, or lack of the required votes, might end with no resolution at all which would be a disaster. The government authorised me, however, to go ahead with putting our own draft resolution to the vote if I felt certain — repeat 'certain' — of success. I was asked to make a reassessment of the situation and report back. I analysed the new situation caused by the American threat to use its veto, and became more convinced that the United States would not subject its prestige to any set-back. It would not use its veto, but was merely playing a tactical game.

At that time the United States Delegation at the U.N. had three Ambassadors, Ambassador Goldberg and two deputies. One of these, Ambassador Pedersen, came to see me with the suggestion that we should convene the Council immediately and put the draft of the United States to the vote and have the matter finished. At that time cables were still going back and forth between me and my Government and no final stand had been determined. I did not know what the final position of my Government would be and considered it premature to think in terms of a quick meeting and speedy adoption of a resolution. I was playing for time. It was Friday.

I did not want to discuss the subject with Ambassador Pedersen and thought that this meeting with me was purely coincidental since we met at the entrance of the United Nations General Assembly just by the escalator. I told him: "Sorry, Dick, I am standing with you over here as a friend, but since you have an official request, please ask the head of your delegation to see me." He replied: "But Ambassador Goldberg is in Washington. He is coming in one or two hours time."

I replied: "All right. If you do not want to wait until he arrives, have Ambassador Buffum (the number two U.S. deputy at the U.N.) see me. After all, you are number three in the U.S. delegation."

I saw that Ambassador Pedersen was very much upset, which I regretted, but I wanted more time, and since I was the head of Jordan's delegation, I felt I should insist on my right.

Two hours later I met Ambassador Goldberg, who apologised for the incident. He had been in Washington and he had only just arrived back in New York. I told him that his information about my receiving instructions on their draft was not exactly accurate and that my Government would contact me during the weekend to give me instructions.

"Why this hurry?" I asked. "How about having the meeting on Monday? Today is Friday. The day is almost over. Tomorrow you have your weekend and I am, as the complainant, not in a hurry."

He said: "Let us see how things work out."

I wished him a nice weekend to emphasise that there would be no meeting during the coming two days and also to convey the message that I would not be available for consultation during that time.

In order to avoid further pressure, I accepted an invitation to speak before a group of Canadians of Arab descent. I flew to Ottawa without telling any of my colleagues, although Ambassador El-Kony of Egypt, my home and my office, knew where I was. During the weekend Goldberg called Agha Shahi, the Pakistani Ambassador and pressed for a meeting. As a member of the Security Council Ambassador Shahi was entrusted with presenting the draft resolution on Jordan's behalf. He tried to reach me and was informed that I was in Canada. He wondered why I should have left all the burden on him and disappeared to Canada. I arrived back on Sunday at 8 o'clock and went to my office which I had asked my staff to man to see if any cables had arrived. Leaving the elevator I met Egypt's Ambassador El-Kony, a seasoned diplomat who, with some of the best contacts in the United Nations, brought me up to date on what had been going on during my short absence.

I was more than happy about the contents of the telex I found. Before going to Canada I had briefed my Government on the new developments, and had explained what would happen if we agreed to drop the reference to the principle of non-acquisition of territory through war from our resolution, or agreed not to put our draft to a vote, which amounted to the same thing. Any retreat, at that stage, would have been disastrous. I also assured my Prime Minister and Foreign Minister that I had every reason to believe from past experience that the U.S. State Department, a master of manoeuvres when it comes to the Arab-Israeli problem, would have to think twice before exercising its veto on the question of Jerusalem, because of its spiritual value to both the Christian and Moslem worlds. I had assured my Government that we had more than enough votes to get the resolution adopted.

The new cable did not give a clear-cut endorsement of the stand I had suggested, but did not oppose it either. My Government was especially careful, because the question was on Jerusalem, the Holy

City, and they wanted the strongest possible resolution to be obtained from the Security Council but, on the other hand, did not want me to end up with no resolution at all.

I asked the Security Council to convene and cabled my government explaining that the situation in the UN was far from gloomy and that I was almost certain that the U.S. was just manoeuvering. In the end, I assured them, with some determination on our part, our draft would pass.

The American delegation, and particularly Arthur Goldberg, were shocked to hear my request that our draft resolution sponsored by Pakistan should be put to the vote first. In the end, thirteen members voted for our resolution[4] and only two members, the United States and Canada abstained. So I was right; the U.S.A. did not use its Veto. This was on 21st May 1967. The Pakistani delegation co-operated to the very end with us, in achieving our success, because the late Zulfiqar Ali Bhutto, then Foreign Minister, had given specific instructions to the permanent representative of Pakistan to give us all the support we needed.

The resolution incorporated the principle that there could be no acquisition of territory by force and urgently called "upon Israel to rescind all such measures already taken and to desist forthwith from taking any further action which tends to change the status of Jerusalem." It became clear that even if we assume, for the sake of argument, that Resolution 242 was vague regarding any part of the occupied territory, the new resolution, 252, clarified every vagueness vis-à-vis Jerusalem.

3

Later I was recalled to Amman. At Amman airport I saw the Mayor of Jerusalem, Mr El-Khatib and many dignitaries standing in the airport lounge. The Mayor whispered in my ear: "We are going to have a big reception in your honour. Almost all distinguished figures, among them all diplomats, are invited." He told me that the former Prime Minister of Jordan Suleiman Bey Nabulsi, now President of the Committee for Saving Jerusalem, would speak on this occasion. "Why all this?" I asked.

He answered: "The Americans are trying to remove you from

---

4. Security Council Resolution No.252, dated May 21st 1968; The 13 votes in favour were: Algeria, Brazil, China, Denmark, Ethiopia, France, Hungary, India, Pakistan, Paraguay, Senegal, United Kingdom and the U.S.S.R. There were as I have already stated, two abstentions, Canada and U.S.A.

9. Informal conversation before the Security Council meeting of 9-10th November 1967 between (left to right) Abdul Monem Rifai, Jordan's Minister of State for Foreign Affairs; the author; Mohammed Awad El-Kony, Permanent Representative of the UAR to the UN and Mahmoud Riad, the UAR Foreign Minister.

10. *Left to right, Tewfic Bouattoura, Permanent Representative of Algeria, Lord Caradon, Permanent Representative of Great Britain and the author, 21st March 1968.*

11. *The destruction at the village of Karameh — its name meant 'dignity' — on March 21st 1968.*

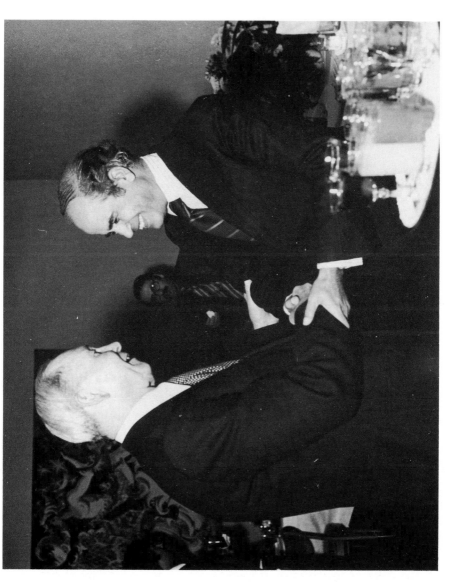

12. *The author welcomes Soviet Representative V. V. Kuznetsov to the lighter side of life.*

13. *The changing skyline of Jerusalem; in the foreground the Dome of the Rock, in the background tower blocks erected by the Israelis.*

14. *Conversation between Abdul Monem Rifai, Jordan's Ambassador to the UAR, Muhammad El-Aamiry, Minister of Foreign Affairs of Jordan and Arthur Goldberg, American Ambassador to the UN. The author has his back to the camera; 27th September 1967.*

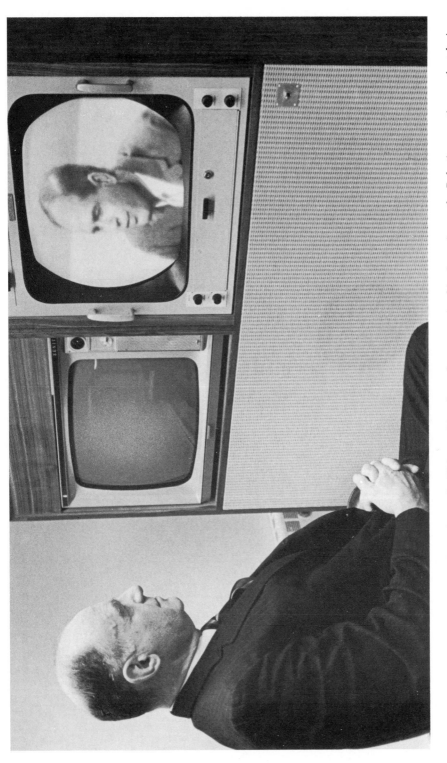

15. Michael Comay, the Israeli ambassador to the UN, watching the author presenting his viewpoint on the Palestine question on the television programme "Face the Nation" in November 1966. The picture was sent to the author by the New York Times.

16. The author, with Abdul Monem Rifai, Jordanian Foreign Minister, and Jordan's ambassador to Washington Abdul Hamid Sharaf meets President Nixon, William Rogers Secretary of State, Henry Kissinger of the National Security Council and Joseph Sisco of the State Department, October 1969.

your post and we want them and everybody to know that we are backing you and appreciate your stand."

The invitations had been sent before my arrival. The American Ambassador called me at my hotel and expressed real regret for his inability to attend the reception given in my honour, for he had a previous commitment. I knew that 4th July is a special day for Americans, but I appreciated his thoughtfulness and thanked him for his call.

The following day I attended the large reception given in my honour. Suleiman Bey Nabulsi who was well known for his nationalist stands, made a forceful speech thanking me for my efforts in the United Nations. He attacked American imperialism and asked the United States to cease this unbecoming behaviour. In reply I thanked him and all those who had organised and had attended the reception, adding that our rights were stronger than all American pressure and intimidation.

The next day I had an audience with His Majesty King Hussein and explained the United Nations situation to him. I found that he was fully informed. On many problems, including the Jerusalem debate matters, because of American pressure, became complicated during discussions so much so that the Jordanian stand in the United Nations called for special directives from the King. His Majesty's guidance was of great help to me and gave me strength in those difficult debates.

His Majesty asked me to go back to New York and I left the following day.

In the United Nations lounge colleagues came to greet me with surprised looks on their faces. One was the Indian Ambassador, who asked me what on earth I was doing there. He told me: "Arthur Goldberg informed everybody that you were not coming back. And here you are."

I said: "But why?"

Another colleague answered. "The U.S. asked for your removal and so it was to be!"

I replied: "You see, I am here, and I am here to stay".

While we were chatting Arthur Goldberg passed by and came to shake hands. I was very nice to him. So was he to me.

I could well understand the Israeli representatives' behaviour, but to this day I cannot understand how American conduct in the deliberations of the Security Council could serve the interests of the United States of America.

After I returned from Amman the question was brought up again. The Council convened its meeting once more to consider further the failure of Israel to implement its Resolution 252 and censured Israel in the strongest terms for its failure to abide by the will of the Council and reiterated its request, stating in Resolution No.267 of 3rd July 1969 that it:

> *Censures* in the strongest terms all measures taken to change the status of the City of Jerusalem;
> *Confirms* that all legislative and administrative measures and actions taken by Israel which purport to alter the status of Jerusalem, including expropriation of land and properties thereon, are invalid and cannot change that status;
> *Urgently calls* once more upon Israel to rescind forthwith all measures taken by it which may tend to change the status of the City of Jerusalem, and in future to refrain from all actions likely to have such an effect;
> *Requests* Israel to inform the Security Council without any further delay of its intentions with regard to the implementation of the provisions of the present resolution;
> *Determines* that, in the event of a negative response or no response from Israel, the Security Council shall reconvene without delay to consider what further action should be taken in this matter.

Today, despite huge majorities for resolutions censuring Israel the situation remains the same. Changes continue to be made in Jerusalem altering its character, re-shaping its appearance, anything and everything to isolate it and change its status. The American veto is there to prevent any further condemnations, let alone sanctions.

There is a wider and more sinister aspect to this question. No one who attempted to defend the Holy City could escape the Israeli smear campaign. Since the debate at the United Nations General Assembly in 1947 which led to the recommendation to partition Palestine into Jewish and Arab States, the Zionists had succeeded in sacking or removing many Ambassadors from their posts and this success scared others. Today many colleagues, though representing the Christian world which has a vital interest in the Holy City, only whisper to us in the United Nations or in social gatherings about the Holy City. Unconsciously, they whisper even when there is no third person present, afraid to talk. Some Ambassadors from the Christian world have made mild speeches on Jerusalem at the United Nations, their caution being brought about by pressure from groups in the United States. This I believe is very bad and is not beneficial to world Jewry. Similar circumstances where people were

150

afraid to speak out facilitated Hitler's rise to power in the 1930s.

Now, when neither the findings of the international body entrusted with the task of determining proprietary rights in Jerusalem, nor the elementary principle of international law that acquisition of territory by conquest or war conveys no rights, nor the declaration of the General Assembly in two resolutions deploring Israeli behaviour in Jerusalem in the strongest terms, nor the Security Council's decisions affirming this stand have met with anything but complete indifference on the part of Israel.

In the face of this, it remains to be seen whether the United Nations, faithful to its tradition, prestige and authority will take more effective measures — namely invoking Chapter VII of the Charter that imposes sanctions, economic, political or others — to ensure that Israel abides by the will of the world community.

Chapter 11

A New cabinet and New Foreign Minister and More American Pressure

"I do not believe in dictation. Jordan is a sovereign state. We respect its sovereignty. All that we expect is to be consulted before a decision in Amman is taken."

Arthur Goldberg

Subsequent to the 1967 War, a new cabinet had been formed in Jordan, with a new Foreign Minister, who was new in the real sense. He had no experience in foreign affairs, although he was a decent man with good intentions to do anything that could advance Ambassador Jarring's mission. He was thinking of preparing a paper on the implementation of Resolution 242. In that mood he arrived in early September in New York to attend the regular session of the General Assembly.

It was his first visit to the United Nations. We discussed the Agenda of the General Assembly and agreed on the time for him to make his major speech, as all the foreign ministers do. He expressed a desire to visit Dean Rusk, U.S. Secretary of State for Foreign Affairs, but said that before then he would like to call on Ambassador Goldberg.

I said that, being a Foreign Minister, his first visit or courtesy call should be to Dean Rusk. He disagreed, being of the opinion that he should first prepare the ground for such a meeting through those to whom the State Department and the White House listen. He added: "We all know the strong relationship now existing between President Johnson and Ambassador Goldberg."

I said that if this was indeed the case it was easy and that I could arrange for him to see Ambassador Goldberg immediately. At the time we were sitting in the U.N. Indonesian delegates' lounge, facing the entrance to the General Assembly. At that moment the meeting of the Assembly had been adjourned; when I saw Ambassador Goldberg coming out I went over and asked him to meet my Foreign Minister.

Ours was an informal meeting. After listening to the Minister requesting U.S. support so that efforts for peace in this area could make some progress, Ambassador Goldberg realised what the Minister was after. He immediately started speaking from a position of strength. He declared that if the Foreign Minister wanted the friendship and support of the United States he should know that friendship was a two-way street. The Foreign Minister replied: "We realise that and we are the friends of the United States." Then he added: "That is why I am here to see you."

Ambassador Goldberg answered pointedly; "But your ambassador should himself show this friendship in his speeches to the various organs of the United Nations. He keeps attacking the United States."

I was sitting listening to all this, but made no comment. My new Minister was taken by surprise. He looked at Goldberg and said very quietly he did not mind solving this matter first. He agreed to discuss all the matters at a special private meeting in the small conference room adjacent to the Security Council Chamber at 4.00 p.m. the following day. It was postponed to a later date, apparently because the U.S. Ambassador wanted to prepare for it.

I presumed I was to attend. It was customary, after all, to have the Permanent Representative join his Foreign Minister in all meetings. However, my Minister asked me not to join them. "Your absence will help," he said. I did not like the idea, but had to agree. He went, accompanied by a member of the delegation, to meet Ambassador Goldberg while I attended the meeting of the General Assembly.

A few minutes later my colleague who had accompanied my Foreign Minister came to say that the Minister now wanted me to attend the Goldberg meeting. I said to him: "We did not arrange for this." There was now nobody to replace me in the General Assembly and there was also the possibility of voting any minute.

"Please explain this to the Minister."

He went back and told the Minister what I had said, and then returned to ask me to arrange for a replacement in the General Assembly, drop everything and come over because the U.S. Ambassador had refused to say anything in my absence.

"I am a Judge, Sir," he told my Minister. "How can I criticise the attitude of a college at the U.N. in his absence?"

I must admit that the meeting was carefully planned. Ambassador Goldberg had brought with him his State Department man Joseph Sisco and his deputy, William Buffum. Sisco sat on his right and Buffum sat on his left. He started with a kind of warning, or it could have been a threat. "Mr. Minister, your security and future are most important to all of us."

What the Ambassador meant by the term "all" I still don't know. He continued: "We are friends of the King and we are the friends of Israel also. We try to serve both parties. But the stand of your Ambassador, Dr. El-Farra, here, affects our relations. His speeches against us affect public opinion. Our public opinion is very sensitive. It is difficult for us to explain the position of Jordan towards us. Had your Ambassador in Washington uttered these recriminations against our citizens,[1] we would have ordered him to return to Jordan as *persona non grata* within twenty-four hours because this is intolerable. He then added: "I respect El-Farra as a person, but we are speaking about principles and how to improve our relations. Let me quote some of his statements in the United Nations."

Goldberg started quoting extracts from my speeches, from a file his office had prepared. He laid particular emphasis on one quotation from a speech I delivered before the Security Council on 31st May 1967, that is five days before the Israeli invasion:

> "Only last Sunday we witnessed a parade (in New York) by supposedly American citizens who carried an Israeli flag in one hand and an American flag in the other. I have just heard a reference to conflicting interests. I was wondering, in case of a conflict of interest between the United States of America and Israel, where their loyalty would be, with the Israeli flag or the American flag? The behaviour of citizens of a country is an internal matter and comes squarely within the domestic juristiction of a member state. But I submit that when the behaviour affects the interest of other members states, I am

---

1. He was referring to Zionist pressure groups, supposedly American citizens.

entitled in sitting here to discuss the behaviour of pressure groups which are working against the interest of the Americans, a peace-loving people. The parade called for war against the Arabs. I saw in the parade many of the same faces that were in an earlier parade on Fifth Avenue to champion peace (in Vietnam)."[2]

Ambassador Goldberg was always sensitive about any reference by me in the United Nations to American Zionists. He wanted nothing to reflect on the loyalty of Jewish citizens in the United States, and always answered every reference I made to Zionists. This is what he had replied on this occasion:

"My Government had no constitutional right to curtail the exercise by its citizens of the right of free speech and free press which is basic to our conception of a democracy. My Government takes cognizance of the opinion of its citizens in formulating its foreign policy. It, however, as a government, declares its foreign policy within its own constitutional processes, and statements on this subject have been made by our President and by me representing our government to the Security Council. These statements, I frankly and readily agree, are an appropriate subject for debate in this Council. Every member of the Security Council is free to agree or disagree with our statements. Indeed, that is the prerogative of every member of the United Nations. But it does not serve the cause of harmonising the action of nations for representatives of any country to make references to what any of our citizens in the exercise of their constitutional rights may say or legally do with respect to their views about a grave situation which we are considering. We all read the world press. Citizens of all countries are expressing their views about this grave situation which is indeed highly understandable and natural under the circumstances. But we do categorically reject the right of any representative in any way to express an attitude with respect to the exercise by our citizens of their convictions in the matter.[3]

Every one of the quotations cited by Ambassador Goldberg before my Foreign Minister had its own background. Take, for

---

2. Security Council Meeting no.1345, 31st May 1967

3. Security Council Meeting no.1346, 3rd June 1967

instance, the statement I made before the Security Council on 26th July 1966, when Jordan was the only Arab member of the Security Council, so that I was duty bound to defend Arab interests.

On 25th July 1966 Israeli air attacks on Syria had caused much destruction of houses and property while many Syrians were killed and wounded. At the same time as the air attack Joseph Sisco of the U.S. State Department was in Israel, having lunch with high officials. What was he doing there? Ambassador Goldberg read the following extract from my remarks of 26th July 1966:

> "The new crime of blowing up houses and the air attack on Syria now being considered by the Security Council are also not new to the history of Zionism. The looting and blowing up of the King David Hotel by the Zionists on 22nd July 1946 — that is, during the British Mandate — is a living example of Zionist brutality. In that dastardly incident over one hundred innocent Christian and Moslem Government officials were killed.
>
> "By the way, it was in the new King David that the United States Representative, Mr. Joseph Sisco, the United States Under-Secretary of State for U.N. affairs, who arrived in Israel on the very day of the attack on Syria, had a luncheon with Israelis from the Israeli Foreign Ministry ... They had a lengthy meeting and it will be interesting for this Council to hear the views of Mr. Sisco on the matter ... He may have first-hand information on the item which we are now considering."

Ambassador Comay of Israel had answered with a big smile on his face. He said that of course Mr. Sisco had had lunch with the officials of Israel at the time and place mentioned by me. But, he asked: "What is wrong with that?"

I answered that the question was not who invited whom for lunch at the King David Hotel in Jerusalem. The whole world knew who paid for such a lunch. The question is what was discussed at that luncheon? Was there a relationship between this meeting and that air attack?

An American audience was then in the gallery of the Security Council. They thought that the matter of who paid for the lunch was very amusing. They laughed. The American media made a meal of it for themselves and made it headline fodder the following day: "Who paid for lunch?"

This had upset Ambassador Goldberg and upset the State Department even more. How did I know about the visit, they wondered. Who had communicated this information to me? Had it been the Jordanian or the Syrian intelligence? Ambassador Fedorenko of the Soviet Union had taken up this matter. He asked Sisco to explain his mission and wanted to know the part played by the C.I.A. Other members also started to ask questions.

In the afternoon, and a few minutes before the President of the Security Council convened the meeting, Joe Sisco who came to replace Ambassador Goldberg temporarily, put both of his hands on my shoulders and pressed them hard, the same way as I was pressing him in debate. Jokingly he said to me: "Will you take your hands off my shoulders? You read a great deal into my visit to Israel."

"This is in your favour," I replied. "I am making you famous in the United States."

He responded: "This will not help me. In the first place, I am not a politician. Secondly, I have no Jewish voters in my state."

Being in charge of United Nations affairs in the State Department at that time Sisco attended almost every serious Security Council debate. When on one occasion I had exposed the U.S. support of Israel and the tax-exempt donations which instead of going to the U.S. Treasury, the Zionists sent to Israel, Joe came to see me. He shook hands, smiled, then said: "You son of a gun. You are the only Jordanian I know who attacks the United States and gets away with it."

I looked at him and said: "Tell me, Joe, how many Jordanians do you know? I know you only know me and Minister Rifai."

He smiled and repeated: "You son of a gun. You always have an answer!"

This conversation of course was before he became a "peace-maker" with Henry Kissinger and others, when he became acquainted with other people in Jordan, Lebanon, Egypt and Syria.

It remains to explain that my source for the information I presented to the Security Council about Joseph Sisco's luncheon with the Israeli officials was not all that surprising. It was not given to me by either the Syrian or the Jordanian intelligence. During my long stay in New York I came to know that most Israeli papers reach Times Square the day following publication. When any Israeli attacks on our territories or people took place I used to rush the following morning to get the "Jerusalem Post" in English. Some-times, for more information, I obtained Hebrew newspapers and asked some of my Palestinian friends who knew Hebrew to translate what was relevant to me. This was a secret source of information which I never disclosed to my American colleagues.

2

The next quotation which Ambassador Goldberg now chose to read to my Foreign Minister was on a more serious matter, concerning the Palestinian resistance.

Israeli armed forces had attacked Jordan and caused much destruction and many casualties. The question had been brought up before the Security Council in 1966. In my speech I warned the Council that Israel was preparing for war with neighbouring Arab states. I said that these acts of provocation had one aim — war.

In response to the complaint to the Council, the United States and the United Kingdom, permanent members of the Security Council, tabled a draft resolution in a way which would make the Palestinian resistance share the responsibility for the Israeli attack. I objected to any reference to the resistance in the resolution because no proof whatsoever had been presented to this effect. The two co-sponsors, out of their lack of knowledge about Fateh,[4] produced their drafts, which stated that:

> "Either the Al Fateh or the Al Assifa organisation has been responsible for a long series of destructive raids into Israel."

Of course, Fateh organisation existed at that time along with its military arm, Al-Assifa. Both were branches of the same organisation. There was no such thing called "The Assifa organisation" and a separate one called "Al Fateh". Luckily these facts were not, at this stage, known either to the United States or to the United Kingdom despite their well-known intelligence organisations. It follows that neither Ambassador Goldberg nor Lord Caradon of Britain knew the difference or the relationship between Fateh and Al-Assifa. I was happy to know that as yet, the two Big Powers despite the strength of their intelligence did not know that Fateh and Al-Assifa were one. With this as a background I made, on 4th November 1966, the following statement attacking their draft resolution which so greatly annoyed Ambassador Goldberg that he now raised the matter with my Foreign Minister. This is what I had said:

> "...In their draft resolution the United Kingdom and the
> United States noted that either the Al Fateh or the Al Assifa

---

4. Due to the lack of knowledge about this organisation at the time even the spelling of its name was uncertain.

organisation has been responsible for a long series of destructive raids into Israel ... This is an either/or paragraph. We are supposed to note a statement of fact. Yet on the face of it, this paragraph embodies a statement of doubt. It does not impute responsibility to Al Fateh nor to Al Assifa, but it is simply an either/or proposition.

"Why did not the co-sponsors stick to one of the two organisations? Why did the United Kingdom representative and you, Mr. President, the United States representative, not make up your minds as to which of the two organisations is responsible? Or are they both responsible and how did you reach this conclusion? What are your convincing facts? Ambassador Goldberg is a learned Judge, and when he presents a case we expect that all the evidence will be weighed by him as a Judge.

"...And if the machinery in the area could not establish this claim as a fact, how can the United Kingdom and the United States representatives sitting thousands of miles away from the area come here and say that it is either Al Fateh or Al Assifa? And if in their complaint the Israelis condemn the unknown, how come the United States and United Kingdom are more certain than the Israelis? Is it an attempt by one of the two cosponsors to capitalise on the incident in an election year and thus be more pro-Israel than the Israelis? All these are important questions because they expose the real motives."

It was after one such meeting that Chief Adebo of Nigeria was presiding over the Security Council. He used to call representatives who wanted to speak by name rather than by title. I had earlier in previous statements referred with emphasis to the Palestinian organisation "El-Fateh". Apparently the name "El-Fateh" stuck in the President's mind and when I asked for the floor a second time he unconsciously — or deliberately, I don't know — said "I call on Ambassador El-Fateh of Jordan." This invited loud laughter from members and non-members of the Security Council sitting at the back of the chamber, the audience, ambassadors, diplomats and members of the press sitting in the gallery. Only one member sitting facing me on the other side of the horse-shoe shaped table did not think it was funny. It was the Israeli representative.

Ambassador Goldberg next brought to the attention of my Foreign Minister a statement I had made in the U.N. General Assembly on the refugee problem. Attempts had been made to limit and restrict the activities, of the U.N. Relief and Work Agency,

UNRWA, in an attempt to put pressure on the host countries to integrate and settle the refugees within their own borders, thus putting an end to the refugees' right to repatriation. I warned that this behaviour would feed the resistance and would cultivate more instability in the Arab East. In my statement to the General Assembly of the U.N. on 10th November 1966, I said, in part:

> "Tenthly, my delegation believes that there is in existence a plan to limit and restrict the activities of UNRWA stage by stage. There is no attempt to bring pressure to bear on the host countries to integrate and settle the refugees within their own borders, contrary to the letter and spirit of the United Nations Charter, to the determination of the refugees and to their inalienable right to return to their home. This explains the attempt of some Governments to perpetuate the problem by reducing their contributions to UNRWA at a time when the Agency was undertaking a rescue operation. We believe that the policy implications of financial decisions are as important as the financial implications of policy decisions. The hearing staged before the Senate Sub-Committee on Refugees and Escapees, and the questions raised by members of that Sub-Committee as to the effectiveness of UNRWA, as well as the present policy of the United States in the Middle East, are manifestations of the existence of such a plan...

> "There is no doubt that recent developments in the area were the natural reaction to the inaction and unfortunate behaviour of certain great powers, particularly the United States of America and the United Kingdom, with regard to the problem as a whole, and this specific item in particular. When people find that no progress is being made towards an equitable solution, but rather that there is continued attempt to break down the responsibilities of UNRWA in order to shift them to the host countries, certainly they must revolt, and challenge such measures with all the means at their disposal."

> "We are witnessing these challenges today. The unfortunate development in the area, which I warned against then, are the result of American policy vis-à-vis this problem and the refusal of Israel to repatriate the refugees to their homes."

3

On 13th November 1966 a savage attack had been made by Israel against Jordan. Regular Israeli forces crossed the demarcation line and destroyed houses in the Jordanian villages of Samou', murdering in cold blood and injuring many Jordanian citizens in what became known as the Samou' incident. The State Department issued press releases which did not reflect the reality of the situation. On 16th November 1966 I made a statement before the Security Council, as a complainent. Part of this Ambassador Goldberg now referred to in his conversation with my Foreign Minister:

> "...The immediate reaction in the United States reflected in Press Release No. 4975 of 13th November 1966 was unfortunate to say the least. The United States attempted to find justification for the attack. Moreover, and I say this with regret, the United States continues to treat the question of Palestine — it has done so from the very beginning to the present time — as a domestic issue. Its policy therefore, vis-à-vis the problem has been no deterrent to the Zionist criminals who cross demarcation lines to kill and butcher.
>
> "But now that all the facts of the case are crystal clear, now that we have heard a valuable report from the Secretary-General, now that the United States can see a rapidly deteriorating situation in a small country, a friendly country, a peaceful country, in Jordan, we should like to hear what the United States representative, you, Mr President, as ambassador of the United States and representing the United States, has to say on this question."

Ambassador Goldberg next had much to say about my speech to the Security Council on 21st November 1966 and he read out a lengthy part. All that he quoted was true. But I had a rising feeling, listening to all this, that it was unfair for Judge Goldberg to interfere in Jordanian internal affairs in such a manner. After all, I had been representing a sovereign state, and he had no right to cross-examine my Foreign Minister about speeches made by his Ambassador. The Minister did not stop him and I thought perhaps I should still show patience and wait until Goldberg's monologue of complaint petered out.

This was the part of my speech to which Ambassador Goldberg gave special emphasis:

> "According to the 'New York Times' of last Saturday highly placed sources in Washington insist that the United States' policy toward Israel remains one of friendship, aid and

protection — as it has been since Israel's birth eighteen years ago.

"Now what does this insistence of friendship, aid and protection, by highly-placed sources in Washington at this very stage of our deliberations, mean? Was it made to help members around this table form an opinion, or an estimate, as to the position of one of the permanent members of the Security Council, or was it intended to calm the nerves of the aggressor, facing certain condemnations and requests for sanctions? And, if the answer to our request is reassuring Israel of friendship, aid and protection, is the Council in a position to adopt any measures which would deter aggression?

What I have already stated is the deduction of any reasonable man from the article itself, and the quotation attributed to 'highly-placed sources' as well as other circumstances not known to members of this Council.

If, through the Chair of this Council, Mr President, you would permit me to address you as the representative of the United States of America. If this appraisal is a mistaken one, it would give me and my delegation pleasure to be corrected, because I must stress the point that these statements have been of grave concern to my government and to other Arab governments in as much as they may reflect on the position to be taken by the United States on the question before the Council, and on the Palestine question as a whole.

We cannot ignore the fact that forty-six of the tanks that invaded Jordan were American Patton tanks, which were for defensive purposes! They were used for invasion ... for invading Jordan — which Mr. Comay, to meet United States requirements, chose to call a 'defensive operation'. They too were delivered in conformity with the policy of friendship, aid and protection — but used for murder and destruction."

My Foreign Minister realised from the text that my statement was about the Samou' invasion, where over half of that village was completely destroyed with scores of men, women and children murdered, with many other casualties reported officially by the U.N. Secretary-General.

This was all that Ambassador Goldberg had to say about my speeches in 1966. I thought he had at long last finished. But apparently he had still more to complain about for 1967.

Indeed I would have been naive not to expect him to say more about this, the year of the so-called Six Day War, the year in which

Ambassador Goldberg in New York acted in concert with the Reston brothers, one in the White House and the other in the State Department. Together they played a key role in support of Israel. I did not want to stop the Ambassador and raise an objection to more of this stuff, or to mention Jordanian sovereignty. I therefore whispered to my Foreign Minister and asked him to stop Goldberg. "We've had enough," I said.

The Minister, however, wanted to listen to more of the same. He received everything he had heard calmly. He certainly was very amused.

Sure enough, Ambassador Goldberg paid special attention to what I had said during the Six Day War. On 7th June 1967 Jordan announced its acceptance of a cease-fire. A cable was sent to this effect to the Secretary-General which was read in the afternoon meeting of 8th June 1967.

Every member of the Arab delegation to the U.N. was shocked at this announcement. I was sitting in my seat in the Security Council waiting to see what the Council would do. The Foreign Minister of Morocco, Ahmed Benhima, (then Morocco's permanent representative to the United Nations) came up and asked me on no account to leave the forum to Abba Eban, the Foreign Minister of Israel, nor to the 'tenacious Arthur Goldberg.' "This is the time for speaking. Please do. Say anything! Jordan is a friend of the United States. Let American public opinion know what a big power did to a friend."

I explained to him my view that the cease-fire had been announced and that was that. "I have nothing to say."

He said emphatically "No, this is not right! I know you do not mean it. I shall go and put your name to speak after Ambassador Goldberg."

Arthur was at that moment taking the floor and blaming those familiar U.S. punch bags, the Arabs, as well as the Soviet Union, for what had happened. In effect, he was saying "we told you so."

When he had finished the President gave me the floor. This is part of the statement I made then, afterwards read to my Foreign Minister by Ambassador Goldberg in his deep desire to describe me as an 'undesirable' advocate of my country's cause:

"The generous United States help given to Israel through all kinds of tax-deductable donations, the arms, the American Patton tanks given for defensive purposes but used for invasion, the heavy machinery and the stronger aerial cover enabled Israel to acquire more of our lands and displace more of our people. But it will not enable Israel to conquer our strong spirit, our faith and our determination."[5]

By the following day, 9th June, Israel had violated the cease-fire. We wanted the Security Council to condemn Israel for invading Arab territories and committing an act of naked aggression. Judge Goldberg had departed from the main issue and came out with a suggestion that the machinery in the area should investigate who violated the cease-fire. I thought that if I left this diversion unanswered we might end up condemned by the Security Council for violation of the cease-fire. I had to answer him and this is what the Judge quoted from my statement to my Foreign Minister, while I was listening with a surprised look on my face:

> "I have listened with interest to the statement just made by Judge Goldberg of the United States. I was astonished to hear Judge Goldberg speak about impartial investigation of cease-fire violations by the Secretary General with adequate machinery. I was astonished because I was hoping — apparently against hope — that Judge Goldberg would proceed to bring first issues first. I was hoping that Judge Goldberg would ask the Council to establish the facts about the aggression and who committed the act of aggression now being considered by the Council? Who invaded land and occupied towns and villages, destroyed buildings, and killed inhabitants?....
>
> I was hoping that Judge Goldberg, a learned Judge, a man of law, would be able to come here as the representative of a great Member of the United Nations, a responsible member — and I would quote him when I say "the greater the power the greater the responsibility" those were his words — and deal with the crux of the matter.
>
> But Judge Goldberg did not come to the crux of the problem; the act of war committed against my government, against my people, against innocent civilians of Jordan.
>
> There is another question. I keep hearing a statement repeated time and again that the United States government is committed to protect the territorial integrity of all nations. I keep hearing the words 'all nations'. But when Jordan was invaded, when thousands were killed, I did not hear anything

---

5. Security Council Meeting no.1351, 8th June 1967.

about this commitment other than a speech in the Council repeating the very same statement: we are committed to all members of the Middle East, to all nations in the Middle East.

I have to say this. We are a country friendly to the United States. We have to be careful about the sensitivity of a great power, because we are a small Member. We have to be careful about choosing our terms, because we need the support of all great Powers. But what is going on cannot be defined or described with sweet words."

The following day the Security Council met but no attempt whatever was made to put an end to the Israeli occupation of our lands. Again I made a speech. What he clearly thought to be my intemperate references to the United States provoked Ambassador Goldberg. He of course referred to it now. This is what I had said:

"Pages of newspapers have been used to mislead American public opinion. These pages speak about peace. One of them states: 'Israel wants peace.' They have the word 'peace' spelled wrongly: It should be 'piece'. They do want piece! One piece was the part invaded in Jordan which was occupied. That is piece number one. Piece number two is Gaza. Piece number three is part of Syria. Piece number four is Sinai...

".... Here in the Security Council instead of taking immediate action we are having a discussion about law, legality and illegality. That discussion took place yesterday. Today when the facts have become very clear as presented by the Secretary General we see a different approach. We find the United States coming to the Security Council to say that: '... it could not render a judgement on the basis of allegations by one of the parties.'

"The United States will not render a judgement on the basis of allegations by one of the parties. These are not allegations now. They are facts that have been presented. But I do not doubt that the Council has not forgotten that in October of last year the United States — Ambassador Goldberg to be exact — submitted to the Council a draft resolution condemning a State on the basis of a one-sided investigation. Later we received more information."

The Security Council had ordered a stop to war in one part of the Arab East though Israeli violations of the cease-fire continued. The war continued in another part namely Sinai, the Gaza Strip and the

Golan Heights. No immediate action to put an end to this war was taken by the Security Council because of American tactics. We wanted action, but the behaviour of the U.S. invited inaction. Arab members had appealed to the Council to take more serious and effective steps. Then Ambassador Goldberg made a statement advising the members of the Council not to make 'inflammatory statements.' I of course had attacked his negative stand, which upset him a great deal. He did not want us even to show our resentment at what was going on in the highest organ, the Security Council — the body responsible for the maintenance of peace and security in the world.

In our meeting he cited a part of my statement which had offended his susceptibilities:

> In many of his interventions, the representative of the United States, Ambassador Goldberg, advised the members of the Council not to make inflammatory statements. This suggestion is intended, if we understand it correctly, to cultivate peace, but since the behaviour of the Zionists within the United States is directly connected with the question of peace, it would be greatly appreciated and greatly helpful at this important stage if the United States representative would condemn Zionist practices in the United States which, even in this delicate situation, are playing a most destructive role....
>
> The Zionists have gone to the extent of threatening the lives of Arab ambassadors who are fulfilling their duties in this august body. One wonders whether this also comes under freedom of expression or freedom of speech.
>
> This wholly un-American activity of the Zionist group within the United States violates United States tradition. It was for this reason that I spoke about a curtain between us and the people of the United States, imposed by Zionism. It is this curtain which makes many Americans unaware of the Palestine tragedy ...
>
> We were asked not to make inflammatory statements. Ambassador Goldberg said that what is needed here is not hot words. Thus we are expected to be silent while our people are being slaughtered in the invaded area. We are asked not to call a crime a crime; we are advised to avoid explaining the terrible acts of genocide committed against people...
>
> We agreed that hot words alone are not the meaningful answer to hot deeds. We may not have other means at present, but we can only hope that through honest and sincere words we

can open a closed door, and that we can lift the dark curtain so that truth be not a stranger in the land of Jefferson and Washington.

How can we, the delegation of Jordan, a small member of the United Nations, find mild and soft language to describe the American napalm bombs used by the Israelis against our people and our heroic small army, which has fought without adequate machinery, without air cover, but with every sacrifice, with all courage, with manliness and determination? And with this and many other Israeli atrocities, how can we find an excuse for American politicians who, for cheap political gains, exploit the suffering and losses inflicted upon us and the acts of genocide committed against our people?[6]

Ambassador Goldberg's opposition to my attitude during the June war of 1967 was that I had compared Nazism and Zionism. He was equally annoyed when I had shown in one of my statements that the United States was trying to accommodate Israeli aggression.

The United States had submitted a draft resolution to the Security Council. We opposed it, claiming that it enabled Israel to make political gains through force. It amounted, we said, to encouragement of the aggressor. Of course what happened later proved that our fear had much justification. It was this kind of support which in the end brought about more wars, causing yet more human suffering. It was Israeli arrogance and financial and military American support to Israel which brought all this about. Ambassador Goldberg underlined all my words very strongly during his lengthy 'presentation' to my Foreign Minister. Other statements of 13th and 14th June 1967 which he now complained of read as follows:

"Jordan has been considered a friend of the United States. But I regret to say that Jordan was betrayed by its so-called friends. We are assured that the territorial integrity of all nations in the Middle East would be protected. We were told that the movement of the Sixth Fleet in the Mediterranean was intended to put that policy into effect, to stop the aggression from whichever side it came from. But when Jordan was invaded and a substantial part of its territory was illegally occupied, the Sixth Fleet kept silent. One cannot but wonder

---

6. Security Council Meeting, no. 1359, 13th June 1967.

whether the Sixth Fleet was there to protect Jordan or to facilitate the task of the invaders ...

...If the United States government is to ignore the legitimate rights of the Arabs, if the United States government intends to have expediency as its guiding principle, then this will pose a challenge to every Arab.

In conclusion, let me make it very clear that Jordan is not happy about the part so far played by the United States and some other powers here in the Security Council vis-à-vis our cause. If this United States policy continues, some politicians in America may win Zionist and so-called Jewish votes in the United States, but the American people as a result, will definitely — and I repeat, definitely — lose all their interests and friends in the Arab East."

...But despite the assurances about the territorial integrity of all nations of the Middle East, nothing was done to prevent an act of aggression against Jordan. Of course, the Sixth Fleet was there. It was manoeuvring to show its presence. But when we found that we had become subjected to aggression and that the Sixth Fleet stood idly by doing nothing to protect the territorial integrity of Jordan, we wondered whether it was intended to safeguard the members of the Middle East or whether it was there as an assurance for the Israeli aggression.

...My delegation feels that the United States, with the ship 'Liberty' standing there for a purpose, had good reason to believe that the Israelis were contemplating aggression against Jordan."

On the Zionist movement and Zionism this is what the Ambassador chose to quote from the statement I made to the Security Council on 13th June 1967: I said:

"...Both Nazism and Zionism hold to the concept of the fifth column. The Nazis used to have a fifth column, and the Zionists in the United States have pressure groups; they have a city within every city and they have a town within every town.

They have a pressure group within every single branch of the United States Government. These are facts. Let the Israelis refute a single one of them. Therefore, a movement of this destructive purpose should not be permitted to function against the interests of both the Arab people and the American people; a movement which has this expansionist design aimed at displacing my people, expanding in our lands,displacing

more of our people, acquiring more of our towns and cities —
this movement should not be permitted to function in the
United States."

June 14th, 1967

...As we see it, the United States draft resolution
accommodates the invader and occupier, It enables Israel,
through force, to acquire political gains. It amounts to
encouragement of the aggressor....

The question arises: Why is the United States government
changing its attitude and stand? Is it because the United States
is now more involved in this problem than it was in 1956, one
indeed wonders. Is is permissible or compatible with the
principles of the Charter to permit Israel to use as a bargaining
point a gain achieved by means of force? Mr. Goldberg — who
is not at the meeting this evening — is a jurist and can clarify
this question. Both the American nation and the Arab nation
are entitled to know."[7]

The reader may wonder just why did Ambassador Goldberg
choose to raise all these matters with the Minister of Foreign Affairs
of Jordan? Or why did the Ambassador of Jordan single out the
United States in his speeches? These are proper questions.

In my speeches I was presenting my country's case and referring
to a genuine peace. I referred to many countries which took stands
in violation of their obligations under the U.N. Charter. The United
States had a special responsibility under the Charter and, what is
more, it was consistently ignoring the victim and doing everything
possible to accommodate the occupier. Take, for instance, the
attitude of Ambassador Goldberg himself. Speaking in May 1967
(i.e. before the Israeli occupation of parts of our homeland), he said
to the Security Council that restoration of the *status quo* was the first
essential to peace.

"I said that the short-range problem was restoration of the
status quo ante in the Strait of Tiran — the status which has
existed for eleven years — so that the Council, enjoying the
breathing spell, the cooling-off period, that the Secretary

---

7. Security Council Meeting, no. 1359, 13th June 1967 and 1361, 14th
June 1967

General has suggested, could consider the underlying problems and arrive at a fair, just and honourable solution of these problems."[8]

After the occupation of our territories the policy of the United States had suddenly changed. Students of international law will certainly ponder the utter inconsistency between the U.S. policy announced in May and that announced in June of the same year, that is after the Israeli victory. This latter statement said:

"What the Near East needs today are new steps toward real peace, not just a cease-fire which is what we have today; not just a fragile and perilous armistice, which is what we have had for eighteen years; not just withdrawal which is necessary but insufficient."[9]

Prior to the hostilities, Ambassador Goldberg had stated to the Council that meaningful peace negotiations could not take place unless the Gulf of Aqaba was re-opened to Israeli shipping, thereby restoring the *status quo ante*. He added that it would not be possible to negotiate and explore the underlying causes of the Arab-Israeli dispute in the tense atmosphere created by the closing of the Gulf of Aqaba.[10]

Following the Israeli victory the United States adopted an entirely contrary position. Ambassador Goldberg called the *status quo ante* a "prescription for renewed hostilities."[11]

It is this attitude which brought about the inaction of the Security Council, which encouraged Israel to refuse to withdraw and, in fact, to undertake more arrogant steps, invasions and wars. So much so that Israeli later arrogantly and openly invaded and occupied Southern Lebanon.

Israel now insists on individual negotiations, i.e. under duress. This is the kind of negotiation they had with Anwar Sadat of Egypt and with the Lebanese while a substantial part of their country was under occupation. This is what the Rt.Hon. Sir Anthony Nutting called the doctrine of "divide and conquer" and these are what he

---

8. Security Council Meeting, no.1344, 30th May 1967.
9. Security Council Meeting, no. 1358, 13th June 1967.
10. Security Council Meeting, no. 1343 29th May 1967.
11. General Assembly Document no.A/PV 1527 dated June 30th 1967 at 16-17.

called "conquerers' terms."[12]

Over an hour had passed during this lengthy recital of my "offensive speeches". Ambassador Goldberg was still enjoying the patience of the Jordanian Foreign Minister and continued reading excerpts of my statements in the Security Council and to the General Assembly. My note to my Minister that he should stop Goldberg in full flood had not helped. My Minister believed, apparently being led to do so by the American Ambassador in Amman, that Ambassador Goldberg was the one who could make it or break it so far as Jordan was concerned. The Minister, therefore, wanted him to continue.

I whispered to the Minister that, out of respect for my country and to myself, I refused to continue sitting there listening to Goldberg's charges and attacks on the Government and its policy. "I shall stop him and answer him if you do not want to do it," I said.

By that time the Minister himself had started getting impatient. He said to me very quietly: "Do answer him but do so carefully." I said:

> "Ambassador Goldberg has exploited the Minister's courtesy and patience to the very end. I am not sitting here to receive attacks and charges from the distinguished representative of the United States. I represent a sovereign state. All my speeches and my interventions and the draft resolutions I tabled in the Security Council and in the General Assembly are upon specific instructions from my government. That is why I have been the representative of the government of Jordan for over seven years. What my colleague Ambassador Goldberg has been saying for over an hour now amounts to intervention in our domestic affairs. Certainly, our policy is dictated by our interest. It would do the State Department good to consider its own policy vis-à-vis our problem with Israel. Any objective analysis of the American attitude would show understanding and agreement with the Jordanian stand that Ambassador Goldberg is complaining against."

I ended my statement saying: "Friendship is, Mr Ambassador, as you said earlier, a two-way-street."

---

12. See Anthony Nutting, The Tragedy of Palestine from the Balfour to Today", an address delivered at the annual conference of the American Council for Judaism, 2nd November 1967.

Ambassador Goldberg now said that he had never intended to intervene in the domestic matters of Jordan. However, he had thought that the idea behind the meeting was to air differences and start a new kind of mutual understanding. "This I think is enough, I shall not cite more of Ambassador El-Farra's speeches," he concluded.

The Foreign Minister said that he was a new Minister, "but everybody has a high regard for Dr El-Farra. His stands to my knowledge reflect the government's position and policy." He ended by saying that he would, however, study all Ambassador Goldberg had said.

He then turned to the American Ambassador and declared: "Let us turn to the present problem. What can you do for your friends?"

Ambassador Goldberg replied: "We are a democratic country. We are not Israel. You help us and give us a chance to help you. This is our stand."

The Minister asked: "Is your complaint against our press, our radio or our public opinion?"

Ambassador Goldberg replied: "No, only against what goes on in the international field. Right here."

The Minister: "Then it is against Dr El-Farra?"

Goldberg: "Exactly."

At this point Joe Sisco joined in. "Whatever Dr El-Farra says is carried by TV, radio and the press. As you, Mr Minister, said before Dr El-Farra joined us here, and you are quite right, the Egyptian Foreign Minister, Mr Riad, attacked us today. He attacked no other state. This makes it difficult for us to do anything for their case."

The Minister: "The Jordanian people like the United States. Nothing is written or published in Jordan against the U.S. I am sure your Ambassador in Amman reports all this to you."

Joe Sisco replied: "I am most happy that your people love America but the problem is here."

Ambassador Buffum then contributed to the dialogue: "Even members of the United Nations do not understand why Dr El-Farra stands against us. The continued strong attacks of Jordan on the U.S. make assistance to you impossible. Speeches are important for either improving or worsening relations."

The Minister: "Yes. Irresponsible government policy or talk can affect friendly relations."

Here I was happy because the Minister spoke implicitly about American policy which invites strong speeches. I wrote a quick note to him not to be so lenient. Why not ask the Ambassador about his stand and that of his government vis-à-vis our rights and Israeli continued occupation of our lands? Why not query the tax-exempt donations? Why not question the military and economic help which actually accommodates Israel's continued occupation? Why not emphasise how the U.S. is accommodating Israeli conquests by acts, deeds and behaviour?

The Minister assured me he would and continued: "I certainly listened carefully to what you all had to say. I hope you will also remember, in passing judgement on our main speeches in the United Nations, your own policy regarding our main problem. Our Ambassador reminded you quite rightly earlier that friendship is a two-way street. Let us during my stay meet again and see how we both can improve understanding. I am sure our Ambassador and all of us would love not to find ourselves in a position having to oppose your policy. We should discuss this matter further. But now tell me what you can do to help us."

Goldberg: "Frankly, let me use an American slang expression, we are running out of gas. We can't do anything. We can't give you integrity. You have to participate in the process to work out the problem. If you start negotiating with the Israelis you may save the situation. We can help you reach an agreement so that you can have the West Bank ... Time is of the essence. We can't impose a prescription on Israel. We only support by sending a special representative. We shall try to get for you the best deal possible."

He added: "Jordan's entering the war was a mistake. It served Nasser. When the war started we spoke with the Russians on the hot line. We said to them: 'Let us both stay out of the complications of this war'."

The Jordanian Foreign Minister stayed with the American group for two hours. Nothing fruitful came out of the meeting. The Minister continually obtained the same evasive answers.

He asked me when we had finished whether his meeting with Dean Rusk would amount to the same thing and with the same result. I answered: "Yes, but it will be more pleasant. On the Arab-Israeli conflict all American diplomats and State Department people speak the same language, but the choice of words is different."

When the Minister met Dean Rusk, he was well received, but nothing encouraging came out of the meeting. Dean Rusk said that the Palestine problem was a problem of lost opportunities and that nothing less than dialogue could help Jordan make progress.

Of course, the Minister was not happy about what he heard. He was keen that I should join him in all his meetings with the various Ministers. He realised that I wanted him to succeed and that I did not want him, at this early stage of his new responsibilities, to put the wrong foot forward.

4

Together with two members of the Jordanian delegation the Minister then went to meet the late George Brown, the Foreign Secretary of the United Kingdom at the residence of Lord Caradon. When the Foreign Minister arrived with his delegation at the room where George Brown was sitting they found him in a happy mood. He looked at the Foreign Minister and asked: "Are you the Foreign Minister of Jordan?"

The Minister replied: "Yes Sir I am."

George Brown pointed at him and said: "You are the one, then. You are the one! Please sit down."

The Minister and his two deputies sat. Lord Caradon was as surprised as anyone by the British Foreign Secretary's next words. He said:

"You, the Foreign Minister of Jordan, have to sit down with Golda Meir of Israel. Negotiate a treaty. But all the time keep the King out of it. You sign a treaty. You may get a bullet after that. But the treaty will last and you will have left behind you a treaty and rendered good service to your country." But, he repeated: "Keep the King out of it."

George Brown went on: "This is what we in England did with Michael Collins of Ireland. We negotiated a treaty. We partitioned Ireland. Michael Collins received a bullet after that, but the treaty has remained till this moment."[13]

He added "It takes a man to take this courageous stand. I see in you that man. Go ahead. Do it."

The Foreign Minister was stunned. He did not knew what to do. He thanked George Brown for his advice, excused himself and left. Brown walked with him to the door where he said emphatically, with a smile on his face: "Mr. Minister, think it over."

Unfortunately, those ideas which the Minister had in mind and wanted to discuss with friends in the United Nations did not find any encouragement either in Washington or from the Foreign Secretary of the United Kingdom. Unfortunately, too, he was relieved of his duties while he was still in New York to be given another position.

---

13. After the Anglo-Irish treaty on 6th December 1921 Michael Collins was quoted as saying: "I have signed my own death warrant." See Robert Kee: *Ireland: A History* p.197, Abacus edition, pub. 1982 by Sphere Books Ltd.

He was not at all happy about the change.

Later, apparently, Anwar Sadat of Egypt was encouraged by the United States to surprise the world, and negotiate with the Israelis. Sure enough, Sadat reached agreement on certain issues and signed a treaty with Israel. And equally surely, he received the bullet which George Brown had predicted. It remains to be seen whether this treaty between Egypt and Israel will last.

5

The meeting between Arthur Goldberg and my Foreign Minister did not achieve its purpose. He thought he could put pressure on me through that meeting, though luckily, nothing happened, and it brought no result. Relations between Ambassador Goldberg and myself, however, continued to be friendly. Socially we were on good terms. When it comes to business, or to be more accurate to U.N. deliberations, we could, of course, hardly see eye to eye. He had his convictions, and I had mine. Having a special relationship with the White House, he was very influential in the State Department. Many times, to impress me, he called President Johnson on the phone and both were speaking on a first name basis. In the State Department, Joe Sisco was always available for any assistance needed. He was a close friend of the Ambassador. Goldberg had such high regard for Joe that he wanted to recommend him as his successor. This did not occur because when his assignment was ending he had lost much of his influence on the State Department and all influence on the White House.

On another occasion, when the Israelis held a military parade in Jerusalem, I again complained on behalf of the Jordan government to the Security Council. The Council considered that the parade would aggravate tension in the area and would have an adverse effect on a peaceful settlement of the problems in the Middle East. Goldberg had told the State Department that I was not consulting with him on the question and because of that "lack of cooperation" the State Department then stated that it could not support Jordan's protest.

At the same time, Goldberg also came to me and complained that my government itself did not consult the State Department on the Jerusalem issue.

When I sent this complaint back to my government in Amman, I was told that in fact the opposite was true. They were in contact with the U.S. government, but the U.S. government had refused to support the Jordanian position. Their lack of support was not because of a lack of contact or consultation, as Arthur Goldberg inferred, but simply because the U.S. government was committed to help Israel on any and every problem relating to the occupied territories. The U.S. claim of lack of consultation was in fact nothing but a pretext to justify their attitude. Jordan, a small country, would not fail to contact and exchange notes on such vital issues with all Big Powers, and particularly with the United States of America.

In 1968 a new development took place, again concerning the disputed Israeli parade in the Holy City, that necessitated a further urgent meeting between myself and Ambassador Goldberg.

On 17th April we met in his office early in the morning. Apparently the United States did not want to take a stand between two "friendly countries" like Jordan and Israel. It, therefore, wanted the matter adjourned until the State Department could contact the government of Jordan, not the first time Arthur Goldberg used this kind of delaying tactic.

He opened the meeting by saying that he had woken up very early that day, which was unusual. He added that I must have done the same. "We both, therefore, need a cup of coffee so we can be awake and the discussion can be fruitful," he commented.

I replied: "This is true."

He then continued: "I am sorry if our last meeting was a little unusual. Your complaint was handled in a very rapid way and the decision of the Security Council was passed at unimaginable speed." Then he paused and commented: "And now you are applying more pressure for more action."

I said: "Frankly, Arthur, what happened the other day was very unfortunate. And to be more specific what you and your government have done was very strange indeed. To my knowledge, it has no precedent in diplomacy. You, on the one hand, complain against me to my government saying that I held no consultation at all with you. Then you turn to me and complain that my government does not contact your State Department and takes decisions and adopts attitudes without your knowledge. This method does not inspire confidence, neither does it lead to genuine trust and cooperation." After a pause I went on: "You said to your State Department, and, through your State Department to my government, that I do not accept consultation. I hope you agree with me that it would have been more accurate to say that I do not accept dictation and refuse submission to the will of a Big Power — any Big Power. Consultation, as you know, was always going on. I contacted you, Bill (Buffum) and Dick (Pedersen) before requesting the Security

Council to convene a meeting. I delayed the meeting of the Security Council on the question of the Israeli parade in Jerusalem by thirty-six hours hoping that your government would use its influence to stop that Israeli violation. Nothing was done. When the case came before the Security Council you wanted the debate to be concluded with a simple statement of regret to be issued by the President of the Council. It was natural for me, and for any reasonable man, to say 'no' to this unique suggestion. Thus the matter was not lack of consultation, but your insistence that we should go along, for the sake of peace, with the American idea of having no action whatsoever taken by the Council. I would like to state my position for the second time. I shall speak very slowly so the gentleman who is taking the minutes of this meeting will take down everything I say so that the State Department will know our position in very clear terms."

I went on to emphasise the point I had so much in mind:-

"Friendship, Mr. Ambassador, is a two-way-street. It has to be mutual. It is Park Avenue. It is not First Avenue. We appreciate your friendship. But you can prove it by practice. I mean by acts, deeds and behaviour. Of course, Jordan will consult the United States of America. But I say on behalf of my government I shall refuse any suggestion that you have the final say about what is and what is not in the interest of my government. This is simple because I know better what is in the interest of my country. We are not a protectorate. We are a sovereign state."

Ambassador Goldberg replied: "Let me explain one thing. I expect that we may disagree. I don't believe in dictation. Jordan is a sovereign state. We respect its sovereignty. All that we expect is to be consulted before a decision in Amman is taken. Your government knows our position on the question of Jerusalem. And in spite of this it presented its complaint to the Security Council. We want to work together and strengthen our friendly relations."

Here I could not resist saying "There is much difference between working together and working as one, and you are the one! Isn't this what you are after?"

Ambassador Goldberg broke in: "On this question of Jerusalem you put us in a dilemma. We could not support your draft resolution and wanted some time to convince Amman of our point of view.[14] You refused and pushed the draft to the vote. Had you asked me for an adjournment of any problem before the Security Council for a reasonable time I would have gladly done so for a friend. But you

---

14. Security Council Meeting no. 1420, March, 1968.

refused the reasonable request of the United States of America for an adjournment."

I replied: "The reasonable thing for me in the interest of my government is not to wait until you put pressure on member states in the Security Council so they would vote against my draft and you would lobby for its failure. I would be very naive Mr Ambassador to accept this request. Thus consultation did take place. The fact that your request was not accepted for the reasons I have just mentioned is something else."

At this stage the Ambassador said: "Let us open a new page."

I said: "By all means."

He then stated that the Security Council was now debating the new stage of the parade problem. Israel had already held its parade. He didn't know what kind of action should be taken and he would suggest an adjournment.

I said: "Again! And why? You knew this was coming up because Israel defied the will of the Council."

I emphasised that things were not quiet in the area. Security Council action was badly needed. The United States as a Big Power should not use such tactics for the sake of peace.

I concluded: "Adjournment is not in the American interest, nor would it be of service to its reputation, let alone its prestige, which is at its lowest ebb in our area."

Our meeting ended with no agreement. The resolution taken by the Security Council against Israel on the question of the parade was never implemented.

6

During 1968, Goldberg and I had a long discussion on how to improve Jordanian-American relations and on how Jordan's attitude towards the United States in the United Nations could be changed. I explained that every small power would love to be on close terms with a Big Power and, in particular, the United States of America. This was only natural, since it needed friendly relations with that power not only in the United Nations, where it has the vote and the weight that goes with it, but also outside the United Nations Organisation. He referred to the earlier meeting with my Minister, and showed understanding of my objection to his reading to the Minister quotations from my various speeches in the United Nations.

I suggested that we should discuss the matter "man to man", and said I would appreciate a copy of the file he had containing quotations from my speeches. He asked one of his aides to secure a copy for me, which I received the same day. It included all the quotations which he had read out to my Minister together with those that he did not have a chance to read, which I was keen to study.

When the United Nations General Assembly Session ended that year, a rumour spread that because Goldberg was helping the Robert Kennedy campaign for the presidency, he was no longer on good terms with President Johnson and that he was about to resign. We never had our "man to man" discussion.

One day I met Goldberg in his office and he told me he had quit. He said that he would now be very independent and that he hoped to maintain contact with me. He offered to do anything that would help bring peace to the area. However we lost contact when a little while later, I was transferred to be Jordanian Ambassador in Spain, later joining the League of Arab States as Under-Secretary.

Ambassador Goldberg was succeeded by George Ball, who came to Jordan to get first hand information on the Middle East crisis. I was in Amman when he arrived. Harrison Simms, then U.S. Ambassador in Amman, had a luncheon on Tuesday, 16th July 1969 in honour of Mr. Ball, and invited the Prime Minister Mr. Bahjat El Talhouni, the Foreign Minister Mr. Abdul Monem Rifai,the Minister of Economy Mr. Hatem El Zu'bi and myself to the luncheon. While chatting socially Ambassador Simms said to Minister Zu'bi : "Your Ambassador in the United Nations, El-Farra, is worse and more difficult for us than Goldberg was for you. He makes violent speeches and whenever he speaks we see on his face the Palestine image."

Hatem Zu'bi did not want to encourage this kind of talk, and replied "Muhammad is not alone in having this privilege. We are all Palestinians and have the Palestine image." I was delighted to hear the Minister's support.

Unlike Simms, Ambassador Ball was most pleasant and charming. In his conversation with me he said that we should meet more often at the United Nations. He assured me that his stand in the United Nations on the Palestine problem would be "constructive, positive, and even-handed," and emphasised that he would talk less in the Security Council and not allow himself to be provoked. And whatever the stand of his predecessor might have been he told me his own would be far from being biased. Our Prime Minister, Talhouni, emphasised the need for a more active role by the United States in the search for peace, saying that a rapid withdrawal was very important and that peace could only be achieved when a positive framework was built on which it could be based.

Indeed Jordan has subsequently made repeated requests to the American Government to make some move towards the achievement of peace. But when some move is made it is usually in the wrong direction, because of the many pre-existing American commitments to the other side. Its manoeuvres therefore create more complications instead of reaching a just solution.

Take for example the signing of the Camp David Accords, when a new President, Jimmy Carter, seemed inclined to push for peace, disregarding Zionist pressure. Under his auspices negotiations between Israel and Egypt started. The President, a man of good intentions but in practical terms lamentably unfamiliar with the Middle East, had a simple and unshakeable faith that peace could be achieved. He could not, or would not, realise the strength of Zionist opposition ranged against him. He was outspoken about the illegality of the Israeli settlements in the occupied territories of the Golan Heights, the Sinai peninsula and the West Bank and said that each was "an impediment to peace". He went further and declared that the Palestinians deserved a "homeland", had "legitimate rights" and should "participate in the determination of their own future".

His aim was a peace conference to be held at the end of 1977 to seek a comprehensive solution to the Arab-Israeli conflict. President Sadat's autumn trip to Jerusalem, when he indicated his willingness to open talks, precipitated twelve months of discussion which culminated in the Camp David Accords. But they were "agreed" on by three ill-assorted negotiators; a persevering Carter squeezed by domestic pressures, the haughty Begin ruled by the conviction that Israel "did not need Egypt's recognition because recognition of Israel's right to exist came only from God" and the dazzled Sadat who felt he enjoyed a special relationship with the United States President.

But though it is debatable whether the Camp David Accords were intended to bring genuine and lasting peace to the Middle East or simply to isolate Egypt and thus further divide the area, the Israelis could not accept this chance for an end to hostility. Begin used the sessions as another opportunity to grab greatly increased economic aid in return for ceding Sinai; Sadat was the one who gave in to all concessions demanded by the unreasonable Begin. Three years later Sadat received the bullet which demonstrated the rejection of the Camp David Accords as unequal agreements, taken under duress and painful to the dignity of proud Egyptians. In the end the treaty has done little for the Egyptians and nothing for the Palestinians.

Chapter 12

The Use of Pressure and Intimidation

*"I think it is about time that somebody should pay some considera-
tion to whether we might not lose the United States."*

James Forrestal
Former American Secretary of Defense.

"This is the American Way, boys. You have to accept it."

United Nations Diplomat.

I have already tried to show the methods used by the Israelis to
intimidate the Palestinian people and force them to leave homes and
lands.

One thing, however, I have not yet mentioned is the pressure
applied in the political field on many international figures or
representatives of members of states at the U.N. who do not see eye
to eye with Zionism: the threats to diplomats, the smear campaigns,
the pressures on governments, the resort to all ways and means to
achieve Zionist goals. Much of this type of Zionist behaviour was
practised in the United Nations during the debate on Palestine in
1947, i.e. before the adoption of the recommendation calling for the
country's partition. Many ambassadors were subjected to this
pressure and the U.N. recomendation for the partition of Palestine
into Jewish and Arab States, dated 29th November 1947, was the

result of such acts of intimidation and arm twisting.

The case of the late General Romulo, the Philippines representative to the U.N., was an example. In a speech to the General Assembly, he warned that the partition of the Holy Land would lead to bloodshed and more violence and emphasised that it defied a basic human right, namely the right of self-determination.

Romulo referred to the right of a people "to determine their political future and to preserve the territorial integrity of their native land." He stressed: As I pronounce these words "without distinction as to race, sex, language or religion", I think of our United Nations Charter; for these are words which occur in that instrument over and over again. And the reason is simple: They look forward rather than backward; ... We cannot believe that the majority of this General Assembly would prefer a reversal of this course. We cannot believe that it would sanction a solution to the problem of Palestine that would turn us back on the road to the dangerous principles of racial exclusiveness and to the archaic documents of the theocratic governments ... The problem of the displaced European Jews is susceptible of a solution other than through the establishment of an independent Jewish State in Palestine.[1]

Prince (later King) Faisal, then Foreign Minister of Saudi Arabia, hugged General Romulo and praised his courage. But when the General walked out of the United Nations building, a Zionist Jew was waiting near the main entrance and attacked him, hitting him on the head and shoulders. President Truman coerced the President of the Philippines to change his stand on the partition resolution. The Philippines, like other small countries, submitted to the will of the United States. General Romulo was asked to leave the United Nations on another assignment; he left for Europe with tears in his eyes.

A new man then came to the United Nations to say "Yes" for Romulo's "No".

Other small members such as Liberia, Belgium and Thailand were frequently subjected to similar pressure. Until that form of duress was used the U.N. recommendation for the partition of Palestine could not get the required votes for adoption. Many innocent diplomats in the United Nations wondered at the time why President Truman would perform such actions for Zionism.

---

1. General Assembly, Second Session Plenary II, pp.1313-15, November 27th 1947

He gave the answer in his memoirs:

"The facts were that not only were the pressure movements around the United Nations unlike anything that had been seen there before but the White House, too, was subjected to a constant barrage. I do not think I ever had as much pressure and propaganda aimed at the White House as I had in this instance. The persistence of a few of the extreme Zionist leaders — actuated by political motives and engaging in political threats — disturbed and annoyed me. Some were even suggesting that we pressure sovereign nations into favourable votes in the General Assembly"[2]

He added:

"As the pressure mounted, I found it necessary to give instructions that I did not want to be approached by any more spokesmen for the extreme Zionist cause."[3]

The diaries of the former American Secretary of Defense James Forrestal tells much about the American pressure used to intimidate member states in the U.N. to vote for partition. Forrestal explained how he tried to have the two American political parties lift the problem of Palestine out of its political context, and how he failed, because of Zionist pressure. He opposed Zionism, saying that "no group in the country should be permitted to influence our policy to the point where it could endanger our national security."[4]

Franklin D. Roosevelt Jr. said that taking the problem of Palestine outside its political context could influence the Democratic vote in some states and thus could make the Democratic party lose the Presidential election and the Republicans win. Forrestal answered: "I think it is about time that somebody should pay some consideration to whether we might not lose the United States."[5]

Having experienced these un-American activities, he found himself compelled to state that "methods used by people outside the

2. *The Memories of Harry S. Truman*, Years of Trial and Hope, vol. ii, Doubleday New York, 1956, p. 158.

3. Ibid, p.160.

4. *The Forrestal Diaries*, Viking Press, New York, 1951, pp.344-45.

5. Ibid, p.364.

executive branch of the Government to bring coercion and duress on other nations of the General Assembly bordered closely on to scandal."[6]

The one-sided policy of the United States, its trampling on legitimate rights, its complete defiance of the principle of self-determination, the scandalous use of its power in the United Nations — all this brought about the partition resolution. This did not lead to peace in the Holy Land but, as the representative of the Philippines had predicted, to more wars and more human suffering. Being illegal and unjust it was tantamount to an invitation to war; the resistance that followed was foreseen by many leading statesmen, including Sir Zafrullah Khan of Pakistan and General Romulo.

I was never sure about the story of General Romulo being attacked by a Zionist outside the U.N. until I, by chance, found myself sitting at a dinner given by Egypt in honour of the Foreign Ministers of Sierra Leone and Dahomey on 11th February 1973 in Cairo. Next to me sat the Philippines ambassador. He confirmed the story, adding that the General had a hug from Prince (later King) Faisal and a hit on the face and shoulders from a Zionist waiting outside.

On 5th August 1968 I had a meeting with U Thant, then United Nations Secretary-General, in connection with the air attack on the town of Salt in Jordan. During this meeting U Thant referred to the refusal of Israel to receive his representative to investigate Israeli practices against the civilian population in the occupied territories. He added that there was a Zionist campaign against him in New York and that some papers referred to the dozens of letters he was receiving containing slanders and vicious attacks. He said that Zionist pressure would not intimidate him. He was neutral and the whole world knew this. I told him of the letters addressed to me and the telephone calls my staff had been receiving.

U Thant suddenly looked at me and said: "I have been thinking of you all the time these days. I am worried about you. Your life may be in danger. One of those American 'nuts' may subject your life to danger. You should be careful, alert and take necessary precautions, especially at night."

Other kinds of pressure used on me personally, and on my staff, are interesting. Every time I appeared before the Security Council to present a Jordanian complaint against the Israeli occupying

---

6. Ibid, p.363.

authority, warning of an Israeli war or calling attention to some situation threatening international peace and security, my office was subjected to intimidation in different forms.

A stream of filthy telephone calls would be received by my poor Australian secretary, Sandra. Before she could say a word the caller would hang up. She could not stand this for long and resigned. Other secretaries worked for a while and left for the same reason, simply because some American Zionists, who are supposed to be U.S. citizens, made life for them in my office miserable, or difficult, to say the least. They all resigned. Later the same Zionist machinery was turned on me. On dozens of occasions in June 1967 Zionists in New York would recognise me and shout: "This is the Ambassador of Jordan," then insult or threaten me whether when I was walking on Fifth Avemue or shopping in a department store. They recognised me because of my participation in Security Council debates, which during the June so called Six Day War, were televised.

When all the insults and slanders failed, those so called Americans resorted to other forms of intimidation. On 11th September 1969, only a few seconds before leaving my office to appear before the Security Council to speak on the question of Jerusalem, and to address it on the Israeli burning of our Holy Shrine Al-Aqsa, a cable was handed to me. At first I thought it was carrying my instructions from my government. However it turned out to be from the Jewish Defence League of Meir Kahane who was then living in Brooklyn, New York. Here is the text of that wire:

"Hold you directly responsible for any anti-Jewish terror acts. In event of such acts, consider you legitimate target for deserved punishment."[7]

I brought this to the attention of the Council. I reminded it that the same Jewish Defence League had appeared on TV in New York, in uniform, with their leader on 4th September 1964. I was surprised to receive threats by telegram. Previously, I had also received threats of assassination from an organisation called the "Minuteman".

I explained to the Council that if I referred to this abnormal situation facing Arab members of the United Nations in New York, it was not only to mention the atmosphere in which we were living, but also to remind every single person around the table about our

---

7. Security Council Meeting, no. 1509, 11th September 1969.

people within the occupied areas, about the captives of the Israelis whether in the Gaza Strip, on the West Bank, in the Golan Heights, in Sinai or in my own town of Khan-Yunis.

I wanted Council members to know the kind of treatment we receive in our host country, the United States, so I read the cable in the Security Council. Ambassador Goldberg rushed to me and requested the original text of the wire, saying that he needed it in order to file a complaint with the police. Some colleagues thought I would use it in court in a claim for damages (similar to Sharon's case against "Time" magazine), against both the Jewish Defence league and Western Union which had communicated a criminal threat to me over its wires. They did not realise that it was not my nature to exploit the situation; I gave Judge Goldberg the original of the wire and kept a photocopy.

The President of the Security Council was astonished to hear of the threat and commented: "In connection with the reference made by the representative of Jordan in his statement today about the terrorist threats against Permanent Representatives of Member States of the United Nations, I, as President of the Security Council, consider it necessary to state that the question raised by the representative of Jordan has a bearing upon the common interests of all member States. I deem it necessary to draw this matter to the attention of the Secretary General of the United Nations and I should like to ask him to study the matter, together with the representative of the United States, so that the necessary measures can be taken."[8]

What I have just related refers to what the Israeli and United States Zionists did after the Israeli occupation of Palestinian lands. But even before the occupation of those Arab lands, Israeli arrogance and love of power brought about similar acts of ruthlessness against other neighbouring Arab States. Take for instance the case of the Zionist attack on the Syrian Delegation to the United Nations in New York. This was a case which I brought to the attention of the Security Council of which Jordan was then a member.

What are the facts?

On 14th October 1966 at noon, while I was speaking on a complaint presented to the Security Council by Israel against Syria, thirty Zionists, American citizens, entered the office of Ambassador George Tomeh, the head of the Syrian Delegation. I reported to the

---

8.   Ibid

Council: "This is a problem for the United States delegation. But it is my duty to refer to the pressure groups which work everywhere, even here in the United Nations. Everywhere there are pressure groups defending and working for a foreign state."

While I was speaking a note was passed to me informing me that Zionists had taken all the office files and destroyed them. These were the files and the documentation used by the Ambassador in his speeches. Ambassador Tomeh used to make lengthy speeches on the Palestine problem before the various organs of the U.N. They were distinguished by their clarity, scientific approach and reliable citations.

The police had come to the Syrian office but had not chased out the Zionists. They were still refusing to leave. I warned: "It is a most serious matter when pressure groups come to our offices. Here in the Security Council we are discussing United Nations jurisprudence, whether or not there has been an act of aggression (committed in the area) and now we have a fifth column, pressure groups in the United States, going to our offices and committing a naked act of aggression. I bring these facts to the attention of the President of the Security Council, the Secretary-General of the United Nations, and the U.S. Delegation, on behalf of Arab Delegations that are here now."[9]

Ambassador Arthur Goldberg, speaking for the United States said:"I too, have received information relating to the same incident as that just mentioned by Ambassador El-Farra. I deeply regret and in no way condone any illegal action directed against any Mission accredited to the United Nations. Having just received the information in question, I have, on behalf of my government and on my own behalf, directed that the full force of the law be applied to rectify the situation — and that shall be done."[10]

Ambassador Tarabanov of Bulgaria said he was "most upset at hearing what was said by the Representative of Jordan with regard to what happened at the office of the Permanent Mission of Syria." He said:"This is a very serious matter, especially because it was deliberately organised to coincide with the meeting of the Security Council. Measures must be taken by the United Nations and by the United States to ensure that our work can be carried on in this forum without the fear that the offices of our delegations in New

---

9. Security Council Meeeting, no. 1305, 14th October 1966.

10. Ibid.

York will be threatened by anyone, for this is not conductive to calm discussion."[11]

Ambassador Fedorenko of the U.S.S.R. also intervened, to say: "We for our part, because of our own responsibility, share the concern expressed by the representative of Jordan and we ask you, Mr President, to take all measures which it is in your power to take by dint of the Charter and the Rules of Procedure to protect our Missions from this kind of illegality."[12]

Ambassador Goldberg reported to the Council at a later stage that "The intruders ... have been arrested and removed by the Police on the complaint of the United States Government made and signed by me. They will be prosecuted in accordance with our laws."[13]

Ambassador Goldberg "profoundly regretted" and apologised to the Syrian government for this highly regrettable incident.

We never heard about the matter again neither did we hear any further about the judicial action mentioned by the Ambassador. One thing was certain. The documents, correspondence and cables between Ambassador Tomeh and his Government never came back, either because they were completely destroyed or because they were taken away. Similar acts of intimidation, however, continued in different forms including physical attacks.

2

On 3rd November 1968, Ambassador and Mrs El-Kony of Egypt and Ambassador Bouattoura of Algeria paid me a visit. Bouattoura had a warning for me:

> "There is a strong campaign organised by Israel, America and Western Delegations against you. Israel says as long as El-Farra is here there is no hope for any progress. He is the wrong person in the right place."

I asked: "What does this mean?

He answered: "They meant you are the wrong person in the right place for negotiations." He then asked me to be careful: "Beware;

---

11. Ibid.

12. Ibid, p.61

13. Ibid

you might be in danger."

El-Kony said:"You are stronger than they are and they know this very well."

Bouattoura added: "They all know your strong popularity in the Arab homeland. And because they cannot put pressure to have you transferred, they may turn to your personal life. Be careful."

I answered: "This is a great honour for me to feel that America and Western Powers and with them Israel are all working to undermine me and hurt me. This is a kind of decoration which will reinforce my conviction, determination and will."

It remains to be said that I, the one called the "wrong person in the right place", left the U.N. many years ago. The problem continues to be as bad and complicated as ever. This is because of the Israeli reliance on U.S. accommodation and blind support to its racist-oriented desires for power through expansion.

3

All kinds of methods were used to assist Israel's cause in the U.N. where she had many friends. Some members supported Israel not out of conviction but for other reasons. The Israelis often relied on such support and took it very much for granted.

I remember one day the Israeli delegation asked a certain ambassador to attend the Special Political Committee in order to vote on a vital aspect of the Palestinian question. When he arrived he discovered that many speakers had registered to speak before the vote would be taken. He did not want to listen to the speeches, since he was not interested.

He went to a neighbouring bar to have a few drinks before the voting process started, and an Israeli envoy accompanied him. A young Israeli girl was asked to watch the debate and call both of them from the bar when the voting started. Of course, the Israeli stayed with the Ambassador to make sure he would not leave the area. Half an hour or so later the young lady came rushing to call them.

The voting was by roll-call. By the time the Ambassador reached his seat the name of his country was being called. It so happened that the delegation who preceded him had said "abstention".

He wanted to say "yes". Instead, he said, "absent", then he said "abstain".

We all laughed. The Israeli rushed up to remind the Ambassador that the vote needed was a "yes" to favour Israel's case, not "absent" or "abstain". It was too late. The result was anounced. It was not, on that occasion, what Israel was after.

4

On the 1967 war some U.S. information media was used to mislead Arab delegates in the United Nations. I remember on 5th June 1967 when the Arab group debated the Israeli war in the Security Council we, the representatives of the Arab group in the United Nations, were led to believe that our armies had been able to check the Israeli attack and score victory. News reaching the United Nations headquarters confirmed this belief. Meanwhile Radio transistors carrying the "pleasant news" were brought down to the Security Council and the General Assembly lounge on the second floor. Many United Nations officials sympathetic to Israel left their offices and were to be found in the two lounges, tuned to the uninterrupted broadcast from a local radio station. Meanwhile, United Nations diplomats rushed in to hear the news. All dispatches communicated the same line and the diplomats never realised that it was not true. With all good intentions, they congratulated us on our so called victories and on our armies "wonderful performance" in the field.

Having received no information to the contrary from our capitals, we believed the news to be true. But the transistors became very noisy — too many and too loud. Never in any United Nations crisis, whether that of Cuba, Hungary, the 1956 Tripartite aggression against Egypt or Vietnam did such a campaign of transistors take place. With the passage of time I started to doubt what I heard. The noise became unbearable and annoying.

I wanted someone to stop it. I went to Ralph Bunche, the Under-Secretary, and asked him to explain why the United Nations civil servants were leaving their offices and assembling in every corner of the two lounges. Why had this happened now? I requested him to see to it that all transistors be withdrawn so that the diplomats would have some badly needed peace, Bunche agreed, and asked the Security Officer to request all officials with radios to leave the lounges and go to their offices. Only then did a quiet atmosphere return.

5

There was of course, a much pleasanter side to our life in New York, brought home to us by daily encounters with the warm-hearted, buoyant, sympathetic and ever-generous ordinary people of America.

One day in the late summer of 1969, for example, a colleague and dear friend of mine Ambassador Mohammad El-Zayyat who represented Egypt, whose country was also a victim of Israeli occupation, received information that more violations of the cease-fire had been committed by Israel against his country. We listened to the TV evening news. They mentioned something of this sort but did not give more details. We, therefore, had to wait for the *New York Times* for more information. We could not rely on cables from our capitals to reach us because sometimes they never arrived. To be on the safe side, we thought that it would be of great help if we waited for the first edition of the *New York Times*, which arrives on the newspaper stand on 86th Street and Lexington Avenue at about 11 pm. In a small coffee shop two yards from the newspaper stand we sat and started anxiously examining the newspaper. Meanwhile the waitress came to take our order. She looked at us with sympathy and said: "You guys can have something with the coffee and the tea. You will have to pay half a dollar each anyway. Why not take a piece of cake since you are paying for it?" We realised that the considerate waitress was under the impression that we were reading the *New York Times* looking for jobs and wanted to see what was on offer so that we could go very early to beat others for the job. The Ambassador said to her, "No, coffee is all I want. I know we'll pay that minimum, but don't worry." We read the news about our area, drank what the waitress offered us, paid her what she wanted, and walked out. We used to come almost every night and she came to know us and much about our problem. She became very sympathetic. We discovered eventually that she was an American of Irish decent. I was greatly pleased by her genuine sympathy and said to my colleague: "God bless the Irish."

6

It is wrong to imagine that everything was serious and hectic at the United Nations. We ambassadors had our own social gatherings in receptions, luncheons and dinners.

On the occasion of Human Rights Day on 10th December every year, for example, Dr Hammarskjöld when U.N. Secretary-General, used to arrange a very enjoyable evening. Dress was formal, with movie stars and singers participating.

One day Ambassador Goldberg contacted his friend President Lyndon Johnson and suggested that, as a public relations exercise, it would be a good idea if the President would do what no other president had done in the past, namely, invite all the Ambassadors accredited to the U.N. to visit the White House. The U.N. Ambassadors, not being themselves accredited to Washington, would much enjoy such an invitation as well as being suitably impressed. The idea appealed to the President, and he gave Goldberg the green light.

We all accepted and on the day assembled at La Guardia Airport ready for the four Army jets which landed at the airport to pick us up. An army sergeant walked towards us, then said: "Line up, boys".

I was standing with Ambassador El-Kony and Lord Caradon; but we all felt most embarrassed to hear this, even more so when the American sergeant continues: "Four lanes, boys, not one!"

We started lining up in four lanes. Then the sergeant said: "Lane number one should proceed to jet number one. It is the first jet on this side."

The orders kept coming: "Lane number two should proceed to jet number two. Lane number three should proceed to jet number three. And the last lane, number four, should proceed to jet number four."

We all carried out the "military instructions" nicely. Some of us remembered how we used to line up thus every morning when we were going to classes. We performed the same drill when we reached Washington to seat ourselves in the four big waiting buses. But by that time many ambassadors had forgotten what their lane number was. It was all a little confusing. It was very funny seeing scores of ambassadors stuffed into every bus where more than one continent was represented. My colleagues all had the same impression and there was unanimous agreement that this was not good public relations. One colleague had a good sense of humour and said: "This is the American Way, boys. You have to accept it."

In the White House the President, together with Vice-President Hubert Humphrey and U Thant, stood to receive us.

Ambassador Goldberg was there to introduce us to the Vice-President, while the Chief of Protocol was announcing the name of each ambassador and his country to the President.

When Ambassador Goldberg tried to introduce me to Humphrey, he saw the Vice-President greet me most warmly. Goldberg asked him whether he had known me before, and Vice-President Humphrey answered: "Yes, we have been good friends since I was a senator."

While waiting in line to meet President Johnson a guard wearing a U.S. Air Force uniform came and whispered to each of us: "If you want to have a good picture with the President make sure to stand on the yellow line facing the President." But it was no easy matter to find where the yellow line was and in the few seconds available also look at the face of the President!

One of the members of the American delegation to the United Nations introduced me to President Johnson's daughter, Linda. She told me that she was greatly impressed by the Jordanian pavilion at the World Fair. "It was so beautiful, I saw it three times," she explained. I told her how happy I was to hear this and expressed the hope that the next time she came to New York she would give me the pleasure of showing her the United Nations. I said this after Linda had offered to show me round the White House and explain the historical background of every room. She explained what treaty was signed where and provided a commentary on some of the events that had taken place in the White House. She also pointed out the decorations made by Jacqueline Kennedy in the various rooms.

Special guides took the rest of the ambassadors in groups around the White House. When I by-passed them under the special escort of the President's daughter, my colleagues were most surprised and impressed.

Other occasions could be much less formal. Thus at every opening session of the United Nations General Assembly, so many Foreign Ministers come to New York that the big city looks like a capital of the world.

In every session many parties are usually given in the United Nations dining room, on the fourth floor of the United Nations Headquarters. One country may have a reception to celebrate its national day. An Ambassador may give a party, reception or dinner, in honour of his foreign minister. Another diplomat may wish to have a gathering with friends and colleagues at his residence. Talking shop at such parties is not encouraged. After all, diplomats have discussed United Nations matters all day long. Light conversation is the order of the day.

7

One evening I had a dinner at my residence in honour of a colleague who just got married for which I invited ten couples. It was a formal "black tie" dinner. Ambassador Charles Yost, then the Permanent Representative of the United States at the United Nations, was invited to this dinner but on the day he had to go to Washington to attend a White House meeting. He delegated Shirley Temple Black, a former movie star, to attend my dinner on his behalf for she had been appointed by the President of the United States to represent his country during the General Assembly session. Of course, I welcomed Shirley with her husband, Mr. Black. The United Nations Protocol which usually helps in preparing the seating arrangement for such a dinner had to do a fast job on the seating list so that it was rearranged to include Shirley's husband. Being a representative of a Big Power she was placed opposite the Russian Representative, Ambassador Jacob Malik. No politics were discussed. Malik was well known for his sense of humour, and he was cracking jokes all evening. Arabic food was served. It was very pleasant gathering. Shirley liked Arab food and agreed with Jacob Malik on one thing that Arabic food was "exotic".

At the conclusion of the United Nations Session on 11.12.1968, Shirley revealed to Judy Klemersrud of the *New York Times* her experiences in the United Nations during that session with a movie star flavour. She made reference to my dinner and said:

> "When recounting the time the pine nut lodged in my throat at the Jordanian Dinner, I started to black out. But then I thought to myself: 'I am a representative of the United States, and I am the only one here, and I can't die. If I do, nobody will believe that somebody didn't do something to me on purpose.' Finally the nut went down."[14]

Shirley, who had sat across from Jacob Malik also recounted how she presented him with what she called her "jovial idea" She said:

> "I suggest that there be only women on the Security Council." She said "he hasn't expressed himself on that idea".

Another luncheon reflects how great statesmen act when facing an embarrassing situation. Lord Caradon, the Permanent Representative of the United Kingdom to the United Nations, had a luncheon party at his residence in honour of his foreign minister, George Brown. Ambassador El-Kony of Egypt and myself were among the guests.

Lady Caradon worked hard on the preparations, for that party and decorated the dining table very nicely. She had in the centre of the table a big basket full of fresh fruit with more fruit going down on both sides of the table. Some of the grapes on the table were not

---

14. *N. Y. Times* of 12th December 1968

real but false grapes made of plastic.

While waiting for the last course George Brown entered into a discussion with me about the Palestine problem and the need for a solution. I reminded him that the policy of the United Kingdom was mainly responsible for the displacement of the people of Palestine and that it was his government's duty to push for peace. I emphasised the conflicting British promises given to the Arabs and the Jews and how Britain cheated the Arabs. With his usual cold blooded attitude George Brown did not show any objection to what he was hearing. He was staring all the time at the beautiful grapes facing him. He tried to pull one off. It was not easy and he did not realise that it was plastic. He tried harder. Lady Caradon was looking and certainly was not happy about what she was witnessing. Finally the minister succeeded in pulling the grape from the stem. He put it in his mouth, crushed it, and only then realised that it was artificial. By that time most of us were watching George's struggle for the grape. To cut down embarrassment he stood up with a big smile on his face and said:

"Ladies and Gentlemen, I never realised that Her Majesty's Government cheats"

To what extent our conversation about how Britain had cheated the Arabs was in the mind of George Brown when he made his statement to the guests I don't know. Everybody laughed at George's remarks except Sylvia Caradon who was still upset because of her spoiled decoration.

It was customary for the President of the Security Council to have a dinner party for members of the Council in honour of the Secretary-General. This practice started when the late Dag Hammarskjöld was Secretary-General. It is amazing how, sometimes, without preparation, very important decisions are taken on vital issues during such informal social gatherings.

In March 1966 I was President of the Security Council. I had this customary dinner in a hotel. U Thant, who was a good friend of mine, said to members in my presence that that dinner was not "it". I asked why? He said he had been expecting some of those exotic Arab dishes. Sure enough I arranged for another dinner for him at my residence. All members attended. The genuine United Nations spirit — the spirit of "togetherness", was reflected in that dinner. We all were happy, chatting, laughing and enjoying good Arab food.

U Thant and Big Power representatives sat at the head table

prepared for them and the host. The table was decorated with a pink cover, red roses and white and red glasses. Ambassador Fedorenko of the U.S.S.R. took this as a compliment to his country. He was most happy. So whenever an Arab dish was served he would look at it and say to Ambassador Goldberg of the United States and Lord Caradon of the United Kingdom "We have this dish in Armenia." When the second dish was served, he would turn to Goldberg and say "We have this dish in Georgia" and so forth. Lord Caradon looked at Fedorenko and said with his English accent : "Ambassador,! very soon you will say Ambassador El-Farra's cook is Russian." We all laughed.

Before the expiration of U Thant's term members of the Security Council asked me together with other Asian-African members of the Council to contact U Thant and try to convince him to accept another term. He was very adamant in refusing the offer. He blamed the Big Powers for lack of support for him and for the United Nations adding : "I refuse to accept another term and be a mere 'glorified clerk'."

It was at the close of this dinner that I stood to make a surprising toast. After spending a few minutes praising the man dedicated to the cause of peace, I appealed to him on behalf of all members of the Security Council "now present", to accept a new term as Secretary-General.

The pleasent atmosphere that night contributed a great deal to the subsequent acceptance of the Secretary-General's subsequent acceptance of another term of office.

Chapter 13

Zionism and the Jewish State

"A separate national community could not be forcibly subjected to another people in the name of majority rule."

Chaim Weizmann

Over the years I have done much research in attempts to understand the Zionist mind. What is it exactly that Zionist leaders want?

One thing I realised was that the confusion so evident in the utterance of the Israeli leaders and reflected by their representatives in the United Nations was intentional. They were meant to achieve just this: "Confuse everybody and work on your own strategy".

Originally when the Balfour Declaration was issued in 1917 after some considerable pressure from Chaim Weizmann the Zionist leaders declared their satisfaction with the promise of a "national home" in Palestine. This display of satisfaction was assumed and was intended to mislead the international community into thinking that the terms of the Declaration were acceptable and accepted.

To consolidate their gain and to make retreat by the British less possible they planned for continued and unrestricted immigration. This they achieved in practice by simply sending in large numbers of immigrants with no legal papers for entry into Palestine and no regard for quotas imposed by the British who then governed Palestine. Zionists later changed their stand on the Balfour Declaration, claiming that it embodied the promise of a Jewish state whereas in fact the phrase used is "a home" for the Jewish people. This point occupied much time in 1947 where debates concentrated on whether the world had been intended to mean a home for World Jewry or a home only for those Jews already in Palestine. Either meaning of course conflicted with the rights of the Palestinian Arabs in the area. In the end the point was never satisfactorily resolved.

The partition resolution which was the outcome of these debates was passed on 29th November 1947. It established two states in Palestine, one for the Jews there, the other for the Palestinian Arabs there. The resolution fixed the boundaries of each state.

This resolution the Jews already in Palestine, assisted by world Zionist organisations, interpreted as permission to do what they liked and they immediately took matters into their own hands, starting terrorist campaigns against the indigenous population. Fighting and skirmishes across the borders defined by the United Nations took place. Many massacres, including that of Deir Yassin on April 9th, 1948, were committed by Zionist terrorist groups which prompted the United Nations to pass a resolution on 19th April 1947 calling for a cessation of military activities in Palestine and in particular calling on the Jewish Agency and the Arab Higher Committee, the recognized representatives of the people of Palestine at that time, to "refrain, pending further consideration of the future government of Palestine by the General Assembly, from any political activity which might prejudice the rights, claims or positions of either community."

Terrorist activities of this sort made the U.S. Ambassador at the United Nations announce that his government no longer thought that the U.N. partition plan could be carried out. He called for an immediate truce in Palestine to be followed by a temporary U.N. trusteeship.

2

Despite all this, Zionist activists in Palestine and Zionist pressure on the White House forced President Truman to discuss with his advisor, Clark Clifford, the question of recognition of the Jewish State. Clifford knew that the Jewish Agency planned that day, 14th May 1948, to announce the new state i.e. the day the British mandate was to be surrendered. He may or may not have known of an urgent letter to the President from Chaim Weizmann pleading for immediate recognition of the proposed state.

It was also the case that General Marshall, then the United States Secretary of State for Foreign Affairs, had already agreed to *de facto* recognition of a Jewish State, but had felt that that should be done in consultations with the British and French. When President

Truman asked for Clifford's comments, his attitude was crisp and clear. He thought that if America were going to recognise the country it would be best done immediately. The President's response was to authorise Clifford to seek a formal request for recognition.

Clifford telephoned Eliahu Elath at the Jewish Agency head-quarters in Washington and asked whether Elath's people, meaning the Jewish Agency in Palestine, were still determined to proclaim their state today. His answer "I haven't the slightest doubt" led to Clifford's request that he should send a letter requesting immediate recognition of this state by the United States. Elath was almost speechless at the news but, of course, he agreed. He sought the help of Benjamin Cohen, an advisor to the United States State Department, who came to the Jewish Agency's office to draft the request for recognition for a state which was neither yet in existence nor even named. This to Elath was a real problem, the only solution to which seemed to be to use the phraseology of the United Nations partition resolution, "the Jewish state". The letter said:

"My dear Mr. President:

"I have the honour to notify you that the Jewish State has been proclaimed as an independent republic within frontiers approved by the General Assembly of the United Nations in its Resolution of November 29, 1947, and that a provisional government has been charged to assume the rights and duties of government for preserving law and order within the boundaries of the Jewish State, for defending the state against external aggression, and for discharging the obligation of the Jewish state to the other nations of the world in accordance with international law. The Act of Independence will become effective at one minute after six o'clock on the evening of May 14, 1948, Washington time.

"With full knowledge of the deep bond of sympathy which has existed and has been strengthened over the past thirty years between the government of the U.S. and the Jewish people of Palestine, I have been authorised by the provisional government of the new state to tender this message and to express the hope that your government will recognise and will welcome the Jewish state into the community of nations.

Very respectfully yours

199

Eliahu Epstein (Elath's original name)
Agent
Provisional Government of the Jewish State."

The letter was signed on behalf of a government that did not exist, the government of the Jewish people of Palestine. The Jewish Agency's press attaché was instructed to deliver it personally to Clark Clifford. But a few minutes after the press attaché was on his way to the White House Elath heard on the radio that his leadership had declared their state and named it "the State of Israel".

Elath sent his secretary chasing after his press attaché to insert the new name in the letter. She caught up with him at the entrance to the White House where together they removed the letter from the envelope and with a pen crossed out the typed references to "the Jewish State" replacing them with the words "the State of Israel".

Needless to say, this whole process of recognition, its timing and its procedure, were kept secret until the very end. Not even the head of the United States delegation to the United Nations was informed. It was quite a surprise, and very embarrassing, for the entire American delegation at the United Nations.

The United Nations passed the partition resolution in November 1947. Another resolution six months later, on 17th April 1948 called on, *inter alia*, all persons and organisations in Palestine to "refrain, pending further consideration of the future government of Palestine by the General Assembly from any political activity which might prejudice the rights, claims or positions of either community."

When, therefore, the Zionists proclaimed their state, they did so in complete disregard of this resolution which, in effect, froze the situation "pending further consideration of the future *government* of Palestine by the General Assembly". What is more, the letter requesting recognition sent to the American President at his suggestion also violated this resolution of which neither the Jewish Agency in Washington nor the President himself could claim ignorance since the United States had voted for it. American recognition accorded to Israel is therefore an illegitimate recognition without legal basis, of a state which is itself without legal foundation. Its proclamation was a unilateral act, an act which has set the tone of every subsequent Israeli action and the first demonstration of the *fait accompli* policy.

3

Subsequently those same people wanted all Palestine, despite the United Nations Partition Resolution, on the grounds that since the Arab side had not accepted the partition resolution earlier they had no right to seek the implementation of that resolution later. This argument does not hold water. It is true that the Arab States objected to the competence of the United Nations to adopt a resolution which violated a basic principle embodied in its Charter namely the principle of self-determination. This was a constitutional question which the Arabs, as a last resort, wanted the International Court of Justice to adjudicate upon. Unfortunately because of the pressure of the United States, and that of President Truman in particular, the Arab request did not get the necessary votes in the General Assembly. It is clear, however, that this legal process did not deprive the people of Palestine (who were not even parties to the vote) of their right to a sovereign state prescribed by the United Nations in the very resolution which created the Jewish State. No argument can enable the Israelis to go beyond the specific terms of that same resolution nor can they exceed or infringe the rights of others laid down in the resolution, the more so since the United Nations reaffirms this same resolution every year thus reminding the Israelis of its continuing validity.

After this unilateral proclamation the Israelis proceeded to flout every act in the book. It may be recalled that Israel's admission to the United Nations was conditional on its observance of the partition resolution and was granted in the belief "that Israel is a peace-loving country". It was also conditional on the right of Palestinians to return home. Furthermore, it was conditional on observance of the Protocol of Lausanne, signed by Walter Eitan one day before Israel's admission to the United Nations. Almost immediately after Israel's admission Mr. Ben Gurion revoked his country's adherence to the Protocol on the grounds that Eitan had never been invested with the authority to sign such a commitment. It became clear later that signing the protocol was nothing but one of the Israeli tricks to secure admission to the United Nations.

It is therefore a state without legal basis in the position of disregarding all the conventions of decent behaviour which other countries of the world wish to see observed. It spurns to honour any commitment it undertook before acquiring *de facto* recognition, making the United States party to subsequent Israeli behaviour. The request submitted to the White House in May 1948 stated that the Jewish State would be an independent republic "within frontiers approved by the General Assembly of the United Nations in its resolution of November 29,1947." But today it cannot be described as a "peace-loving" state "able and willing to carry out the obligations contained in the Charter".

There were some who foresaw the trouble that the proposed partition was likely to cause, amongst them Count Bernadotte, sent to negotiate a truce in June/July 1948. But he was not allowed to live long enough to implement his solution and meanwhile the Arab voice, which had also predicted trouble, went unheard.

4

As I have already mentioned, the Arab states objected from the very beginning to the right of the United Nations to partition the land against the will of the majority of its people, namely the Palestinian people. To the Arab states, the ideal solution was the creation of a secular state a single Arab-Jewish state in Palestine.

When such a plan was suggested Dr Chaim Weizmann, the former Chairman of the Jewish Agency and the first President of Israel, objected on the grounds that unity could not be imposed without consent. But the consent of whom, of the Jewish minority or the Palestinian majority? What Weizmann really advocated, of course, was that unity could not be imposed without consent, but partition could be so imposed, an argument which makes no sense at all.

In advocating the partition of Palestine in a speech before the United Nations *Ad Hoc* Committee on Palestine Weizmann set out his argument in favour of a state for the Jewish minority in Palestine succinctly:

> "Historical and legal considerations were secondary as compared with immediate realities. In Palestine there was a Jewish community of 700,000 people with its own language, its own religion, its own traditions, its own distinctive social outlook, its own scientific, industrial, agricultural achievements, its own schools and universities. That community was profoundly democratic; it had its own distinctive organization...
>
> "It was confronted with another group, which had reached a different stage of development; which was numerically superior and which had no characteristics in common with the Jewish community. The Assembly has to decide who was to govern that community and who was to regulate its life..."

"A separate national community could not be forcibly
subjected to another people in the name of majority rule..."[1]

The background of those 700,000 Jews is worth examining in
some detail. They were divided into four categories. One category
of Jews had been settled in Palestine for more than twenty years
when the question was brought to the United Nations in 1947.
Another consisted of those who had settled in accordance with the
Mandatory Immigration Regulations and had become Palestinian
citizens. The third category comprised those who had entered
legally but had not become citizens. The fourth category consisted
of illegal immigrants. According to British statistics only about
250,000 Jews were Palestinian citizens. Most other Jews had entered
illegally. It was for that minority of illegal Jewish immigrants that Dr
Weizmann insisted on having a state.

Now, some thirty years later Menachem Begin has refused not
only a state for the Palestinians, but even "self-government" on a
part of their homeland. It is appropriate to compare this rejection
with Dr Weizmann's words above. For in Weizmann's own words a
separate national community could not be forcibly subjected to
another people in the name of majority rule. There, in what is called
Israel, is an Arab-Palestinian community, consisting of over 700,000
people, with its own language; its own religion; its own traditions;
its own schools; it has its distinctive character and organisation, it
has no characteristics in common with the Jewish community and,
guided by Weizmann's advocacy the Israelis should have to decide
either to have a secular state for Jew and Gentile in Palestine
namely Arabs and Jews or abide by Weizmann's thinking and let the
"Arabs of Israel" exercise their right to self-determination. I am
sure, judging from the ruthless policy Israel has up to now
demonstrated towards them and the arbitrary practices to which
they are subjected, these people would choose independence. On
the other hand, after the withdrawal of Israel, the Palestinians in
other occupied Palestinian territories would exercise the same right
to self-determination and, judging from the Jordanian-Palestinian
agreement and geographical and other factors they would choose
confederation with Jordan. Israel should think twice before insisting
on its blind policy because if this continues Israel will be digging its
own grave.

---

1.   18th Meeting of the *Ad Hoc* Committee on the Palestinian Question: 18th
     October 1947, p.124

5

The alleged reason for the Israeli objection to a Palestinian State is one of security. But security cannot be achieved through tanks, rockets and planes, but rather through co-existence, in accordance with the very partition resolution which recommended the establishment of the Jewish state.

The Israelis objected to this because a Palestinian Arab State would put an end to the Zionist dream of expansion. They were always honest about it, even before the creation of an Israeli state, with Zionist Congresses proclaiming their determination to continue their struggle for a Jewish State in "the original boundaries of Palestine".

In 1938, during the debates on the partition scheme of the British Royal Commission (the Peel Commission) at the Twentieth Zionist Congress, Mr Ben Gurion had stated that "No Zionist can forgo the smallest amount of the land of Israel but the point at issue is which of the two routes will lead more quickly to the common goal."

Abba Eban called the instruments obtained through these tactics "opportunities" which were ignored after they had served their purpose, as he points out in his introduction to Dr Weizmann's book, *Trial and Error*.

The Israeli leaders have always refused to recognise the people of Palestine as the central issue in the Arab-Israeli conflict; they now also refuse to accept the fact that the Palestine Liberation Organisation is the representative of the people of Palestine. So far more than one hundred and fifteen members of the family of nations including India, Greece, France, Spain, Austria and Italy have given the PLO full diplomatic recognition. Other European countries will follow. Israel has not as yet accepted this reality and continues to challenge the whole world. It has special reasons for this attitude, as explained by Ben Gurion:

"Our position among the nations is unique, but not because we are a small people: there are smaller states than ours in the United Nations. But we are an isolated people by the very nature of our situation and our history. Every other people has its bonds of kinship with others,whether by virtue of religion, language or race. There are Scandinavian, Anglo-Saxon, Arab, Moslem and Buddhist families of nations and so forth. Israel, however, is not related to any group by bonds of religion, language or race. The countries that are closest to us from a linguistic and geographical point of view are our deadly enemies. And Israel is and will be able to win her place among the nations only by the measure of her achievements, the heroism of her spirit, the example of her democratic regime, and her power to create. The history of Israel ever since ancient days has demonstrated the superiority of quality over quantity, and this superiority has also been shown in the first decade of her revival."[2]

According to a report in the *New York Times* of 29 December 1960 Mr Ben Gurion went so far as to say that:

"Jews who lived outside Israel were Godless and violated the precepts of Judaism every day they remained away from their country. Whoever dwells outside the land of Israel is considered to have no God."

One wonders: does the former prime minister of Israel really believe that God is dead everywhere but in Israel? And are all Gentiles — Christians, Moslems, Hindus and others — Godless. This feeling of superiority and uniqueness, the division of the world into Jews and Gentiles, the call for security that requires more of Arab lands, all this together with the rejection of assimilation brought about Herzl's definition of the Jewish problem as a question of logistics. "A people without a land should be transferred to a land without a people".

Nahum Goldmann, a former President of the World Jewish Congress, who devoted most of his life to help realise the Zionist dream and who occupied important positions in the Zionist leadership for many decades, had the following to say about the Herzl Formula:

"Nothing in this formula, of course, was true: most of the Jews throughout the world were not people without a land, but loyal citizens of their countries, and Palestine — although not as densely populated as it is today — was certainly not a land without a people. Nor has the transfer of nearly three million Jews to Israel solved the Jewish problem in the world, as is unfortunately apparent in the recent resurgence of anti-Semitism, often in the form of anti-Zionism."[3]

---

2. David Ben Gurion, *Jewish Frontier*, September 1958, section 2, p.3
3. Nahum Goldmann, "Zionist Ideology and the Reality of Israel", *Foreign Affairs*, Fall 1978, pp. 70-82.

Prior to the so-called Six Day War of 1967, Levi Eshkol, then Prime Minister of Israel, said: "Israel has no desire for territorial expansion." But after Israeli occupation of yet more lands, her leaders started speaking about the so-called historical borders. Particularly arrogant was Menachem Begin, who insisted that "Israel does not require Arab acceptance because its existence is the affirmation of God's promise and Jewish tradition."[4]

Where in the Bible or the Talmud is there any specific reference to what these borders should be? To quote Nahum Goldmann: "One may legitimately wonder why the Arabs or the Americans should be committed to the promises of the Jewish God.

"Great religious Jewish leaders, with whom I have discussed this issue, state unequivocally that it is contrary to the spirit of Jewish law, in which welfare of any human being is a major commandment, to fight a war and risk the lives of thousands of young Jewish men and women in order to gain territories."[5]

Israel now forcibly occupies all the area allotted by the United Nations to the Palestine Arab State, in utter defiance of the partition resolution and despite the fact that the Security Council determined that the policy and practices of Israel in establishing settlements in the Palestinian and other territories occupied since 1967 had no legal validity and constituted a serious obstruction to achieving a comprehensive, just and lasting peace in the Middle East.[6] When Israeli representatives in the United Nations find no other way to justify their expansion they cite their favourite charge of "discrimination", meaning "against Jews". This, however is unjustifiable, because Islam has always tolerated Jews and Christians as 'people of the book'. They cannot justifiably call this conflict racial or anti-Semitic. Nor can they call it religious, because it is not.

It is ironic that simultaneously with ruthless territorial expansion and unremitting pressure against others, the Israeli Prime Minister Shimon Peres announced his "Marshall Plan" for the Middle East on 9th April 1986. The Israelis cannot hope to woo either the Arabs or world opinion to their side by such means. This is a typical example of Israeli arrogance. Not content with a homeland they must also have a State. Not satisfied with a State, they must dream, within forty years of establishment, of becoming the dominant

---

4. Ibid., p. 75.

5. Ibid., p. 77.

6. U.N. Security Council Resolution No 446, dated 22nd March 1979.

power in the area. Mr Chadli Klibi, Secretary General of the League of Arab States, has expressed the view of the Arab World strongly. "We believe," he said, "that the Peres plan is nothing but an attempt to divert attention from the real quest for peace....without relinquishing the Occupied Territories or doing justice to the Palestinian people ....the Israeli Prime Minister is trying to mystify the western world by asserting that the nature of the final peace settlement in the Middle East can wait." But it *cannot* wait; neither is there any reason why it should.

Chapter 14

Israeli Tactics Inside and Outside the United Nations

"Not only geography and history but logic are against Israel over the long run and the Israelis know it."

James Reston

There is one white and four blue seats for each member country of the Security Council. These are assigned to the Chairman and four members of each delegation around the main semicircular table. Red seats are assigned to other ambassadors and to the advisors of those delegations not represented in the Security Council. When appearing before the Security Council the Israelis, T.V. and media-minded always, made sure that they placed one solitary member of their delegation behind the Chairman. All other assigned seats were, most of the time, deliberately left empty. Many times Abba Eban had only the Israeli Permanent Representative, Joseph Tekoah, sit behind him. I once asked a friend of mine from the *New York Times* why they did this. He explained to me that this was the Israeli way of playing for maximum world sympathy.

The Israelis behave in the Security Council in a manner unique in the United Nations, always trying to look helpless, isolated, unwanted and weak. No other delegation would ever think of using similar methods.

We Arabs, on the other hand, not being acquainted with this means of seeking sympathy, did just the opposite. The Arab complainant always came to the Security Council with all the members of his delegation. They occupied the five seats assigned to them. Other members sat in the red seats behind. Not only this, but many other Arab delegations always rushed to help! They always asked to participate in the debate and made their speeches. So many Arab delegations took part in the debates that it invariably looked as though a particular problem before the Security Council was really between the huge Arab world and 'little Israel'. And with the Israeli's deliberate provocation, still more Arabs came to answer Israeli distortions. That, it appeared, was precisely what Israel wanted. This was the picture as I saw during the many years I spent in the United Nations.

The Israeli line in the Security Council is clear and simple. Israel answers the Arab complaint with a counter complaint, and then comes before the Council to ask it to combine both. The United States then intervenes to seek a 'balanced' resolution that takes into consideration both complaints and the requests of both parties. On every occasion we Arabs were obliged to struggle to make sure that the Council considered each complaint separately and on its own merits. With time the Council became familiar with Israel's tactics, not least because the falsity of Israeli allegations soon became clear.

When it launched its invasion of the Egyptian, Syrian and Jordanian territories on 5th June 1967, Israel at the same time submitted a complaint against those states, claiming that they started the war. The Arab side did not lodge its complaint until twenty minutes later. Today it is public knowledge that Israel started the 1967 War. Israel itself, and many of its representatives have admitted this. Yet the records of the Security Council show that Israel was the first to complain against Egypt, claiming that Israeli forces were defending themselves against "Egyptian aggression".

In answering complaints before the Security Council, the Israeli speaker made every effort to make sure he could divert the attention of the Security Council from the main issue in the complaint towards irrelevant emotional matters which would appeal to the average American or European. These included favourites such as the 'Nazi persecution' and the argument that 'Israel is the only democracy in the Middle East'.

Another popular Israeli ploy was the statement: "The area on which the Jews have established their state is very little compared to the huge area of the Arab world." They also repeatedly reiterated that the "Jews suffered a great deal under the Nazis", going on to ask: "Is it too much to have a little state as our country?"

Of course, this Israeli argument, which is repeated in every U.N. debate is in no way valid. The criterion is not how large was the area of this or that continent or any part thereof, but who were the people to whom the land actually belonged. If the Israeli argument were accepted on a large scale it could warrant, for example, the creation of a state for the Jewish minority in Latin America. Why not? Latin America is a continent with a huge area in which there is a Jewish minority. By the same token, the Jews in Western Europe, also a minority, could invite more Jews to join them from the U.S.S.R. and then claim a separate state in one of the European countries. The Jews in New York could also under the same criterion claim New York State as a Jewish state. Thus, if we are to follow the Israeli logic the whole map of the world would be altered.

The Israeli approach to the question of the media is also different from that of the Arabs. Unlike our side, which confines its activities to making speeches with little and often no attention whatever to the mass media, the Israelis make sure they brief the press fully on their stands in the Security Council, furnishing the media with a press release before the delivery of each speech, and making sure that sufficient copies of each speech reach TV, radio stations and the news agencies before delivery.

I remember in November 1966 when Israelis attacked the village of Samou' in the West Bank of Jordan. At the time of the Security Council debate on the question the CBS television network assigned its programme 'Face the Nation' to cover developments in the Middle East, allotting fifteen minutes to me and fifteen minutes to Ambassador Michael Comay of Israel. Leading journalists were present. Comay appeared first. Then came my turn. So that I should have no advantage over my opponent the TV moderator did not give me a chance to see or hear what he had to say. I was kept in a closed room until the time fixed for Comay's appearance was over. Having finished his part, he however, then went straight to see and hear me.

I stated that the attack on Samou' was a prelude to a major Israeli aggression to occupy all the West Bank of Jordan. I explained why I made that charge and cited my evidence.

Comay immediately afterwards met those members of the press who had been invited to cover the programme to explain himself further, confuse the issue and give an answer to every charge I had made. I never realised that the members of the press were there, welcoming the opportunity of further clarification and more discussion.

The following day a summary was made of what we had both said on TV. What Comay said separately was also carried by the media. The *New York Times* published a nice picture of Comay watching me on TV which was sent to me by the *Times* as a present.

I admit I did not have this Israeli talent. I was unfamiliar with these ways and means of reaching public opinion through such "follow-up" type of information. Public relations to all of us Arabs was something very new. We felt right to be on our side and therefore we felt we needed no proof, no public relations. We were bad advocates for a just cause.

I often wonder whether those who published Comay's denial of Israeli further plans to occupy all of the West Bank of Jordan remember that this did take place on 5th June 1967. We have often lost just causes by default. It is wrong to claim that all the press was unfair. True, there are Zionist pressure groups in big cities. And there is the pressure of advertisement for pro-Israel department stores. There is some influence of shareholders in many places in the media of information. But I know that independent journalists are not told what to write. They form their own ideas. It is our job to use all the means of communication and public relations to make the truth known.

It is however fair to point out that Zionist pressure groups in the United States through intimidation, through their financial strength and through other means, have obliged the U.S. administration to note carefully any developments in the Middle East.

Their influence is such that it seems it is felt even within the U.N. Secretariat. Late in 1968 a top U.N. official came to see me. He told me the U.N. Department of Statistics had completed its Year Book and was about to send it to the printer when new instructions suddenly arrived that the draft should be revised. The word "Palestine" was to be replaced by the word "Israel". The official raised the question that prior to the partition resolution there had been a country called "Palestine". How on earth, he asked, could the United Nations commit a forgery and distort history. The answer was: "Do what you are told. There is nothing we can do about it".

Since I was the Jordanian Ambassador and directly connected with the matter, I decided, at the suggestion of the U.N. official, to do something about this grave act of distortion and try to correct the situation. The same day I saw Secretary-General U Thant and explained what had happened. I discovered that he knew nothing of the matter, nor did the Under Secretary in charge of the department concerned. An investigation took place and things then became clear. Members of the Israeli U.N. staff had used their influence on one key official in the Department of Statistics in order to carry out the required change — i.e. deleting the name "Palestine" and substituting the name "Israel".

U Thant ordered that their "error" be rectified, and the draft of the U.N. Year Book remained as it was, with the word "Palestine".

Many years later, in 1984, at a dinner hosted by the Secretary-General of the League of Arab States, Mr Chadli Klibi, we all talked over an aspect of the Palestine Question. I had been discussing with Mr Brzezinsky his book *Power and Principle* in which he cited President Carter's statement recommending a "homeland" for the Palestinians. Here he had written that the President's statement, made in Clinton, Mass., was "a spontaneous and unexpected public statement."[1]

The President was quoted as saying: "There has to be a homeland provided for the Palestinian refugees who have suffered for many, many years."

Mr Brzezinsky stated in his book that he and Cyrus Vance received "instruction ... directly from Air Force One that no elaboration or clarification were to be issued."

"Nonetheless to reassure the Israelis, I did tell the Israeli Ambassador, Simcha Dimitz, that in my judgement the word 'homeland' 'had no special political connotation.' Mr Brzezinsky thus, despite the President's direct instruction, undermined the whole idea presented by his President and conveyed a different message through the Israeli Ambassador to reassure Israel.

What was published in Brzezinsky's book, however, was only part of the truth. Jimmy Carter's statement was not as unexpected as Mr Brzezinsky had implied. It was meant to serve a purpose, and its timing was well calculated. It was made at a time the Palestine National Council was convening at the Arab League Headquarters in Cairo, and was intended to reassure the Palestinians that there was a new American policy on the Palestine question.

Arthur Lowry, from the American Embassy in Cairo, came to see me at that time in my capacity as Under-Secretary at the League of Arab States. He handed me a copy of the President's statement and expressed the hope that the new development would be conveyed to Mr Yasser Arafat, the Chairman of the Executive of the P.L.O. and the Arab League Committee Secretary-General, Mr Mahmoud Riad.

---

1. *Power and Principle*, Zbigniew Brzezinsky, Farrar, Strauss, Girou, New York, 1983, p. 91.

It was ironic that while Lowry was visiting me in an attempt to reassure the Palestinians of the American 'new policy', Mr Brzezinsky was also meeting Ambassador Simcha Dimitz of Israel in Washington to reassure him that the word 'homeland' uttered by the President had no 'special' political connotation'.

It was this kind of double talk, or the American attempt to ride two horses at the same time, that made United States promises lack credibility in our area. When high American officials speak of the Palestine problem as one of 'lost opportunities' I wonder to what extent American politicians were responsible for that.

At the same dinner I asked Brzezinsky why he mentioned his Washington meeting with Dimitz while saying nothing about Lowry's Cairo meeting. I wanted him to explain why the United States had spoken in two different languages, one to the Palestinians and another to the Israelis. I cited his reference to President Carter's statement which in his book he had said had no 'special' political connotation'. He replied that he used the word 'specific' not 'special'. He explained that that carried no specific *political* connotation, and that the statement did not exclude the specific *historical* connotation, like the fact that the word 'homeland' was incorporated in the Balfour Declaration, which led to the Jewish State. Since some time had passed since I had read his book I was not sure whether he was right in his explanation about the word 'special'. When I went home that night I checked and found that he had indeed used the word 'special' as I had said and not 'specific'. It follows that none of his explanations that evening was of any value.

Brzezinsky, however, avoided explaining why he did not mention the whole story about Carter's 'homeland' statement, i.e. the part the American Embassy played in Cairo, and the message carried to me to be delivered to Yasser Arafat and Mahmoud Riad. Before concluding my conversation with Brzezinsky I stressed that our problem with the United States was one of credibility. The United States should stop exploiting our human problem to accommodate the pressure groups in the United States.

Despite all the tactics, manoeuvres, pressure and intimidation catalogued in this book, there will be no peace as long as there is injustice. It is time that both Israel and the United States, the two strategic partners, ponder this. By double-talk, they cannot achieve peace. The United States, a Big Power, can however promote peace if it stops accommodating Israeli "conquest" and considers the basic facts of the problem.

Man has learned from history that might conveys no right. It imposes a duty on the people conquered by force who come under occupation to resist it until they get rid of the invader. This is a lesson all invaders have learned, and Israel cannot be an exception to the rule. Today we have seen Israel's violence extended to the Lebanon and one wonders which other country is to be the next target for Israeli expansion.

I do not think I can bring this book to a close on a more fitting note than with the remarks of a distinguished U.S. journalist. After an interview with Mrs Golda Meir, James Reston wrote in the *New York Times* of 8th February 1970:

> "Israel appeals to justice and is not just to the Arab refugees; it asks for mercy and is merciless in attack; it cries for a decent order in the world and for principles among nations, yet scorns and even vilifies the United Nations, which despite obvious weaknesses is the only instrument of international order and justice we have."

Reston continued:

> "in this sense, not only geography and history but logic are against Israel over the long run and the Israelis know it."

Conclusion

A whole generation is growing up now in the West for whom the present situation in Palestine represents the *status quo* beyond which it sees no need to probe. For them the Palestinian struggle has no history, no association and little meaning so that automatically there is diminishing comprehension of the magnitude of this long-standing conflict.

The aim of this book is to increase understanding of the several different dimensions this problem has acquired. I hope that the episodes in the long story of "corridor diplomacy" I have recorded will bring home to the reader the way in which international voting alliances are formed and may be influenced. Though nations may work together at a time of crisis — for example to achieve the resolutions adopted as a result of the crisis arising out of the 1956 Tripartite Aggression — it is not a corollary that such cohesive action will continue to cement them together for any length of time. But, ironically, the determined stand of two countries, Israel and its ally, the United States, shows what can be achieved by a refusal to shift. With only some rare exceptions the United States of America has stood behind Zionism, the political philosophy opposed to a Palestinian nationalism which it sees, and presents, as a threat to its goals. But it does not follow from this that the rest of the world must tacitly accept the new situation the Israelis have brought about by their compulsive desire to acquire, illegally, the territory of others and a wider sphere of influence.

Raids which have escalated in size and horror to the point where they become massacres, wars which have resulted in a refugee problem of considerable magnitude and a bloc of countries fiercely opposed to country which by its deeds and practices behaves like a foreign body in their midst is the legacy left by the U.N. Partition Resolution of 1947. Those Palestinians who have to leave their homeland have an uncertain existence elsewhere, whether it is in refugee camps or working in 'foreign' countries. Those who remain in the Gaza Strip and West Bank are not only denied any degree whatsoever of self-government but also have to watch the insidious take-over of their territory as Israeli settlements burgeon in areas where they have no legal right to be.

Israel today seeks nothing less than the total disappearance of the Palestinians — apparently by whatever means, however crude. This attitude bears a remarkable resemblance to Hitler's "Master Race" theories, against which the world united in World War II, their triumph. Nevertheless, these same theories, emanating from another part of the world, are today radiating outwards with appalling speed — not least because Israel enjoys the support of the United States — moral, economic and military.

But it seems that it is with impunity that the emerging new master race pursues its murderous policies. Israel is the embodiment of Zionism and Zionism was condemned on 10th November 1975 by the United Nations General Assembly "as a form of racism and racial discrimination." Furthermore, Israel is in flagrant breach of every promise it made before admission to the United Nations and is patently not a "peace-loving" nation "able and willing to uphold the principles of the Charter." Nevertheless, many Israeli policies are both connived at and condoned by its strategic partner, the United States of America which offers it complete support together with all kinds of aid from the latest jet-fighter down to the smallest item in the Army Quarter-Master's store.

At the time of writing evidence of 'anti-semitic' practices — this time against the Arabs — is emerging in the United States. The influence of the Zionist lobby there would seem to be sufficiently strong for its leadership to be able to push the American government into associating with it in such practices. This is a sinister development indeed and one which, it will be unwise for the U.S. government to ignore since the Arabs, already cognisant of the root cause of instability in the Middle East, can hardly be expected not to react strongly against clear signs of racial discrimination.

It is time that not only the United States and Israel realise that the basic concept of Zionism is wrong, but that world opinion too comes to take a more positive attitude, bringing pressure to bear on the protaganists to cease provocation and to abide by the conditions to which they agreed in 1947. Only when the United States stops accommodating Israeli intransigence and only when the Israeli leaders change their hearts and minds and stop ignoring the reality of the existence of people of Palestine can an atmosphere conducive to peace be created. And no matter how long the Israelis rely on twisting facts and distorting the truth, the truth will eventually

216

prevail.

The Palestinians will never abandon the fight and their determination to continue the struggle is well expressed in the words of the late Musa Alami, a prominent Palestinian leader, to an official of the U.S. State Department Elliott Richardson in May 1970.

> "If you continue in this policy of animosity to the Arabs and of subservience to the Israelis, then the time will come when you will be driven out of the Middle East....not only your economic interests, your diplomatic mission and others will suffer, but no American will ever again be able to walk in the streets of the Arab world, and none of your puppet agents or friends will remain there either....and this will come about very soon."

It is worth pondering this statement.

Index

Page numbers in **bold** refer to illustrations.